CLOSE THE DEAL

CHENG & TSUI PUBLICATIONS OF RELATED INTEREST

Pop Chinese
A Cheng & Tsui Handbook of Contemporary Colloquial Expressions
By Yu Feng, Yaohua Shi, Zhijie Jia, Judith M. Amory, and Jie Cai
Paperback   0-88727-424-2

Cheng & Tsui English-Chinese Lexicon of Business Terms (with Pinyin)
Comp. by Andrew C. Chang
Paperback   0-88727-394-7

Open for Business: Lessons in Chinese Commerce for the New Millennium
By Jane C.M. Kuo
Volume 1 Text & Exercise Book Set, 2nd Edition   0-88727-456-0
Volume 1 Audio CDs   0-88727-411-0
Volume 2 Text & Exercise Book Set   0-88727-359-9
Volume 2 Audio CDs   0-88727-410-2
Conversations DVD (Volumes 1–2)   0-88727-500-1

Startup Business Chinese
By Jane C.M. Kuo
Paperback   0-88727-474-9

China Scene
An Advanced Chinese Multimedia Course
By Hong Gang Jin, De Bao Xu, and James Hargett
Textbook & Workbook   0-88727-330-0
Audio Cassettes   0-88727-332-7
VHS Video Cassette   0-88727-333-5

Please visit **www.cheng-tsui.com** for more information on these and many other language-learning resources.

CLOSE THE DEAL

在商言商

Yu Feng · Xiaoxue Dai · Miranda Chen-Cristoforo

冯禹　戴晓雪　陈念湘

Advanced Chinese for Creative and Productive Business

CHENG & TSUI COMPANY · Boston

Photographs by Xiaoxue Dai.

18 17 16   3 4 5
3rd Printing

ISBN: 978-0-88727-437-4

Published by
Cheng & Tsui Company, Inc.
25 West Street
Boston, MA 02111-1213 USA
Fax (617) 426-3669
www.cheng-tsui.com
"Bringing Asia to the World"™

Library of Congress Cataloging-in-Publication Data

Feng, Yu.
    Close the deal : advanced Chinese for creative and productive business / Yu Feng, Xiaoxue Dai, and
    Miranda Chen Tahnk.
        p. cm.
    Includes index.
    ISBN 0-88727-437-4 (pbk.)
    1. Chinese language—Textbooks for foreign speakers—English.   2. Chinese language—Business
Chinese.   I. Title: Advanced Chinese for creative and productive business.   II. Dai, Xiaoxue.   III. Tahnk,
Miranda Chen   IV. Title.
PL1129.E5F46 2005
495.1'82421'02465—dc22

                                                                                              2005049712

Printed in the United States of America

Contents

目录

Publisher's Note vii

Introduction ix
    前言

An Introduction to Golden Bridge Consulting Group xiii
    背景介绍：美国金桥商务咨询公司

Lesson 1: Conducting a Market Survey 1
    第一课：市场调查

Lesson 2: Recruiting Talent (Human Resources) 17
    第二课：人力资源（招聘）

Lesson 3. Seeking a Business Partner 37
    第三课：寻找合作伙伴

Lesson 4: Creating an Advertising and Promotion Plan 53
    第四课：广告策划

Lesson 5: Investing in Real Estate 65
    第五课：投资房地产

Lesson 6: Investing in Stocks 81
    第六课：股市投资

Lesson 7: E-commerce 97
    第七课：电子商务

Lesson 8: Seeking Approval from Environmental Protection Authorities 111
    第八课：环保审批

Lesson 9: Resolving Contract Disputes 127
    第九课：合同纠纷

Lesson 10: Intellectual Property Rights 143
    第十课：知识产权

Lesson 11: Added Investment. 157
    第十一课：追加投资

Lesson 12: Mergers and Acquisitions 177
    第十二课：企业并购

Lesson 13: Financial Audit 191
    第十三课：财务清查

Lesson 14: Life Insurance 205
    第十四课：平安保险

Lesson 15: Business Strategy. 217
    第十五课：企业战略

Lesson 16: Establishing a Restaurant Chain. 229
    第十六课：餐饮连锁店

Appendix: General Notes on Business Communication
    I. Meeting for the First Time. 239
    II. Using Proverbs, Aphorisms, and Quotations. 243
    III. Getting Closer. 245
    IV. Addressing a Businessperson 247
    V. Getting Straight to the Point…or Evading It 249
    VI. Disagreeing and Refusing 250
    VII. Exerting Pressure on the Other Party 251
    VIII. Talking During Business Meals. 252

Vocabulary Glossary 253

PUBLISHER'S NOTE

China is fertile ground for foreign investment and foreign joint business ventures, and the increasing number of textbooks focusing specifically on business Chinese attests to that fact. But this book's approach, using a series of case studies to teach Chinese business communication, is new and distinctive. *Close the Deal* will actively involve and challenge students as they refine their Mandarin Chinese language skills in a wide range of applied business contexts, from resolving contract disputes, to developing a business strategy, to establishing a franchise overseas. And the appendix features an extensive list of expressions to help learners master the different levels of social formality and know exactly what to say in various business contexts—skills that spell the difference between mere proficiency and real mastery of Chinese. To augment the text, we offer a companion website and supplementary audio files.

THE CLOSE THE DEAL COMPANION WEBSITE

A companion website at **www.cheng-tsui.com/resource_center/close_deal_companion_site** contains additional resources and updated information for both students and teachers. On the student site, you can find detailed information related to the lessons, the English translations of some very difficult parts of the textbook, and links to important websites related to the Chinese economy and Chinese business. On the teacher site, which is accessible only to teachers of the course, there are suggested tests and other teaching resources.

AUDIO INFORMATION

Readers have access to free audio files that correspond to the text. To access the audio, simply visit **www.cheng-tsui.com/resources** and follow the instructions. For technical support, please contact **support@cheng-tsui.com** or call 1-800-554-1963 (toll-free) or 617-988-2400.

ABOUT THE CHENG & TSUI ASIAN LANGUAGE SERIES

The Cheng & Tsui Asian Language Series is designed to publish and widely distribute quality language learning materials created by leading instructors from around the world. We welcome readers' comments and suggestions concerning the publications in this series. Please send feedback to our Editorial Department (e-mail: **editor@cheng-tsui.com**), or contact the following members of our Editorial Board.

INTRODUCTION

前言

Imagine that you are on the 53rd floor of a skyscraper in Shanghai representing an American company in negotiations with a potential Chinese partner. Your first sentence—an apt idiomatic expression with flawless pronunciation and tonal inflection—shocks your Chinese counterparts, and your convincing analysis shatters any doubts they may have had about such a young foreigner. You even bring them a contract draft beautifully written in formal Chinese. The negotiations quickly end in success. A dream? This textbook is designed to help you make that dream come true.

We believe that the best way to learn business Chinese is by interacting with Chinese businesspeople in real business settings. Since we cannot move our classroom to a business site, the next best alternative is to turn the classroom into a simulative business environment, in which students are motivated to achieve business goals. All of the lessons, exercises, and tests are designed for this pragmatic purpose. The companies directly involved in simulative business tasks in this book are fictional, while some of the companies whose names appear throughout the book as background/reference are real. Tokio is the actual English name of a real Japanese insurance company.

TOPICS

Doing business in or with China may take a number of forms. The capacity of one textbook to deal with these many forms of business is, of course, limited. Therefore, in selecting the topics of our lessons, we keep in mind what our students will do in the business world after their graduation: investment banking, international consulting, business law, etc. We discard old topics, such as purchasing Chinese silk and crafts, and pick up topics such as e-commerce, intellectual property rights, and business mergers that reflect the new Chinese economy in the context of globalization and the IT revolution.

LANGUAGE POINTS

Besides important business terms and expressions, we pay close attention to the following:

- different styles of language and their respective business functions,
- word collocations that demonstrate language maturity,
- idiomatic phrases/proverbs frequently used in business talks, and
- some general rules of business communication that are conventions of the Chinese business world.

EXERCISES

The exercises in this book are challenging and exciting. For each lesson there are four types of practice: two oral exercises and two written assignments. The oral exercises will culminate in a role-play. Students play the roles designated in the lesson to complete an assigned business task. The most important written assignment is a composition. Students are required to write business emails, advertising plans, contracts, market surveys, and other simulative business documents. The compositions should not only be perfect in linguistic structure but also appropriate and feasible in terms of real business practice.

HOW TO USE THIS TEXTBOOK

There are in total 16 lessons, and these lessons vary in length. The shorter ones should be taught in one week while the longer ones should be taught in one-and-a-half to two weeks. The entire textbook is designed to cover one year in a university course, or can be completed in an intensive summer course. Each lesson has at least two parts, or texts: a conversation and a written document. Some lessons have two conversations and two written documents. Since business activities always involve both speaking and writing, learners are advised to pay equal attention to both parts. In the beginning of each lesson, there is a brief introduction to the background and business tasks that will be covered. The introduction and all the main bodies of the texts are on the accompanying audio. Students are expected to have listened to the lessons before they come to the classroom, so that they are prepared for the lectures and ready to participate in the drill and discussion sessions.

TEXTS

The underlined words or phrases in the texts appear in the vocabulary list immediately following each lesson. The bolded parts of the texts indicate items explained in the Notes and Explanations section that follows the vocabulary list.

VOCABULARY LIST

While the lessons are in simplified characters only, we provide traditional characters in the vocabulary list. Proper names that do not need to be memorized are italicized. We include them in the vocabulary list only to provide learners with their pinyin forms, as they often contain infrequently used characters. The English translation of each word, phrase, and expression is based on its meaning in the context of the lesson. If necessary, we explain other important word meanings in the Notes and Explanations section. The [cl.] notation means "colloquial."

NOTES AND EXPLANATIONS

The items in the Notes and Explanations section are grouped by type and are therefore not in order of their appearance in the texts. There are following groups:

1. Business and Other Professional Terms.

In this part we explain some terms that may require more than a simple English translation. We also highlight some special structures exclusively used in business expressions. If the usage of a business term is difficult, we provide learners with two examples: the first example is from the current lesson, and the second example is from another lesson or an external context. Otherwise, we just explain the meaning of the term. The notation 【课文】 denotes an example from this book, and the notation 【补充】 denotes an example from an external context. The ability to understand and utilize these terms may distinguish an experienced professional from an amateur. Therefore, learners should pay careful attention to them.

2. Formal Expressions

Some of these are used only in formal writing while others are used in both formal writing and formal speech. We provide learners with two examples of each expression: one from the lesson in which it appears and the other from an external context. These expressions are crucial to a professional businessperson, especially a high-ranking one.

3. Colloquial Expressions

By colloquial we mean a style that is more informal than the standard spoken Chinese that prevails in textbooks for elementary and intermediate Chinese. In the real business world, businesspeople purposely use this style to establish a level of friendliness and informality with the other party. Examples are provided for each of the expressions. Understanding the stylistic differences between them and using them in the proper situation are very important.

4. Other Patterns and Word Collocations

Choosing a correct verb to describe the action of a sentence or choosing a correct adjective to modify a noun demonstrates language maturity and excellence. We also include in this group some common patterns that are neither very formal nor very colloquial. Examples are provided for each item.

5. Important Idiomatic Phrases/Proverbs

In the Chinese business world, these phrases and proverbs are very frequently used. For each of them, we provide the original or superficial meaning as well as the contemporary meaning and usage. Since many of these are self-contained parts of conversation or writing, examples are provided only for some shorter ones whose usages are not straightforward.

CLASS DISCUSSION

After each lesson, there are a number of questions directly or indirectly related to the lesson. Some questions are intended to see if students have really understood the text. Others are intended to stimulate learners to think more profoundly and creatively in order to solve real business problems. These questions should be answered orally in the drill and discussion sessions. Students are expected to have prepared before coming to the sessions.

EXERCISES

The exercises typically include the following components:

1. Fast Oral Translation

Students are required to listen to an audio recording of a paragraph in Chinese consisting of about eight sentences. There is a fifteen second interval between one sentence and the next. Translations must be completed before the next sentence is read. After that, students will listen to an audio recording of a paragraph in English and should translate it into Chinese in the same way. This exercise calls for quick processing skills. Teachers shall not provide the text to students. A similar kind of translation will be an important part of the final oral examination.

2. Role-play

Most of the role-play exercises should be done in pairs, where each student plays the role of a different party in a business negotiation. Some should be done in groups of three or more. Teachers will supervise the performances of the students. A similar kind of role-play will be another important part of the final oral examination, but then one party will be played by the teacher.

3. Rephrasing Sentences

This part may be either in the form of separate sentences or in the form of a short paragraph. Although the meanings of these sentences are clear, the expressions are not appropriate for a professional or business context. Students are required to improve them by using the words and phrases learned in the current lesson or previous lessons. For some very difficult sentences, key words are given. For all the others students must find proper words and phrases from the lessons themselves. In a few of the lessons, another exercise is substituted, such as filling in the blanks or searching for information on the Internet.

4. Composition

Students are required to write many different types of business documents, including emails, proposals, market surveys, and contracts. All the writings require creativity and imagination. We advise learners to form a group of two or three students and complete some of the written assignments together. Others should be done by students individually.

ACKNOWLEDGMENTS

There were numerous challenges to composing this book, not the least of which was obtaining information on Chinese market realities not captured in reference materials. We received invaluable assistance from individuals around the world, and wish to express special thanks to Brady Armstrong, Joseph Casey, Xiaobo Dai, Shengli Feng, Jimmy Gao, Xi Guo, Jiang Han, Ellen Hays, Boquan He, Pengyu He, Wenze Hu, Aimin Li, Jinyu Li, Mingang Liu, Kevin O'keeve, Joseph Tahnk, Jusheng Wu, Kaibin Wu, Li Wu, Weishan Wu, Weijie Zhang, and Wei Zhao.

AN INTRODUCTION TO GOLDEN BRIDGE CONSULTING GROUP

背景介绍：美国金桥商务咨询公司

Note: Golden Bridge Consulting Group is the name of a fictional consulting company whose activities are featured throughout this book.

Key: The underlined words or phrases in the texts appear in each lesson's Vocabulary List. The bolded parts of the texts indicate items explained in the Notes and Explanations section that follows the Vocabulary List.

美国金桥**商务咨询**公司是一家为美国商家**提供各种商业服务**的公司，在全球设有十多家办事处。1995年，该公司在上海成立了办事处，专门处理和中国有关的业务。王艾琳小姐是台湾人，**毕业于台湾东海大学**，现在是金桥公司上海办事处的项目经理。韩森先生是哈佛大学工商管理学院的硕士研究生，今年夏天来到上海实习。

[handwritten notes:]

shè yǒu include within; incorporate

☆ not in vocab list

gōng shāng guǎn lǐ
business administration

LESSON 1: CONDUCTING A MARKET SURVEY
第一课：市场调查

Background and Business Tasks
背景和任务

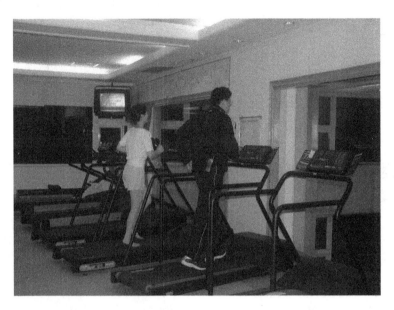

菲特公司是一家专门生产健身器材的公司，希望能在中国**出售**跑步机。该公司的跑步机有高、中、低三个**档次**。哪种产品在中国最有市场？他们委托金桥公司作市场调查。艾琳和韩森带着菲特的样品和宣传材料参加了北京第四届健身产品**博览会**。

note the use of zhuanmen as an adverb

Zui yǒu shì chǎng

Part One: At the Exhibition
第一部分：在博览会上

韩森：　艾琳，你看，来参加博览会的**足有**一百多个厂家，大部份都带来了样品。

艾琳：　看来这个市场发展得很快。我参观了上届博览会，人比这次少多了。不过，你注意到没有，来参观的主要是年轻人，好像中国的中老年人不怎么注意健身。

（正说着，一位老人走了过来。）

韩森：　老先生，您想试试我们的跑步机吗？

— 老人：　嘿，你这小伙子汉语讲得**还真**不错。不过这机器我看着有点儿晕，还是别试了。

艾琳：　您别紧张，就像平常走路一样。

— 老人：　和着这么老贵的一台机器就是为了走路用的？

韩森：　是啊，走路可以健身嘛。它还可以测量您的心跳血压。

老人：　那也不值啊！我天天去公园走路，空气又好，还能会会老朋友，干吗要花这冤枉钱？再说我那屋子小，也放不下这么大的机器啊！

艾琳：　那您今天主要是来看什么呢？

— 老人：　我是冲这个来的。（出示手里的健身球。）再见。

（一位穿西服的男士走过来）

韩森：　先生，这是菲特跑步机的有关材料。

唐立：　谢谢，这是我的名片。

艾琳：　哦，唐先生是蓝海健身俱乐部的经理，**幸会，幸会**。

唐立：　哎，这材料不是说还有一种能自动调整局部氧气含量的多功能高档跑步机吗？怎么没有样品？

艾琳：　那种机器折合人民币要八万左右，公司认为在中国大陆恐怕没有什么市场，所以就没带来。

唐立：　我对中低档不感兴趣。要是买中低档，不如去买国产货。你看见没有，那边儿的那家浙江公司，**批发价**只有三千来块，也是电子控制的。

艾琳：　那您觉得这种电脑控制的高档品最适合您的俱乐部的需要？

— 唐立：　跟你这么说吧，我们买的一律是进口高档，不然的话会员就不来了，人家就是**冲着高级设备来的**。

韩森： 这么说您觉得八万不算贵？

唐立： 这个价格可以接受，我们去年买的德国划船机比这个还要贵。我们的会员费是每年两万五千元。问题是产品的质量好不好，售后服务怎么样？我们可不愿意买便宜货，一年得修好几次。

艾琳： 菲特的质量在美国是一流的，这个您可以放心。

☆ 唐立： 这跑步机器真是美国原装的还是在马来西亚组装的？

韩森： 只有低档机是在墨西哥生产的，中高档都是地道的美国货。您的俱乐部有少会员呢？

唐立： 这是**商业机密**，但是我可以这样告诉你，**不说个人会员，光是公司会员我们就有八十多家**，健身房里面很少有空着的时候。

韩森： 对不起，我很想知道你们的会员都是些什么样的人。据我所知，很多北京人的**年均收入**才一万左右，什么人能交得起这么贵的会员费呢？

唐立： 我们的会员当然都是有一定经济基础的，四十岁以下的比较多，有很多是名人呢！像影星、歌星什么的，也有不少是企业的老板和经理。**说正经的**，我今天能不能定货？人家那边的日本公司答应给我八折优惠。

艾琳： 我们可以草签意向书，三天之内菲特会给您正式报价。

唐立： 有你这句话就行了，我们不必**草签协议**，**我说了算**，至少要六台电脑跑步机，得保证在30天内到货。

韩森： 好，您放心。

（一位女士走过来。）

安娜： 嘿，古得冒宁。

艾琳： 小姐，您早。

安娜： 菲特的总部是在芝加哥吧？

韩森： 您一张嘴我就知道您是行家。

安娜： 这位先生真会说话，实不相瞒，我是北京最大的银龙健身房的设备经理，今天来就是要采购最先进的健身设备，我早就听说你们的产品不错。

艾琳： 是啊，刚才蓝海的唐先生一下子就订了六台高档跑步机。

安娜： 蓝海**算什么**？我们的规模是他们的十几倍，我们要是看好了，一订就至少要五十台。（看说明书）我觉得你们的高档产品还不够先进，最好能让健身者一边跑一边接受背部按摩，还应该配上专门的音响和灯光。我听说日本有一种机器除了能加氧气还能散发原始森林中的松树的自然气味。

韩森： 真没想到，你们中国的消费者比美国人的要求还高。

安娜：　是啊，**真不知道你们美国是怎么回事**。我去年到<u>洛杉矶</u>去了一<u>趟</u>，商店里刚刚在宣传<u>平面直角</u>彩色电视机，这在中国已经流行了十多年了。我把名片留在这儿，要是有更先进的产品，快点儿告诉我。

（一个穿皮夹克的人走过来。）

何飞虎：　<u>**敝人**</u>何飞虎，东北飞虎公司总经理，这是我的名片。

韩森：　幸会，幸会。

何飞虎：　哎呀我的妈呀，闭上眼睛听你的中文简直就跟中国人一样啊！

韩森：　您过奖了。您对我们的产品感兴趣？

何飞虎：　跟你<u>**开门见山**</u>吧，我愿意当你们产品在东北地区的总代理商，怎么样？

艾琳：　在东北，健身器材有市场吗？

何飞虎：　那还用说吗！我们东北<u>人</u>高马大，大家都喜欢锻炼身体。别看我们的人口只有全国的八分之一，可是中国的世界冠军我们占了一半还多呢。光是<u>辽宁</u>这一个省，就有各种体育学校四百多个，你想想这就得卖多少健身器材啊？

韩森：　那您觉得在东北主要应该<u>**推销**</u>哪个档次的健身器材呢？

何飞虎：　高档的太贵，没有人买得起。低档的就是一堆<u>铁疙瘩</u>，用不着买进口货，卖起来也<u>没有什么油水</u>。我觉得最<u>适销对路</u>的是中档货。

艾琳：　谢谢何先生，我想菲特公司会跟您进一步联络的。

何飞虎：　让他们放心，告诉他们日本的"谷口"，韩国的"铁人"都是让我给他们作东北地区的总代理。在东北提起进口健身器材，没有人不知道我何飞虎的，我的销售网遍及大小城市。

Part Two: Survey Results
第二部分：问卷调查结果

（45107张有效答卷，调查对象为前来参观博览会者）

您的年龄

20岁以下	8%	21–25岁	17%
26–35岁	29%	36–45岁	25%
46–55岁	13%	56–65岁	5%
66岁以上	3%		

您的性别

男	64%	女	36%

您的职业

工人	5%	农民	1%
管理人员	50%	学生	14%
教师/医生	8%	文艺工作者	7%
其他	15%		

您的年收入

5000以下	25%	5001–10000	18%
10001–20000	13%	20001–50000	15%
50001–100000	7%	100001–200000	12%
200000以上	10%		

您觉得您的身体

非常好	19%	很好	32%
一般	25%	不太好	18%
非常不好	6%		

您的体重与标准体重的关系

标准体重算法：[身高（厘米）- 100] X 0.9 = 体重（公斤）	
标准 （正负2.5公斤以内）	28%
清瘦 （低于标准2.6–5公斤）	25%
过分消瘦 （低于标准5.1公斤以上）	13%
轻微超重 （高于标准2.6–5公斤）	19%
肥胖 （高于标准5.1–10公斤）	12%
重度肥胖 （高于标准10.1公斤以上）	3%

您常常锻炼身体吗？

每天	24%	每周2–3次	28%
每周一次	22%	很少	26%

您锻炼身体的方式最主要的是

跑步	21%	游泳	8%
球类	19%	太极拳和气功	5%
在健身房健身	22%	其他	25%

您健身的最主要的目的是

体型健美	38%	防病治病	27%
追求时尚	25%	其他	10%

在过去的一年中，您在健身方面的开支是（元）

0	3%	100以下	18%
101–500	16%	501–1000	24%
1001–5000	17%	5001–10000	13%
10000以上	9%		

在今后的一年中，您将考虑购买何种健身器材？

不打算购买	10%	举重器材	8%
跑步机	14%	多功能健身器	29%
球类器材	30%	其他	9%

在购买健身器材时，您首先将考虑

品牌	30%	产地	24%
价格	20%	性能	15%
其他	11%		

您是健身俱乐部会员吗？（包括集体会员和个人会员）

是	24%
不是，但是准备加入	19%
不是，也不准备加入	57%

Vocabulary List

Note: Proper names that do not need to be memorized are italicized. The [cl.] notation means
        "colloquial."

商务	商務	shāngwù	business (service)
咨询	諮詢	zīxún	consulting; consult
设	設	shè	set up; establish
办事处	辦事處	bànshìchù	branch office
该	該	gāi	that; this; the aforementioned
处理	處理	chǔlǐ	deal with
业务	業務	yèwù	business; operations
王艾琳		*Wáng Àilín*	*Aileen Wang, name of a person*
项目	項目	xiàngmù	project
韩森	韓森	*Hán Sēn*	*Hansen, name of a Westerner*
硕士	碩士	shuòshì	Master (degree)
实习	實習	shíxí	internship; apprenticeship
菲特		*Fēitè*	*Fitty, name of a company*
健身器材		jiànshēn qìcái	exercise equipment
档次	檔次	dàngcì	grade (of a product)
委托	委託	wěituō	entrust
样品	樣品	yàngpǐn	sample
届		jiè	session
博览会	博覽會	bólǎnhuì	exhibition; show
跑步机	跑步機	pǎobùjī	treadmill
晕	暈	yūn	dizzy
测量	測量	cèliáng	measure
血压	血壓	xuèyā	blood pressure
冤枉钱	冤枉錢	yuānwàngqián	wasted money
冲	沖	chòng	toward
出示		chūshì	show
健身球		jiànshēnqiú	marble balls for hand exercise
局部		júbù	specific area; localized
氧气	氧氣	yǎngqì	oxygen
含量		hánliàng	content

多功能		duōgōngnéng	multifunctional
折合		zhéhé	convert
浙江		Zhèjiāng	a province south of Shanghai
批发	批發	pīfā	wholesale
划船机	划船機	huáchuánjī	rowing machine
马来西亚	馬來西亞	Mǎláixīyà	Malaysia
组装	組裝	zǔzhuāng	assemble
墨西哥		Mòxīgē	Mexico
草签	草簽	cǎoqiān	sign (an agreement) provisionally
意向书	意向書	yìxiàngshū	letter of intent; memorandum of understanding
报价	報價	bàojià	quoted price; quote
行家		hángjiā	expert
☆ 实不相瞒	實不相瞞	shíbùxiāngmán	let me be candid with you
规模	規模	guīmó	size; scope
采购	採購	cǎigòu	purchase
背部		bèibù	back
按摩		ànmó	massage
☆ 原始森林		yuánshǐ sēnlín	virgin forest
○ 平面直角		píngmiàn zhíjiǎo	flat-screen — *not in Pleco*
皮夹克		píjiákè	leather jacket
敝人		bìrén	I; me
○ 我的妈呀	我的媽呀	wǒde māya	[cl.] Oh my God
开门见山	開門見山	kāiménjiànshān	get straight to the point
✗ 人高马大	人高馬大	réngāomǎdà	tall and well built
辽宁	遼寧	Liáoníng	a province in Northeast China
推销	推銷	tuīxiāo	promote the sale of
☆○ 铁疙瘩	鐵疙瘩	tiěgēda	[cl.] iron chunks
油水		yóushuǐ	[cl.] profit
☆ 适销对路	適銷對路	shìxiāoduìlù	suited to market demand
谷口		*Gǔkǒu*	*name of a company*
问卷调查	問卷調查	wènjuàn diàochá	survey questionnaire
清瘦		qīngshòu	thin
消瘦		xiāoshòu	emaciated
时尚	時尚	shíshàng	fashion

Notes and Explanations

Note: The notation 【课文】 denotes an example from this lesson or another lesson in this book.
The notation 【补充】 denotes an example from an external context.

1. BUSINESS AND OTHER PROFESSIONAL TERMS

商业　　*(business, commerce) vs.* 商务 *(business or commercial service)*

These two words are similar in meaning and sometimes interchangeable. For example, "business Chinese" can be translated as either 商务中文 or 商业中文. However, the latter strongly emphasizes service. Compare the following words:

商业中心 a complex of many retail stores, a commercial center
商务中心 a complex of many business offices, business center in a large upscale hotel

咨询　　*consult, consulting, consultation*

【课文】美国金桥商务咨询公司是一家为美国商家提供各种商业服务的公司。

【补充】我们公司可以为您提供进出口方面的咨询。

【课文】我们就向中国出口商品的问题咨询了有关专家。

经理　　*manager*

Some frequently used word compounds:

项目经理 project manager
总经理 general manager
经理助理 assistant to the manager

出售　　*sell*

A formal equivalent of 卖.

【课文】希望能在中国出售跑步机。

【补充】该公司去年一共出售个人电脑三百万台。

博览会　　*(product) exhibition/show*

Refers to trade exhibitions or shows participated in by many manufacturers/companies.

Related words:

展览会 exhibition

交易会 trade fair, commodities fair

新产品发布会 a conference announcing the release of a new product (typically by a single manufacturer)

档次   *grade (of a product)*

档 means "category" while 次 means "rank" or "order." Conventionally, commodities are divided into the following three categories:

高档 high grade, higher end, expensive

中档 middle grade

低档 low grade, lower end, cheap

批发价   *wholesale price*

Related word: 零售价 retail price.

组装   *assemble*

This term has two related meanings. Its basic meaning is "to assemble," and its extended meaning is the implication that the product is assembled in countries where the cost of labor is low. The antonym of the second meaning is 原装 (made in the original country). For example, if a Kodak digital camera is made in the U.S.A., it is called a 原装 product; if it is made in Mexico or China, it is called a 组装 product. Chinese consumers often believe that although the brand and the model are exactly the same, a 原装 product's quality is much better than a 组装 product's quality.

年均收入   *average annual income*

Related word: 人均收入 per capita income.

到货   *be delivered to the customer*

Related word: 出货 already out of the factory and on the way to the customer.

推销   *promote the sale of*

Related word: 推销员 salesperson.

2. FORMAL EXPRESSIONS

该   *this or that*

【课文】该公司在上海成立了办事处......
【课文】参与该课题的研究和撰写工作。（L2）

V＋于＋*Place Word*

This word order differs considerably from the common spoken Chinese word order. When we say somebody did something somewhere in common spoken Chinese, the word order is: preposition (在/从/etc.) + place word + action verb. In formal Chinese, however, the word order is: action verb + 于 + place word.

【课文】毕业于台湾东海大学＝从台湾东海大学毕业
【补充】陈先生毕业于北京大学。
【补充】王先生先后就职于联想公司和方正公司。（就职于......＝在......
工作）

幸会   *(I am) so fortunate (to have the opportunity) to meet (you)*

A very frequently used formal greeting. Mainly used when meeting an unfamiliar person. For more explanation, please read **General Notes on Business Communication I.**

敝人   *I, me*

A disparaging way of referring to oneself used when first meeting someone. For more explanation, please read **General Notes on Business Communication I.**

何   *why, how, what*

A frequently used question word in formal expressions.

【课文】您将考虑购买何种健身器材......
【课文】韩先生何出此言...... (L6)

3. COLLOQUIAL EXPRESSIONS

足有   *be fully...(a certain quantity), be as much as...*

【课文】来参加博览会的足有一百多个厂家。
【补充】这一产品给菲特公司带来的利润足有三亿美元。

还真　　*really (with a tone of surprise)*
　　【课文】你这小伙子汉语讲得还真不错。
　　【课文】现在还真有一个上好的机会。（L5）

☆　和着　　*turn out to be*
This colloquial expression is used to indicate that one has discovered a fact.
　　【课文】和着这么老贵的一台机器就是为了走路用的？
　　【补充】和着我干了半天一分钱也拿不到！

冲着……来的　　*coming and doing something for the sole purpose/consideration of*
　　【课文】人家就是冲着高级设备来的。
　　【补充】他想跟你结婚是冲着你的钱来的。

不说……光是……　　*without even mentioning…, just…alone (already a large quantity)*
　　【课文】不说个人会员，光是公司会员我们就有八十多家。
　　【补充】在美国上学很贵，不说学费，光是买书每年就要上千块钱。
　　【补充】来参加博览会的外商很多，不说欧洲和美洲的，光是日本商人就来了三百多。

说正经的　　*be serious*
After some casual conversation, a speaker uses this phrase to show that he wants to focus on serious business.
　　【课文】说正经的，我今天能不能定货？
　　【补充】说正经的，你们到底同意不同意我做你们的总代理？

说了算　　*have the authority to make the final decision (what the person says counts)*
　　【课文】我说了算。
　　【补充】你们公司到底谁说了算？

算什么　　*be nothing (literally, "what does it count for?")*
　　【课文】蓝海算什么！
　　【补充】日本车算什么！英国车才是高级车。

真不知道……是怎么回事   *really don't understand what's with (something/somebody)*

【课文】真不知道你们美国是怎么回事……

【补充】真不知道他是怎么回事，平常作业做得不错，可是一考试就不及格。

没有什么油水   *not much profit in it, not lucrative*

【课文】卖起来也没有什么油水……

【补充】现在中国饭馆太多了，没有多大油水。

4. OTHER PATTERNS AND WORD COLLOCATIONS

提供服务   *provide service*

【课文】美国金桥商务咨询公司是一家为美国商家提供各种商业服务的公司。

【补充】我公司向世界各国企业提供一流的翻译服务。

商业机密   *business secret*

机密 means secret/confidential information. The word before it must be disyllabic.

【课文】这是商业机密。

【补充】有时候国家领导人的身体状况也是国家机密。

草签协议   *sign an agreement provisionally*

The object of 草签 can be 协议, 合同, 意向书，合约, etc. (It must be a two or more syllable word.)

【课文】我们不必草签协议

【补充】这两家公司草签了一项合作协议。

5. IMPORTANT IDIOMATIC PHRASES/PROVERBS

开门见山   *get straight to the point*

Literally, "As soon as the door opens, the mountains can be seen." It means to come straight to the point. Often used as a verb or as a modifier.

【课文】跟你开门见山吧

【补充】我很喜欢你这种开门见山的风格，这样可以节省很多时间。

See **General Notes on Business Communication V.**

6. A Note on the Names of the Two Main Characters

The two main characters in this textbook are 王艾琳 and 韩森. You may wonder why in most parts of the book we call them 艾琳 and 韩森 since the former is a first name while the latter sounds like a last name. Please note 韩森 here is Hansen's Chinese name. 韩 then is his Chinese last name. There are some general rules governing how to address people by their names. If A and B have a close relationship, A will address B by B's given name only. However, if B's given name is only one syllable, A should then address B by B's full name instead. In other words, the number of syllables in one's name matters. We may not call 韩森 by his Chinese given name 森 unless we are extremely intimate with him. For more rules on addressing businesspeople, please read **General Notes on Business Communication IV.**

Class Discussion
课堂讨论

1. 中国保健市场最近几年有什么变化？
2. 为什么北京人的年均收入只有一万左右，但是却有不少人可以交两万会费参加健身俱乐部？
3. 分析一下唐立和安娜有什么不同。
4. 北京的市场和东北的市场有什么差别？
5. 在你看来，在中国市场上，菲特公司最有希望的是哪个档次的产品？
6. 为什么在美国平面直角彩电上市比中国晚得多？
7. 你觉得何飞虎是不是可以信任的代理商？

Exercises
练习

Part One: Fast Oral Translation
第一部分：快速口译

Listen to an audio recording of a paragraph in Chinese. There is a fifteen second interval between sentences. Translate each sentence orally before the next sentence is read. Then listen to an audio recording of a paragraph in English and translate it into Chinese in the same way.

A. From Chinese into English
一位中国健身器材公司经理介绍市场情况。

B. From English into Chinese
An American CEO is analyzing the Chinese home appliance market.

PART TWO: ROLE-PLAY (MARKET SURVEY FOR SKI EQUIPMENT)
第二部分：角色表演（滑雪器材市场调查）

An American ski equipment company hopes to sell its products on the Chinese market and they ask Golden Bridge Consulting Group to conduct a market survey for them. One student acts as the project manager at Golden Bridge and another student acts as the manager of a sporting goods store in Beijing. Discuss skiing and the ski equipment market in China.

美国一家生产滑雪器材的公司希望能在中国销售滑雪器材，请金桥公司为他们做市场调查。一个同学作金桥公司的经理，另一个同学作北京健身器材商店的经理，交流现在中国的滑雪器材市场情况。

PART THREE: REPHRASING SENTENCES
第三部分：改写句子

Using the words given in parentheses, rephrase the following sentences so that they are appropriate for a professional or business context. If no specific words are given, use the words and phrases you have learned in this lesson.

1. 现在中国的大城市和小城市都有健身俱乐部。（遍及）
2. 金龙公司是1997年成立的，这家公司主要是卖价钱比较便宜的电冰箱、洗衣机这类东西，每年卖出的东西大概有六百万元。
3. 我觉得开书店赚不了多少钱，不如开个咖啡厅。（油水）

PART FOUR: COMPOSITION (MARKET SURVEY)
第四部分：写作（问卷调查表）

Design a survey in Chinese for the American ski equipment company mentioned in Part Two of the exercises. The survey will ascertain the potential of the sport of skiing and the ski equipment market in China. You should ask at least 15 questions in the survey.

LESSON 2: RECRUITING TALENT (HUMAN RESOURCES)
第二课：人力资源（招聘）

Background and Business Tasks
背景和任务

Attending a job fair.

威力是一家**生产并销售**高科技医疗仪器的美国**公司**，正筹备在上海**开设在业务上独立运作的分公司**。公司领导层认为，当前最重要的是挑选最合适的人选担任总经理。他们委托金桥公司**代为**寻找合格人才。金桥公司**通过公开招聘和猎头的方式**展开搜寻工作，经初步筛选，艾琳和韩森将对下面两位候选人进行面试。

17

Part One: Interview Transcript A
第一部分：面试记录（一）

地点：　金桥公司

朱建国：　你好！我找艾琳小姐和韩森先生。

秘书：　噢，他们已等候你**多时**了。**这边请**。这就是艾琳小姐，这位是韩森先生。

朱：　您好！我叫朱建国。（一一握手）

艾琳：　您好！

韩森：　您好！

朱：　真不好意思，今天下雨，路上堵车堵得厉害，我的司机想办法抄近道，**才算**只耽搁了十分钟。

艾琳：　我理解。上海的交通一到雨雪天就麻烦了。请坐，请坐。

（秘书端水进来）

朱：　（接过水）谢谢！

秘书：　不客气！

艾琳：　我们可以开始了吗？

朱：　好。

韩森：　我们看了你的简历，请你先介绍一下你的工作经历好吗？

朱：　我从78年进嘉华股份公司开始说起吧，那时公司还叫上海第四精密仪器厂呢。我在那儿做了近20年，从普通工人开始做起，由于表现不错，领导也很重视提拔年轻干部，所以我被层层提升，负责的工作也越来越重要。在我离开公司的时候，我已是公司的董事和副总经济师了。我主要负责企业的战略规划，参与收购兼并的谈判、方案制订、修改和实施等。在这期间，我一直利用业余时间学习，95年得到了硕士学位。三年前，也是经过一家人才中介公司的介绍，我跳了槽，到丰瑞电子通信公司**担任总经理一职**。

艾琳：　你的工作经历很有意思。你喜欢你目前的工作吗？

朱：　当然。

韩森：　那么你喜欢你工作的哪一点呢？

朱：　作为总经理可以全面运作一个企业。我们公司现在业务相对稳定，待遇方面也不错。

艾琳：　既然你很喜欢现在的工作，待遇也不错，为什么还想来威力工作呢？

朱： 中国有句老话，"**人往高处走，水往低处流**"。丰瑞公司具有一定的知名度，但**毕竟是合资，和威力这种跨国公司根本不能同日而语**。所以，虽然都是总经理，但含金量是不同的。我想尝试一个更具有挑战性的位置。

韩： 那你以前的工作经验和现在要竞争的位置有哪些联系呢？

朱： 不管是合资公司还是外资公司的总经理，基本的工作范围都差不多。总经理人选必须懂得经济核算。我本科学的是经济，现在又是高级经济师。总经理还要懂管理，我是一个管理系的硕士，又负责过企业生产和资本的运作规划。我想我在现在的公司能做好总经理的职位，换了一个新公司，同样也能做得很好。

艾： 如果让你**招兵买马**的话，你会选什么样的人做下属呢？

朱： 我会找有理想、有责任心、有一技之长的人来组成一个团队。

韩： 如果有人比你年轻，知识结构也很完善，你会不会用他？你怕不怕今后这会对你造成威胁？

朱： 我敢肯定地说我会用这样的人。如今的竞争说到底就是人才的竞争。我觉得我的长处**在于**实际经验要比年轻人丰富，而且我也在不断地学习新的知识。如果以后我的部下能力比我强，我愿意让贤。2000年西方很多有名的公司**首席执行官**更换了，他们一旦发现有比自己能力强的人马上交权，动作很迅速。这个道理很简单，如果公司业绩不好，他自己继续干可能工资是拿到了，但期权股价下跌，自己**蒙受的损失**反而更大。

韩： 那你觉得你自己有什么短处没有？

朱： 有，人贵有自知之明。我想我的形象略差。虽然五官端正，但长得只有三块豆腐高（艾琳笑），很容易被人耻笑："瞧，武大郎开店"。但是历史上有很多杰出人物的身材也都不高，如果只看外表，就可能**埋没人才**，对吧？

艾琳： 我同意。**千军易得，一将难求**。埋没人才是最大的浪费。好，今天我们就先谈到这儿。谢谢您。

朱： 也谢谢您给我这个机会。

韩： **光顾着说话，您水还没喝呢。**

朱： **不了**，我得赶回去开会。再见！

艾琳、
韩森： 再见！

Part Two: Resumé A
第二部分：简历（一）

应聘职位：总经理

个人概况

姓名：	朱建国
性别：	男
出生日期：	1960年9月1日
职位：	总经理
职称：	高级经济师
社会兼职：	上海海陆咨询专家库特聘专家

教育情况

1985.9–1988.12	沪江函授学院工业经济系大专毕业。
1989.9–1991.12	华理经济系经济管理专业，专升本毕业，获经济学学士学位。
1992.9–1995.7	上海管理学院企业管理系，在职硕士研究生，获硕士学位。

工作经历

1998.4–至今	丰瑞电子设备有限公司总经理 主要职责：公司的生产、销售、进出口业务、财务、人事行政等全面管理
1978.12–1998.3	嘉华股份有限公司 历任工人、劳资科奖励员、**厂办**副主任、主任；股份公司总经理、办公室主任、公司董事、副总经济师。

主要职责

- 负责企业生产、资本运作规划
- 负责企业长、中、短期战略规划
- 兼任董事会秘书，负责上市公司的信息披露

个人专长

在企业管理、经济管理、企业财务管理、企业战略管理方面有很多实践，有一定的实际操作能力。

- 在企业兼并、重组、改制等理论和实践的结合方面做过不少研究和探索。
- 曾在国家相关的经济类核心杂志上**发表过多篇专题研究报告和论文**，有一定的理论功底。
- 1996年曾被上海市政府经济委员会《企业管理指南》课题组选为课题研究成员，参与该课题的研究和撰写工作。
- 1997年被上海海陆咨询公司特聘为咨询专家库成员。
- 有一定社会联系面，并持有B级驾驶执照。

Part Three: Interview Transcript B
第三部分：面谈记录（二）

地点：　　上海凯旋大厦商务厅201

张文彬：　（敲门）：您好！有位艾琳小姐约我来这儿面谈。

艾琳：　　您好！我就是艾琳，您来得很准时。这位是我们公司的韩森先生。

张：　　　Nice to meet you, Mr. Hansen.

韩森：　　您好！我们坐下谈吧。根据我们得到的信息，您很年轻，以前并没有担任过任何公司的高层领导职务。您怎样能让我们相信您能**胜任**这家美资公司的总经理呢？

张：　　　虽然现在上海有不少"**海归**"，但是在美国拿到MBA的并不是很多，我觉得是否具有现代化的管理观念比经验更重要，尤其是这家美国**独资**公司，更需要熟悉美国管理**模式**、通晓英文的人才来管理。我也想指出，目前我所在的大华有限公司是一家非常有实力的公司，货运部是公司的最重要的部门之一。

韩森：　　如果让您来**坐这把交椅**，您将怎样来**实现您的理想**呢？

张：　　　公司的成功**与否**是用数字来衡量的，公司的业务指标逐年上升，**就是总经理的业绩所在**。为了实现预定的目标，我将实行欧美**扁平化**的企业组织管理模式，让高级管理人员**各司其职**，各显所能，以保证公司有效地运行。我目前所在的公司仍采用金字塔的管理方式，摆脱不了传统的领导模式，我认为这会影响公司的工作节奏和效率。

艾琳：　　您目前的工作是主管运输，而这家公司是医疗仪器公司，二者之间似乎存在着很大的差距啊！

张：　　　我有机械工程专业的学士和硕士学位，精密仪器是我的**老本行**。而且我想作为经理，管理比专业知识更重要。我想我未来的角色，当然是我的假设，需要我做更多的前瞻性的思考。我觉得我可以利用我在大华的经验，实现管理的电脑化，也就是说，要把各种数据输入电脑，这样就可以非常清楚地了解生产、销售、送货等各个环节的情况，做到奖惩分明。通过这个方法计算出每个职工的薪酬，这样大家才会**服气**。

韩森：　　您能不能谈谈您打算用什么方法来开拓国内的医疗仪器市场？

张：　　　很简单，一靠广告，二靠价格。美国公司有雄厚的经济实力，可以投入大量资金宣传产品，并且在必要的时候通过低于成本的价格来促销，让竞争对手不得不退出市场。

韩森：　　刚才您谈到薪酬问题。那么您对自己的薪水的期望值如何呢？

张：　我希望我得到的工资能高于我现在工资的百分之三十。

艾琳：　不低啊！

张：　我相信我的实际能力会证明**物超所值**。

艾琳：　好，您还有什么其它问题吗？

张：　我本来以为你们大概会用英文来问我问题。另外，我想我的<u>上司</u>不会知道我来这里面试的吧？

韩森：　放心，我们会替您<u>保密</u>的。

Reading the bulletin boards at a Shanghai job fair.

Part Four: Resumé B
第四部分：个人简历（二）

个人概况

姓名：张文彬　　性别：男　籍贯：浙江

出生年月：　1970年5月16日

联系电话：　65146231(家)

电子信箱：　zhangwenbin@163.net

通信地址：　上海市江苏路85号201室邮编 200093

工作经历

2002.8–现在　大华有限公司货运部总监

- 负责整个公司产品的送货服务工作。
- 任期内通过对运货路线的最优化设计和管理的电脑控制，送货效率提高了35%以上。

1997.7–1999.7 横丙有限公司上海分公司工程师

- 负责上海分公司的机械调试维修。
- 参与分公司的产品质量管理。

1995.2–1997.6 沪宁工学院讲师

- 从事机械工程专业的教学及科研工作
- 担任班主任和系辅导员

教育背景

1999.9–2002.6　　美国加州卡森大学工商管理学院硕士研究生，获MBA学位。

| 1992.9–1995.2 | 上海交通大学机械工程系研究生，93年获工学硕士学位。 |
| 1988.9–1992.7 | 中国科技大学机械工程系机械学专业本科，90年获学士学位。 |

计算机水平

- 通过上海市计算机等级水平考试（二级）
- 精通Windows 操作及Office常用组件的应用

英语水平

- 通过国家英语六级考试
- 托福 590；GRE 1400
- 良好的英语口语沟通能力

兴趣爱好

游泳、书法、乒乓、茶艺、烹饪等

Vocabulary List

人力资源	人力資源	rénlì zīyuán	human resources
威力		*Wēilì*	*name of a company*
销售	銷售	xiāoshòu	sale
医疗仪器	醫療儀器	yīliáo yíqì	medical apparatus and instruments
筹备	籌備	chóubèi	plan; prepare
运作	運作	yùnzuò	operate
人选	人選	rénxuǎn	choice of persons
担任	擔任	dānrèn	hold the post of
招聘		zhāopìn	invite applications for a job; recruit
猎头	獵頭	lìètóu	head-hunting
搜寻	搜尋	sōuxún	hunt for; seek
筛选	篩選	shāixuǎn	screen and select
候选人	候选人	hòuxuǎnrén	candidate
秘书	秘書	mìshū	secretary
堵车	堵車	dǔchē	have a traffic jam
抄近道		chāo jìndào	take a shortcut
耽搁	耽擱	dāngē	delay
简历	簡歷	jiǎnlì	resumé
嘉华	嘉華	*Jiāhuá*	*name of a company*
股份公司		gǔfèn gōngsī	joint stock company; incorporated company
精密		jīngmì	precision
提拔		tíbá	promote
战略	戰略	zhànlüè	strategy
董事		dǒngshì	member of the board of directors; trustees
规划	規劃	guīhuà	planning
参与	參與	cānyù	participate in
收购	收購	shōugòu	buy; purchase
兼并	兼併	jiānbìng	mergers and acquisitions
实施	實施	shíshī	implement
中介公司		zhōngjiè gōngsī	agent; agency
跳槽		tiàocáo	make a career change; job-hop

丰瑞	豐瑞	*Fēnguì*	*name of a company*
通信		tōngxìn	communication
待遇		dàiyù	remuneration
含金量		hánjīnliàng	percentage of gold; quality
尝试	嘗試	chángshì	attempt
招兵买马	招兵買馬	zhāobīngmǎimǎ	enlarge an army; expand personnel
下属	下屬	xiàshǔ	subordinate
责任心	責任心	zérènxīn	sense of responsibility
一技之长	一技之長	yìjìzhīcháng	professional skill; specialty
团队	團隊	tuánduì	group
让贤	讓賢	ràngxián	yield one's position to someone more capable
首席执行官	首席執行官	shǒuxízhíxíngguān	CEO
更换		gēnghuà	change; be replaced
业绩	業績	yèjī	performance
期权	期權	qīquán	stock options
蒙受		méngshòu	incur; suffer
五官端正		wǔguānduānzhèng	have well balanced facial features
耻笑	恥笑	chǐxiào	mock; sneer
武大郎		Wǔ Dàláng	a fictional person known as a dwarf
杰出	傑出	jiéchū	outstanding
外表		wàibiǎo	appearance
埋没		máimò	bury; overlook
职称	職稱	zhíchēng	the title of a technical post
专家库	專家庫	zhuānjiākù	think tank; committee of experts
特聘		tèpìn	special appointment
沪江	滬江	*Hùjiāng*	*name of a college*
函授学院	函授學院	hánshòu xuéyuàn	correspondence college
专升本	專升本	zhuānshēngběn	rise from three-year college status to four-year college status
有限公司		yǒuxiàngōngsī	ltd.
获	獲	huò	obtain
历任	歷任	lìrèn	have successively held the posts of
劳资科	勞資科	láozīkē	payroll office
奖励员	獎勵員	jiǎnglìyuán	staff in charge of bonus distribution
厂办	廠辦	chǎngbàn	office of the factory director

主任		zhǔrèn	chief; director
上市		shàngshì	IPO (initial public offerings) listed on the stock market
披露		pīlù	disclosure; make public
重组	重組	chóngzǔ	restructuring
核心杂志	核心雜誌	héxīn zázhì	an officially rated top national magazine
功底		gōngdǐ	foundation
指南		zhǐnán	guide
课题组	課題組	kètízǔ	research group
撰写	撰寫	zhuànxiě	compose and write
驾驶执照	駕駛執照	jiàshǐ zhízhào	driver's license
凯旋大厦	凱旋大廈	*Kǎixuán Dàshà*	*name of a prominent building*
张文彬	張文彬	*Zhāng Wénbīn*	*name of a person*
胜任	勝任	shèngrèn	qualified for or competent at
海归	海歸	hǎiguī	those who return from abroad
独资	獨資	dúzī	wholly-owned
模式		móshì	mode; model
通晓	通曉	tōngxiǎo	know well; have a good knowledge of
交椅		jiāoyǐ	director's chair; (leading) position
指标	指標	zhǐbiāo	target; quota
逐年		zhúnián	year by year
扁平化		biǎnpínghuà	leveling
各司其职	各司其職	gèsīqízhí	each one does his duty
各显所能	各顯所能	gèxiǎnsuǒnéng	each shows his special skill
金字塔		jīnzìtǎ	pyramid
节奏	節奏	jiézòu	rhythm
效率		xiàolǜ	efficiency
机械工程	機械工程	jīxiè gōngchéng	mechanical engineering
老本行		lǎo běnháng	[cl.] the profession one has engaged in for years
假设	假設	jiǎshè	suppose; hypothetical assumption
前瞻性		qiánzhānxìng	foresight; farsightedness
数据	數據	shùjù	data
奖惩分明	獎懲分明	jiǎngchéngfēnmíng	strict and fair in meting out rewards and punishments
薪酬		xīnchóu	salary and bonus

服气	服氣	fúqì	convinced
促销	促銷	cùxiāo	promote sale
期望值		qīwàngzhí	expected value
物超所值		wùchāosuǒzhí	value exceeds the price
上司		shàngsī	leader; boss
保密		bǎomì	keep secret; confidential
总监	總監	zǒngjiān	chief operating officer
最优化	最優化	zuìyōuhuà	optimization
横丙		*Héngbǐn*	*name of a company*
工程师	工程師	gōngchéngshī	engineer
调试	調試	tiáoshì	setting up and debugging
维修	維修	wéixiū	maintenance
工学院	工學院	gōngxuéyuàn	institute of technology
讲师	講師	jiǎngshī	lecturer
计算机	計算機	jìsuànjī	computer
科研		kēyán	scientific research
班主任		bānzhǔrèn	head advisor of a class
辅导员	輔導員	fǔdǎoyuán	student advisor
卡森		*Kǎsēn*	*Carson, name of a college*
托福		Tuōfú	TOEFL
烹饪	烹飪	pēngrèn	cooking

Notes and Explanations

1. BUSINESS AND OTHER PROFESSIONAL TERMS

公司　　*company*

In English we have firm, company, corporation and other terms, but in Chinese 公司 is the prevailing word.

股份公司 joint stock company
总公司 company headquarters
分公司 branch company
子公司 subsidiary company
上市公司 listed company

首席执行官　　*CEO*

A direct translation from the English. 首席＝chief; 执行＝executive; 官＝officer. Previously, this position was often called 总裁 (zǒngcái).

厂办　　*office of the factory director*

An abbreviation of 厂长办公室. The members of this office are actually the secretaries, and its head is the chief secretary to the director of the factory.

海归　　*graduates returned from overseas*

An abbreviation of 海外归来留学人员. This is a very new term for those who have studied abroad and then returned to China. Many online articles humorously write it as 海龟 (sea turtle) because it is homophonous with 海归.

扁平化　　*leveling*

This means a company is organized in such a way that there are few mid-level managers.

2. FORMAL EXPRESSIONS

V_1 并 V_2

This pattern should have only one subject but can have two objects. Remember, 并 cannot be replaced with 和, which is a conjunction for nouns.

【课文】威力是一家生产并销售高科技医疗仪器的美国公司。
【补充】董事会讨论了生产新产品的计划并通过了公司副总经理的任命。
(The board of directors discussed the proposal for manufacturing new products and approved the appointment of the vice general manager of the company.)

代为 *perform a task on consignment*
【课文】他们委托金桥公司代为寻找合格人才。
【补充】关于产品的售后服务，菲特公司请飞虎公司代为安排。

多时 *a long time*
Same as the common spoken phrase 很长时间了.
【课文】他们已等候你多时了。
【补充】这个计划已经讨论多时了，但是至今没有取得一致意见。

一一 *respectively; one after another*
【课文】一一握手
【补充】他把产品的性能和价格一一记录下来。

担任……一职 *hold the post of…*
Same as the common spoken pattern 担任……这一个职务.
【课文】到丰瑞电子通信公司担任总经理一职。
【补充】他三年前曾经在大同银行担任总经济师一职。

毕竟是……，和…… 不能同日而语
Literally, 同日而语 means "to be mentioned on the same day." Its meaning is "of the same category" or "on the same level." This phrase is usually used negatively, implying that there is a huge gap between the two things being compared.
【课文】但毕竟是合资，和威力这种跨国公司根本不能同日而语。
【补充】中国的西北地区在改革后也有了很大的进步，但是毕竟缺乏人才和资金，和东南沿海地区不能同日而语。

在于…… *lies in; rests with*
【课文】我觉得我的长处在于实际经验要比年轻人丰富。
【补充】我们都希望西北地区的经济能快速发展，问题在于从何处找到资金。

......与否　　　...or not

The word before 与否 must be a two-syllable word.
　　【课文】公司的成功与否是用数字来衡量的......
　　【补充】一项政策的正确与否应当通过产生的效果来检验。

就是......的...... 所在　　　lies precisely in this

The word before 所在 must be a two-syllable word. This pattern is used to identify and stress the key factor behind a phenomenon.
　　【课文】公司的业务指标逐年上升，就是总经理的业绩所在。
　　【补充】你们只注意学历，不注意经验，这就是问题的关键所在。

3. COLLOQUIAL EXPRESSIONS

这边请　　　this way please
　　＝请往这边来

才算　　　scarcely got the result

This adverb implies something was achieved (often just barely) with great difficulty.
　　【课文】才算只耽搁了十分钟。
　　【补充】那个考试非常难，我准备了两个月，才算考了个及格。

光顾着......还没...... 呢

having been so focused on A that one is not yet thinking about B
　　【课文】光顾着说话，您水还没喝呢。
　　【补充】你光顾着招呼客人了，自己还没有吃饭呢。

不了　　　no thanks

Used to turn down an offer in a gentle way, this is similar to the function of "no thanks" in English. If you simply say 不 instead, it would sound very rude. Note: This phrase is not used in really serious matters (for example, a job offer).
　　【课文】不了，我得赶回去开会。
　　【补充】"晚上我请你吃饭。""不了，我还要准备明天的考试呢。"

坐交椅　　　be the leader
交椅 is a kind of large armchair and is used as a symbol for a leadership position.

【课文】如果让您来坐这把交椅……

【补充】他在著名的金桥公司坐第二把交椅。 (He is the second most senior leader at Golden Bridge Consulting Group.)

老本行　*the trade or profession one has engaged in for years*

本行 means one's "trade," and 老 is added to show that one has a long history of experience in that trade.

【课文】精密仪器是我的老本行。

【补充】你放心，照相是我的老本行，我照的照片你一定满意。

服气　*be convinced; concede willingly*

Usually used when a decision or statement is made very fairly in accordance with objective standards so that nobody can complain or object to it.

【课文】这样大家才会服气。

【补充】日本车的质量就是比国产高，你不能不服气。

4. OTHER PATTERNS AND WORD COLLOCATIONS

开设分公司 / 分店　*to set up a subsidiary company / branch store*

【课文】正筹备在上海开设在业务上独立运作的分公司。

【补充】肯德基已经在中国的二十五个省市开设了分店。

通过…的方式V　*do something by means of...*

【课文】金桥公司通过公开招聘和猎头的方式展开搜寻工作。

【补充】大部分人认为总经理应该通过投票的方式选举决定。

蒙受损失　*sustain or incur a loss*

【课文】自己蒙受的损失反而更大。

【补充】如果让不合格的人来作最高领导，公司一定会蒙受巨大损失。

埋没人才　*overlook talented people*

【课文】埋没人才是最大的浪费。

【补充】文化革命时期毛主席把很多知识分子送到农村去，不知埋没了多少优秀人才。

发表论文　　*publish a paper*
　　【课文】发表过多篇研究报告和论文。
　　【补充】他上大学的时候就发表了三篇论文。

通晓英文　　*have a good command of the English language*
　　【课文】更需要熟悉美国管理模式、通晓英文的人才来管理。
　　【补充】王董事长通晓英文、法文等八种西方语言。

实现理想 / 目标　　*realize a goal*
　　【课文】您将怎样来实现您的理想呢？
　　【课文】为了实现预定的目标……

5. IMPORTANT IDIOMATIC PHRASES/PROVERBS

人往高处走，水往低处流
See **General Notes on Business Communication II.**

招兵买马　　*lit. "recruit soldiers and buy up horses"*
Used to indicate that one is building up his forces to prepare for a big campaign.

千军易得，一将难求
See **General Notes on Business Communication II.**

各司其职　　*each performs his/her own function*
Used to indicate (the requirement) that in an institution the responsibility/duty of each member is very clear.

物超所值　　*The value of things surpasses what's paid for them.*
This phrase often appears in the ads of stores/restaurants.

Class Discussion
课堂讨论

1. 你觉得这两个人谁当总经理比较合适？为什么？
2. 你觉得学历和经历相比哪个重要？为什么？
3. 你理想中的总经理应该是个什么样的人？
4. 选择一个合适的人才还可以从哪些方面进行考察？
5. 中国人的简历和美国人的简历有什么不同？
6. 如果你是艾琳或者韩森，你还会问些什么问题来全面考察这两位应聘者？

Exercises
练习

PART ONE: FAST ORAL TRANSLATION
第一部分：快速口译

Refer to Lesson 1 for instructions for this exercise.

A. From Chinese into English
一位中国经理介绍自己的公司如何发现和吸引人才。

B. From English into Chinese
A representative of an American company is talking with the general manager of a Shanghai hiring agency.

PART TWO: ROLE-PLAY (JOB INTERVIEW)
第二部分：角色表演(招聘面谈)

Student A acts as the interviewer and student B acts as the interviewee applying for the position of general manager of a medical equipment subsidiary company.
一个同学作金桥公司的面试官，另一个同学作想得到这家医疗仪器分公司总经理职务的应聘者。

PART THREE: REPHRASING SENTENCES
第三部分：改写句子

Refer to Lesson 1 for instructions for this exercise.

1. 我们公司主要是卖进口的健身器材，我们也修理这些器材。
2. 那家公司的生意不错，但是和蓝海公司比起来，差得非常非常远。

3. 我们想用猎头的办法找到一位英文和日文都说得好的人来作公司的副总经理。

4. 他没有好好调查就决定在上海开个分店，结果损失特别大。

PART FOUR: COMPOSITION
第四部分：写作

Suppose you want to get a job with a Chinese company. Write a resumé in Chinese for that purpose.

LESSON 3: SEEKING A BUSINESS PARTNER
第三课：寻找合作伙伴

Background and Business Tasks
背景和任务

Northwest Transformer Works.

美国杜尔公司研制了一种**可**广泛用于各种电子设备的微型变压器，它的体积只有普通产品的三分之一，电磁损耗只有普通产品的一半。为了降低生产成本，该公司希望寻找一家中国工厂加工生产这种变压器，核心部件的材料由美国提供，其他材料在中国国内解决。杜尔公司希望这种变压器的生产成本控制在八美元以内，首**批**加工量为50万件。由于杜尔对中国情况了解不多，所以委托金桥公司寻找中国合作厂家。经过初步筛选，艾琳和韩森决定对下面的两家工厂进行实地考察。

Part One: A Brief Introduction to Northwest Transformer Works

第一部分：西北变压器厂简介

本厂建立于1984年，在刘建民厂长的带领下，经过短短十几年的时间，由一个只有几十人的村办小厂发展为西北地区规模最大的变压器专业生产厂家，2000年被评为省级先进**民营企业**，刘建民厂长也**被授予"有突出贡献的农民企业家"的称号。全厂现有职工二千八百余人**，技术**人员**95名，其中高级工程师16名。

本厂的产品包括从大型电力变压器到电脑等家用电器所使用的微型变压器，共计43个**系列**，五百余种产品，除满足我国西部地区的需要外，还远销中亚、西亚、南亚及北非的十多个国家和地区，**年产值**超过两亿元。

本厂的宗旨是**物美价廉**，用户至上。欢迎五大洲的朋友前来洽谈订货。除订购现有产品外，我们还可根据客户的特殊需要设计生产各类专用变压器。

法人代表：刘建民（厂长）
厂址：甘肃酒泉光明路41号，邮政编码400752
电话：8625-7314-4500
电传：8625-7314-4502

Part Two: A Brief Introduction to Tailong Transformer Works

第二部分：泰龙变压器厂

本厂是生产微型变压器的专业厂家，技术力量雄厚，生产设备一流，主要设备**系**由德国引进，曾为日本东芝、夏普，韩国三星等国际著名公司加工生产先进的微型变压器。近年来，本厂以生产笔记本电脑的专用变压器为主，平均每三台国产笔记本电脑中，就有一台的变压器是本厂的产品，所占**份额居国内厂家之首**。

本厂原**为**中新合资泰达电器公司的下属厂，2000年成为具有独立法人资格的股份制企业。现有全职员工一百九十名，临时工一百五十名，年产值近八百万美元。

本厂的厂训是：以质量求生存，以创新求发展。全厂职工团结一心，力争在十年内，成为中国最大的微型变压器生产厂。

法人代表：龙在田（厂长）
联系人：苏锐（销售经理）

厂址：江苏省苏州工业园区先锋路26号
邮政编码：230079
电话：8622 – 3397 – 5888，8622 – 3397 – 5688
电传：8622 – 3397 – 5873
电邮：sales@tailong.com.cn

Part Three: At the Small Banquet Hall of Jiuquan Hotel
第三部分：甘肃酒泉宾馆小宴会厅

刘建民：**欢迎二位不远万里来到我们这儿考察**，给你们介绍一下，这位是我
　　　　厂外事办公室刘宁主任，我的小儿子。这位呢，是我们的公共关系
　　　　处处长张梅女士，我的二儿媳妇。（双方握手寒暄，交换名片。）

刘宁：我们甘肃这个地方**也没有**什么好东西，粗茶淡饭，不过酒泉的酒**倒
　　　**是很有名的，请二位赏光，来来，我们边吃边谈吧？

韩森：谢谢，我不会喝酒。什么时候我们可以到你们的生产车间看看呢？
　　　我们在酒泉只能停留二十小时。

张梅：那太可惜了，我本来是准备带二位游览黄河公园和灵岩寺的。韩先
　　　生，您的汉语说得太棒了！艾琳：**非常感谢你们的盛情安排**。不过
　　　刚才韩森说了，我们的时间实在太紧张了，如果我们能达成协议，
　　　相信以后一定会有机会来观光的。

刘建民：好，好。不过饭总要吃吧？小梅，给厂里打个电话，说美国客人两
　　　　小时就到。

韩森：　刘厂长，您大概已经看过我们的传真了吧？我想知道贵厂是否有加工生产这种变压器的能力，也想知道千件的报价。

刘建民：　能力当然不成问题，不管什么样的变压器我们都可以做。这报价嘛，我们可以商量，但我可以保证，我们的价格绝对是最优惠的。

艾琳：　我想知道，贵厂作为民营企业，是不是要等待上级审批后才能和外商签订合同？

刘宁：　原来是那样，最近这两年权力下放了，一千万以下的项目我们可以自己作主。

Part Four: At Northwest Transformer Works
第四部分：在西北变压器厂

韩森：　你们这条生产线看起来好像很旧了。

刘建民：　旧是旧了点儿，但是我们维护得很好，不会影响生产的。你们也许不知道，这种八十年代的设备是仿苏设计，虽然自动化的程度不高，但是非常稳定，不爱出毛病。艾琳：中国西北的风沙很大，你们的厂房好像并没有特殊的防尘设施啊！

刘建民：　这个没有问题。生产变压器最怕的是湿度大，酒泉是全国最干燥的城市之一，当初建厂的时候已经考虑到这个问题了。而且最近几年，周围植树造林，风沙比过去小多了。

韩森：　厂长，您现在是不是能告诉我你们的报价了。

刘建民：　好，好。我们的报价是每千件三万元。如果年加工量在百万套以上，我们还可以再低百分之十。

韩森：　**您这个价格是离岸价还是到岸价？**

刘建民：　离岸价。我们还不太熟悉跨太平洋的海运业务，最好由美国公司负责航运，这样比较方便。过去我们的出口都是从陆路运到巴基斯坦，再通过那儿的中间商卖到西亚、中东和北非。

艾琳：　您刚才的报价，材料费包括在内吗？

刘建民：　在内。我们这儿离甘肃铝材公司很近，我们有固定的伙伴关系。现在国家大力开发西部，我们这儿会越来越好，希望两位有机会常来。这是我个人送给二位的一点儿小礼物：用酒泉特产的红玉雕的奔马。

艾琳：　非常感谢您的好意，可是我们公司有纪律，不许收客户的礼物。这么贵重的礼物，我们绝对不能收。

刘建民：　哎呀，没关系嘛，不值几个钱。你们一定要收下。

韩森： 谢谢，但是这礼物我们真的不能收。我还想问一个关于运输的问题，从你们这里把产品运到最近的<u>港口</u>怎么走？需要多长时间？

刘建民： 一般是用<u>卡车</u>送到兰州，然后用火车运到<u>连云港</u>。时间嘛，十天半个月应该没有问题吧？

韩森： 到底是十天还是半个月？

刘建民： 你这个小伙子还**挺<u>叫真儿</u>**，我想十二天也许差不多。

韩森： 对不起，我最怕你们说"也许"、"差不多"。

刘建民： 可这公路和<u>铁路</u>不是我能控制得了的啊。去年下了一场大雨，铁路断了三个星期，你着急也没有办法。我们中国人不愿意把话说得太绝。

A locally-made horse carving given by 刘建民 to Aileen and Hansen.

Part Five: At the Guest Room of Tailong Transformer Works
第五部分：在泰龙变压器厂会客厅

苏锐：　怎么样？二位对我们的设备有何评价？可以这样讲，不仅在中国是最现代化的，就是在整个亚洲你也找不出几家。

韩森：　的确不错。我现在想听听您的报价。

苏锐：　为你们加工微型变压器我们必须对整个生产线进行<u>改造调整</u>，还要制造专门的<u>加工机具</u>，而你们的需求量又不是很大，这样成本就比较高了。另一方面，由于国内市场对铝材的需求越来越大，所以价格最近一直在上升。

艾琳：　请您直说吧，每千件的报价是多少？

苏锐：　按照我们的会计师的计算，每千件的报价应该是八万五千元。为了表示同杜尔公司长期合作的<u>诚意</u>，龙厂长指示把报价降低到八万元。要知道，我们这样就只有微利了。请注意，我这里说的是到岸价格。

韩森：　**<u>恕我直言</u>**，你们的报价大大高于我们考察的其他厂家。如果你们坚持这么高的价格，恐怕<u>成交</u>的可能性**<u>微乎其微</u>**。

苏锐：　我非常了解我们的竞争对手。我们的报价从国际上看不会比新加坡和马来西亚高，在中国国内也许是比别人高一些，但是坦率地说，只有我们才能保证高质量，并且保证按时交货。我们的技术骨干都曾经去<u>新加坡</u>**<u>接受过现代管理培训</u>**。我们的竞争对手在这些方面根本无法和我们相比。你想想，一群没有现代管理知识、甚至连字也不认几个的农民能造出先进的产品吗？而且，你们一定已经注意到了，从苏州工业园区到上海港走高速公路只需要一个多小时。另外，如果成交的话，我们会按照常规，给二位千分之二的介绍费，以美元现金支付。

韩森：　这就是所谓"**<u>回扣</u>**"吧？

苏锐：　不，不，这是合法的<u>佣金</u>。除此之外，我们还可以为二位提供其他的便利。什么时候二位想从上海来苏州度假，我们愿意车接车送，提供免费五星级饭店。

艾琳：　价格真的不能再低一些吗？我想杜尔公司无论如何不可能接受高于六万的报价。

苏锐：　如果订货批量再大一些，我们可以考虑六万甚至更低的报价。以现在的批量看，降价的空间十分有限。不过，我会和龙厂长商量，想想办法。我相信，如果杜尔公司和我们合作，一定会非常成功。今天晚上，龙厂长会在苏州最有名的<u>姑苏</u>饭店<u>设宴</u>招待二位，**<u>请务必赏光啊</u>**。

Vocabulary List

杜尔	杜爾	*Dù'ěr*	*Dewar (name of a company)*
研制	研製	yánzhì	research and develop
广泛	廣泛	guǎngfàn	extensive; wide-ranging
微型		wēixíng	mini; micro
变压器	變壓器	biànyāqì	transformer
体积	體積	tǐjī	volume; bulk
电磁损耗	電磁損耗	diàncí sǔnhào	electromagnetic loss
核心部件		héxīn bùjiàn	core component
首批		shǒupī	first lot
实地考察	實地考察	shídì kǎochá	on-the-spot investigation
带领	帶領	dàilǐng	lead
省级	省級	shěngjí	provincial level
民营企业	民營企業	mínyíng qǐyè	non-government enterprise
授予		shòuyǔ	grant (a title of); bestow
贡献	貢獻	gòngxiàn	contribution
企业家	企業家	qǐyèjiā	entrepreneur
称号	稱號	chēnghào	title
职工	職工	zhígōng	employee
余	餘	yú	more than
人员	人員	rényuán	staff
电力变压器	電力變壓器	diànlì biànyāqì	transformer for power network
系列		xìliè	series
远销	遠銷	yuǎnxiāo	sold afar
年产值	年產值	niánchǎnzhí	annual production
宗旨		zōngzhǐ	aim
物美价廉	物美價廉	wùměi jiàlián	excellent goods at modest prices
用户至上		yònghù zhìshàng	the customer comes first
五大洲		wǔdàzhōu	five continents
洽谈	洽談	qiàtán	[formal] to talk (business)
订货	訂貨	dìnghuò	to order (goods)
订购	訂購	dìnggòu	to order; to buy
专用	專用	zhuānyòng	to use for a special purpose

法人代表		fǎrén dàibiǎo	legal person; corporate representative
厂址	廠址	chǎngzhǐ	factory address
甘肃	甘肅	Gānsù	name of a province
酒泉	酒泉	*Jiǔquán*	*name of a city*
邮政编码	郵政編碼	yóuzhèng biānmǎ	zip code
电传	電傳	diànchuán	fax
泰龙	泰龍	*Tàilóng*	*name of a company*
雄厚		xiónghòu	solid; ample
一流		yīliú	first rate; top
系		xì	be
引进	引進	yǐnjìn	import
东芝	東芝	Dōngzhī	Toshiba
夏普		Xiàpǔ	Sharp
三星		Sānxīng	Samsung
份额	份額	fèn'é	quota; (market) share
居……之首		jū zhīshǒu	be rated number one
泰达	泰達	*Tàidá*	*name of a company*
电器	電器	diànqì	electrical appliances/equipment
资格	資格	zīgé	qualification
股份制		gǔfènzhì	joint stock (system)
全职	全職	quánzhí	full time
员工	員工	yuángōng	employee
厂训	廠訓	chǎngxùn	company motto
创新	創新	chuàngxīn	innovation
苏锐	蘇銳	*Sū Ruì*	*name of a person*
江苏	江蘇	Jiāngsū	name of a province
苏州	蘇州	Sūzhōu	name of a city
宾馆	賓館	bīnguǎn	hotel
宴会厅	宴會廳	yànhuìtīng	banquet room
不远万里	不遠萬里	bùyuǎnwànlǐ	do not mind traveling far
公共关系	公共關係	gōnggòng guānxì	public relations
处	處	chù	department, section
握手寒暄		wòshǒu hánxuān	shake hands and greet
粗茶淡饭	粗茶淡飯	cūchádànfàn	simple food and drink

赏光	賞光	shǎngguāng	to accept (an invitation)
车间	車間	chējiān	workshop; workplace
灵岩寺	靈岩寺	*Língyánsì*	*name of a temple*
盛情		shèngqíng	boundless hospitality
达成	達成	dáchéng	reach
协议	協議	xiéyì	agreement
传真	傳真	chuánzhēn	fax
贵	貴	guì	your esteemed
优惠	優惠	yōuhuì	favorable (price); discount
审批	審批	shěnpī	examine and approve
签订	簽訂	qiāndìng	sign (an agreement)
权力下放	權力下放	quánlì xiàfàng	transfer power to a lower level
生产线	生產線	shēngchǎnxiàn	assembly line
维护	維護	wéihù	maintenance
仿		fǎng	imitate
自动化	自動化	zìdònghuà	automated
程度		chéngdù	degree
防尘	防塵	fángchén	dust-proof
设施	設施	shèshī	equipment; facility
湿度	濕度	shīdù	humidity
干燥	乾燥	gānzào	dry
植树造林	植樹造林	zhíshù zàolín	enforest
离岸价	離岸價	lí'ànjià	FOB (Free on Board)
到岸价	到岸價	dào'ànjià	CIF (Cost, Insurance and Freight)
跨		kuà	cross
海运	海運	hǎiyùn	shipping by sea
航运	航運	hángyùn	shipping by air or by sea
陆路	陸路	lùlù	overland
巴基斯坦		Bājīsītǎn	Pakistan
中间商	中間商	zhōngjiānshāng	middleman
材料		cáiliào	material
铝材	鋁材	lǚcái	aluminum
伙伴关系	夥伴關係	huǒbàn guānxi	partnership
开发	開發	kāifā	develop
红玉		hóngyù	red jade

雕		diāo	carve
奔马	奔馬	bēnmǎ	galloping horse
纪律	紀律	jìlǜ	discipline
港口		gǎngkǒu	port
卡车	卡車	kǎchē	truck
连云港	連雲港	*Liányúngǎng*	*name of a port city*
叫真儿	叫真兒	jiàozhēnr	[cl.] be serious
铁路	鐵路	tiělù	railway
改造		gǎizào	transform
加工机具	加工機具	jiāgōng jījù	processing equipment
会计师	會計師	kuàijìshī	accountant
诚意	誠意	chéngyì	sincerity
恕我直言		shùwǒzhíyán	pardon me for speaking frankly
成交		chéngjiāo	strike a deal
微乎其微		wēihūqíwēi	next to nothing
新加坡		Xīnjiāpō	Singapore
马来西亚	馬來西亞	Mǎláixīyà	Malaysia
骨干	骨幹	gǔgàn	backbone; mainstay
培训	培訓	péixùn	training
回扣		huíkòu	kickback
佣金	傭金	yōngjīn	compensation
姑苏	姑蘇	*Gūsū*	*name of a hotel*
设宴	設宴	shèyàn	throw a banquet
务必	務必	wùbì	must; be sure to

Notes and Explanations

1. BUSINESS AND OTHER PROFESSIONAL TERMS

批　　*batch, lot, group*

批发＝wholesale; 批量生产＝mass production.

【课文】首批加工量为50万件。

【补充】我们公司只做批发，不做零售。

【补充】这种新药试验效果很好，明年可以批量生产。

Word Order in Quantitative Statements

When numbers are mentioned in business writing (and also in formal speech), the number and measure word are often placed after the noun. In such a sentence 了 is often omitted when a past achievement is mentioned.

【课文】全厂现有职工二千八百余人，技术人员95名，其中高级工程师16名。

【课文】租用大型广告牌350座。(L4)

【补充】该厂去年共生产汽车3500辆。

【补充】新世纪建筑公司三年内兴建大型商业中心十四座。(New Century Construction Company built 14 mega commercial centers/malls in three years.)

Ownership of an Enterprise/Business

In China's transition from a planned economy to a market economy, the terms of ownership of enterprises are changing, and as a result some of them are not clearly defined.

国营企业

This is an enterprise owned and run by the state. In the past, most of the bigger enterprises in China were of this kind, but since the policy of economic reform was initiated, the proportion of state-run enterprises is declining.

国有企业

This is a fast growing sector as many state-run factories are contracted out, but still owned by, the state.

私营企业

This is a private enterprise. But strictly speaking, only a private business of a certain minimum size can be called a 私营企业. One government document defines the term as "a private business with over eight employees." Enterprises with fewer than eight employees are called 个体户/个体经济. Now some people are challenging these definitions.

民营企业

This is the most ambiguous term. In a broad sense, it may include all enterprises except for state-owned ones. Sometimes even the state-owned enterprises that are under the management of private contractors may be called 民营企业. In a narrower sense, this term excludes foreign invested enterprises and joint ventures. And in the narrowest sense, it refers solely to enterprises with collective non-government ownership. In this sense, it is similar to the outdated term 集体企业, which means "a public enterprise owned by a local community" (such as a People's Commune in the pre-reform era).

年产值   *annual production*

In business writing, 每年 or 每年的 is often abbreviated as 年.
年营业额 annual revenue
年增长 annual increase
年吞吐量 annual amount of total imports and exports (for a port)

法人代表   *the representative of a legal entity (e.g., an enterprise or a corporation)*

Typically this individual is the president or CEO of the enterprise. Sometimes you may hear people say 我是企业法人 or 他是企业的法人. Actually they mean 法人代表.

离岸价 / 离岸价格 *vs.* 到岸价 / 到岸价格   *FOB vs. CIF*

The former is FOB (Free on Board) and the latter is CIF (Cost, Insurance and Freight). Obviously, FOB should be lower than CIF. The following are some related terms:
出厂价格 price does not include shipping (the buyer arranges shipment)
入库价格 price includes shipping and insurance (the product is delivered by the seller to the door of the buyer)

回扣   *kickbacks*

Though illegal, giving kickbacks is a very common business practice. In order to sell their products, many companies offer kickbacks to the purchasers or the decision makers in a transaction to influence their purchasing decisions. Sometimes, the kickback may be as high as 20% of the sale.

佣金   *commission*

In a broad sense, this can refer to all kinds of compensation and commission. In a narrow sense, it only refers to non-employment compensation or commission. For example, if I refer a company to a car dealer, the car dealer will give me a referral bonus or a certain amount of commission from the sale of the car.

2. Formal Expressions

可　　*may*

In written style, 可 is the same as 可以. By contrast, in conversational style, 可 is often used to convey the totally different meaning of emphasis, e.g. 他可聪明了.
　　【课文】美国杜尔公司研制了一种可广泛用于各种电子设备的微型变压器,……
　　【课文】我们还可根据客户的特殊需要设计生产各类专用变压器。
　　【补充】为了保护环境，我们应大力发展可再生能源。

系/为　　*be*

These two formal linking verbs do not have a negative form.
　　【课文】主要设备系由德国引进，……
　　【课文】本厂原为中新合资泰达电器公司的下属厂，……
　　【课文】第一年的费用为两千五百万美元。(L4)

居……之首　　*ranks first; occupies the top position*
　　【课文】所占份额居国内厂家之首，……
　　【补充】美国通用汽车公司的产量现居世界之首。

3. Colloquial Expressions

也＋*negative word*

也 does not have substantial meaning, but makes the tone softer.
　　【课文】我们甘肃这个地方也没有什么好东西，……
　　【补充】他走了一年多了，也不知道现在在什么地方。
　　【补充】″我还想去别的城市看看。″ ″我看你也不用去了。我们杭州是天下最美的地方。″

倒是　　*yet; on the contrary*
A very frequently used adverb that has a few different meanings: it may show contrast, concession, or impatience.

【课文】不过酒泉的酒倒是很有名。(contrast)
【课文】我担心的倒是像可口可乐和百事可乐这样的公司。(contrast) (L4)
【补充】东西倒是不错，不过价钱贵了一点儿。(concession)
【补充】"他说咱们可以把产品卖到美国去。" "我看这倒是一个好办法。"(concession)
【补充】事情到底怎么样了？你倒是快说啊！(impatience)

叫真儿　　*unnecessarily serious*

Also written as 较真儿, it means unnecessarily serious, literal-minded, or intransigent.
【课文】你这个小伙子还挺叫真儿……
【补充】你别太较真儿了，有些事情说不清楚。

4. OTHER PATTERNS AND WORD COLLOCATIONS

（被）授予……称号　　*bestow the title of…(on someone)*
【课文】刘建民厂长也被授予"有突出贡献的农民企业家"的称号。
【补充】东方变压器厂被市政府授予"环境保护先进企业"称号。

满足……的需要　　*meet the needs of…*
【课文】除满足我国西部地区的需要外……
【补充】日本的自然资源根本无法满足其工业发展的需要。

欢迎……不远万里来到……　　*welcome somebody from afar*
【课文】欢迎二位不远万里来到我们这儿考察
【补充】欢迎高先生不远万里来到我公司访问。

非常感谢你们的盛情V　　*thank you very much for your great kindness in…*
The word after 盛情 must be a disyllabic verb.
【课文】非常感谢你们的盛情安排。
【补充】非常感谢你们的盛情款待。

接受……培训　　*receive training in…*
【课文】我们的骨干技术人员都曾经去新加坡接受过现代管理培训
【补充】他在美国接受过电脑技术培训。

请……赏光   *ask somebody to come to a banquet, a party, etc.*

赏光   literally means "grant your brightness." The level of politeness and formality is equivalent to "may we have the pleasure of your company" in English. This is used only in an invitation. Do not use it when accepting an invitation.

【课文】请务必赏光啊。

【补充】 "我已经在王府饭店安排好了一桌酒席，请二位赏光。" "谢谢，我们一定去。" 〔You cannot say 我们一定赏光.〕

5. Important Idiomatic Phrases/Proverbs

物美价廉   *high quality and low price*

This phrase often appears in advertisements.

【课文】本厂的宗旨是物美价廉，用户至上。

【补充】那家商店的商品由于物美价廉很受消费者的欢迎。

恕我直言   *pardon me for speaking frankly*

See **General Notes on Business Communication VI.**

微乎其微   *extremely tiny and small*

Often used as a predicate.

【课文】成交的可能性微乎其微。

【补充】听说有三百多人来应聘，看来我成功的机会微乎其微。

Class Discussion
课堂讨论

1. 这两个工厂各有什么长处和不足？
2. 除了课文中提到的内容以外，还应该了解这两个工厂的哪些情况？
3. 你觉得应该选哪个工厂做合作伙伴？请详细说明理由。
4. 应该对选定的工厂提出哪些进一步的要求和条件？
5. 从课文中可以看到中国商业文化的哪些特点？

Exercises
练习

 PART ONE: FAST ORAL TRANSLATION
第一部分：快速口译

Refer to Lesson 1 for instructions for this exercise.

   A. From Chinese into English
   一位中国经理向外商介绍自己的工厂。

   B. From English into Chinese
   An American manager is talking with the director of a Chinese factory.

PART TWO: ROLE-PLAY (NEGOTIATING WITH DIRECTOR LONG)
第二部分：角色表演（与龙厂长谈判）

Student A acts as Director Long, and student B acts as a consultant from Golden Bridge. They are discussing the fee and other conditions that need to be met in order to work together.
一个同学扮演龙厂长，另一个同学扮演金桥公司的代表，在姑苏饭店讨论加工价格和条件。

PART THREE: REPHRASING SENTENCES
第三部分：改写句子

Refer to Lesson 1 for instructions for this exercise.

   1. 欢迎你们从那么远的地方到我们这个地方来谈生意。
   2. 我明天在巨龙饭店请你们吃饭，你们一定要去啊！
   3. 我们公司的产品质量在中国是最高的。
   4. 我们公司每年生产600万台洗衣机。
   5. 因为我们的洗衣机质量高，价钱又便宜，所以不但在中国国内卖得很好，而其已经卖到很多亚洲和欧洲国家去了。

PART FOUR: COMPOSITION
第四部分：写作

Write an email or fax to one of the two factories to suggest further requirements and conditions.

LESSON 4: CREATING AN ADVERTISING AND PROMOTION PLAN
第四课：广告策划

Background and Business Tasks
背景和任务

美国布蓝克公司希望在中国推销该公司生产的"蓝色风暴"健身减肥饮料，委托金桥公司了解中国市场的广告现状，找到最有效的宣传方式。**为此**，金桥公司找到了一家北京广告公司。

Part One: At the General Manager's Office of Ever-Victorious Advertising Company in Beijing
第一部分：在北京百胜广告公司总经理办公室

许志一：　欢迎二位光临，我已经看了你们送来的传真，非常希望能够<u>真诚</u>合作，为蓝色风暴在中国**打开一片天地。**

艾琳：　布蓝克公司是一家非常有实力的饮料公司，他们想了解在中国市场上，哪些形式的广告效果比较好。

许志一：　我想这个问题不难回答，外商在中国作广告，一般都比较重视电视、大型广告牌以及报纸和杂志。

韩森：　您**能否**分别谈谈这些形式的利弊？

许志一：　电视广告无疑是最强有力的广告形式，我想在你们美国也是这样吧？你要知道，当电视播出黄金时段的电视剧的时候，中国观众的<u>收视率</u>有时会**高达**百分之六十以上，大街上的行人都会变得非常少。可是，这时插播的广告，费用高得惊人。而且，影视<u>代理</u>公司通常要求你在电视剧拍摄的时候就**投入一部分资金，**如果这个电视剧拍得不理想，或者没有**通过广播电视局的**<u>审查</u>。要是真发生了这样的事情，那你的钱就**白扔了。**你知道，在中国不像你们美国那么自由，所有的电视剧都必须送到北京来审<u>查</u>。

艾琳：　那路边的广告牌效果如何？我们在大街上看到了许多广告牌，有些还是电动的。

许志一：　我觉得广告牌投入不多，效果不错，关键是看你的广告设计是不是能吸引人。不过我要告诉你，北京和其他一些大城市正在讨论，可能会禁止交通要道边上的电动广告和特别<u>性</u>感的广告，因为据研究，这些广告可能会造成司机分心，**引发交通事故。**

韩森：　有这么严重吗？在公共汽车的车身上作广告是不是也有问题？

许志一：　有的城市**明文规定**不许在汽车车身上作广告，但是有的城市就没有问题。至于报纸和杂志上的广告，最有影响力的是晚报，比如上海的《新民晚报》，北京的《北京晚报》，广州的《羊城晚报》，天津的《今晚报》等。读者都有几百万，甚至**上千万。**但是，不像中央电视台覆盖全国，晚报都是地方的，所以作广告要分别和各个晚报谈判，比较麻烦。

韩森：　现在中国市场上有没有比较畅销的健身饮料，他们的广告作得怎么样？

许志一： 前两年有几种面向孩子和老人的特需产品，后来很快就<u>走下坡路</u>了。所以现在真是机会难得。我担心的倒是像可口可乐和百事可乐这样的公司，如果他们推出健身饮料，别人就很难竞争了，你们一定知道这两种可乐一直是中国人最熟悉的美国品牌。

艾琳： 如果您<u>接手</u>蓝色风暴的广告，您的策划方案的中心会是什么呢？

许志一： 这个……我其实现在不应该说，不过为了表示诚意，就谈一谈**大概**吧。我会作<u>立体化</u>的<u>全方位</u>宣传，让蓝色风暴在很短的时间内成为**<u>家喻户晓</u>**的品牌。

韩森： 什么叫立体化？什么叫全方位？

许志一： **<u>说白了</u>**，就是各种方法一齐上，电视、报纸、广告牌都要作，而且还要有别的特殊方法。

艾琳： 你说的特殊方法是不是<u>赞助</u>一支体育代表队？

许志一： **英雄所见略同**。我想最好是赞助中国<u>体操</u>队。虽然爱看足球的观众可能更多，但是体操是力与美的结合，而且中国体操的成绩比足球好得多。还有呢，我会找一些有名的医学和<u>营养学</u>的专家在报纸上写文章，**肯定蓝色风暴的作用。**

韩森： 他们肯写这样的文章吗？

许志一： 有句中国的俗话你可能还没学过，**"有钱能使鬼<u>推磨</u>"**。除了这些，我还有一些更重要的<u>点子</u>，不过今天我就不能说了。

艾琳： 你觉得做这样的广告，<u>预算</u>大概需要多少。

许志一： 头两个月至少要投进人民币**一点五个亿。**

韩森： 这么多！

许志一： 这可不算多，**谁不知道**健身饮料是暴利产品，成本也就是售价的十分之一。你想想，中国有十三亿人，每人买一瓶饮料，你的广告成本就足够了。不过，我说的预算只是正常的广告，如果你要把外国的名人请来，像<u>老虎伍兹</u>这样的，效果会更好，但是那得额外<u>加钱</u>。中国自己的明星也不是给**俩钱儿**就能<u>打发</u>的。

艾琳： 谢谢您许先生，我会向布蓝克推荐您作他们的广告代理人的，请您尽快准备广告策划书吧。

Part Two: A Promotion Plan
第二部分：广告策划书

产品名称：蓝色风暴健身饮料
生产公司：美国布蓝克股份有限公司
中国大陆地区广告代理人：百胜国际广告公司
广告宣传口号：蓝色风暴，<u>席卷</u>全球
广告<u>文案</u>诉求：蓝色风暴是力与美的完美结合，要想保持健美的体型和<u>充沛</u>的精力，不要喝<u>苏打水</u>，而要喝蓝色风暴。

媒体计划：

第一，在中央电视台体育频道的黄金时段体育新闻前播放30秒钟的广告片。广告片分A、B两个<u>版本</u>，<u>隔日交替</u>播放，持续两个月。A片**拟**请美国高尔夫球<u>大师</u>老虎伍兹为主角，背景为美国纽约、洛杉矶、法国巴黎等大城市，B片拟请中国体操队的男女全能冠军作主角。（广告片设计另文说明）

第二，在北京、上海、广州主要街道，<u>京津高速公路、京石高速公路、沪宁高速公路</u>租用大型广告牌350座。租期一年。

第三，在《北京晚报》、《新民晚报》、《羊城晚报》、《今晚报》等30个主要大城市的晚报的体育版刊登半页广告。持续两个月。

第四，赞助中国国家体操队（三年，每年人民币一千万），**要举行高调正式仪式**，请美国公司总经理亲自出席，邀请各主要媒体参加仪式。

第五，邀请中国知名大学的营养学教授撰写文章，在主要媒体上发表。内容主要是强调苏打水对健康不利，蓝色风暴是科学的健身饮料。

第六，当第一批蓝色风暴在市场上露面的时候，采用有奖销售的形式。奖品为各种档次的健身器材和名牌运动服装。

广告预算：第一年的费用为两千五百万美元。

Vocabulary List

策划	策劃	cèhuà	plan
布蓝克	布藍克	*Bùlánkè*	*Brank, name of a company*
蓝色风暴	藍色風暴	*Lánsè Fēngbào*	*Blue Storm, name of a product*
减肥	減肥	jiǎnféi	slimming
饮料	飲料	yǐnliào	beverage
百胜	百勝	*Bǎishèng*	*Ever-Victorious, name of a company*
光临	光臨	guānglín	"grace with your presence"; be present
真诚	真誠	zhēnchéng	earnest
利弊		lìbì	advantage and disadvantage
收视率	收視率	shōushìlù	viewership rate
插		chā	insert
代理		dàilǐ	agent
审查	審查	shěnchá	examine for approval
性感		xìnggǎn	sexy
明文规定	明文規定	míngwénguīdìng	stipulate in explicit terms
覆盖	覆蓋	fùgài	cover
特需		tèxū	special need
走下坡路		zǒu xiàpōlù	decline
接手		jiēshǒu	take over; handle
立体化	立體化	lìtǐhuà	multidimensional
全方位		quánfāngwèi	all aspects
家喻户晓	家喻戶曉	jiāyùhùxiǎo	well known to all
说白了	說白了	shuōbáile	simply put
赞助	贊助	zànzhù	sponsor
体操	體操	tǐcāo	gymnastics
营养学	營養學	yíngyǎngxué	nutritional science
推磨		tuīmò	turn a millstone
点子	點子	diǎnzi	(smart) idea
预算	預算	yùsuàn	budget
暴利		bàolì	huge profit
老虎伍兹		Lǎohǔ Wǔzī	Tiger Woods

额外	額外	éwài	extra
打发	打發	dǎfa	send on errands
席卷	席捲	xíjuǎn	sweep across; engulf
文案诉求	文案訴求	wén'àn sùqiú	central theme/goal (of a text)
充沛		chōngpèi	plentiful
苏打水	蘇打水	sūdǎshuǐ	soft drinks
版本		bǎnběn	version; edition
隔日		gérì	every other day
交替		jiāotì	in alternation
拟	擬	nǐ	suggest
大师	大師	dàshī	great master
京津		Jīngjīn	Beijing to Tianjin
京石		Jīngshí	Beijing to Shijiazhuang
沪宁	滬寧	Hùníng	Shanghai to Nanjing
			（沪＝上海； 宁＝南京）
高调	高調	gāodiào	high-pitch; high-profile
仪式	儀式	yíshì	ceremony

Notes and Explanations

1. BUSINESS AND OTHER PROFESSIONAL TERMS

高达   *as high as*

Parallel terms: 长达，多达.
Very frequently used in economic reports.

【课文】中国观众的收视率有时会高达百分之六十以上。
【补充】去年中国电子产品出口的增长高达百分之三十。

上 #   *up to, as many as*

The number must be a whole counting unit （百，千，万） of at least a hundred. You cannot say 上十 or 上二百万.

【课文】读者都有几百万，甚至上千万。
【补充】北京有上百家五星级饭店。

个亿

The measure word 个 between the number before it and the 亿 (a hundred million) after it seems unnecessary. However, many professional businesspeople use it in conversation to highlight the large sum.

【课文】第一年至少要投进人民币一点五个亿。
【补充】我们投资了三个亿，但是两年的回报却还不到一百万。(We invested 300 million but the return over the past two years was less than a million.)

2. FORMAL EXPRESSIONS

拟   *to plan*

A formal expression used mainly in writing.

【课文】A片拟请美国高尔夫球大师老虎伍兹为主角，......
【补充】为了尽快完成新产品的研制，我们拟从建设银行贷款五千万元。
(In order to complete the R&D of the new product, we plan to take out a loan of 50 million RMB from the Construction Bank.)

为此   *for this reason; therefore*

An adverb functioning as a connector in formal writing or speech.

【课文】为此，金桥公司找到了一家北京广告公司。

【补充】我们在做计划时忽略了一个非常重要的问题，公司为此付出了极大的代价。

能否   *can or cannot*

＝能不能 The verb following it must be of two characters or duplicated.

【课文】您能否谈谈这些形式的利弊？

【补充】现在还不知道双方能否达成协议。

至于   *as for*

Used to transition to a sub-topic.

【课文】至于报纸和杂志上的广告，最有影响力的是晚报

【补充】今天我们只讨论价格问题，至于交货时间，我们可以在明天继续讨论。

3. COLLOQUIAL EXPRESSIONS

白 + *V*

Mainly used in conversation, this strange adverb has two contradictory meanings:

1) efforts made or money spent did not yield a result
2) something was obtained without making an effort or spending money

【课文】那你的钱就白扔了。(You are just throwing away money.)

【补充】我们白等了他两个小时。(We waited for him for two hours in vain.)

【补充】工作人员个个白吃白拿，结果饭店很快就倒闭了。(All the employees ate and stole from the restaurant without working. As a result, it went bankrupt very quickly.)

说白了   *simply put*

【课文】说白了，就是各种方法一齐上

【补充】所谓"广告策划书"，说白了，就是用什么样的广告来推销产品的计划。

谁不知道　　*everyone knows*

Same as 大家都知道。 Used to lead off a rhetorical question, giving it an attention-grabbing twist as compared with a plain statement.

【课文】谁不知道健身饮料是暴利产品，……

【补充】我可不想去你们那儿工作，谁不知道你们公司很快就要关门了！

俩钱儿　　*a couple bucks*

A very colloquial expression.

【课文】中国自己的明星也不是给俩钱儿就能打发的。 (Even China's own stars will demand a considerable amount of money to do your bidding.)

【补充】商店里的空调已经坏了三年了，你也不花俩钱儿修修，这会影响你的生意的。

4. OTHER PATTERNS AND WORD COLLOCATIONS

打开……天地　　*open up a new prospect*

The object can also be 市场, 局面 (here its meaning is the same as 天地), etc.

【课文】为蓝色风暴在中国打开一片天地。

【补充】我们要让自己的产品尽快在中国打开市场。

【补充】令人高兴的是本公司已经在短期内打开了局面。

投入……资金　　*invest/expend funds*

The object can also be 成本 (cost), 心血 (painstaking efforts), etc.

【课文】公司通常要求在电视剧拍摄的时候就投入一部分资金。

【补充】我们为此投入了相当大的成本。

【补充】培养大型企业的管理人才是需要投入一定的心血的。

通过……审查 / 检验　　*pass the examination or inspection*

【课文】（广告）通过广播电视局的审查。

【课文】所有的电视剧都必须送到北京来审查。

【补充】这种新的饮料已经通过了卫生部门的检验。

引发……事故/问题　　*cause an accident/problem*

【课文】这些广告可能会引发交通事故。

【补充】产品质量不合格，将引发很多问题。

明文规定　　*explicitly stipulate; explicit regulation*

Used either as a verb or a noun.

【课文】有的城市明文规定不许在汽车车身上作广告，……

【补充】合资公司的外资最多只能占百分之四十九，这有明文规定。
(There is an explicit regulation that foreign investment in a joint venture cannot exceed 49%.)

大概　　*probably; outline*

In most cases, 大概 is an adverb meaning "probably." However, it can also be used as a noun meaning "a brief outline." Used in this sense, it is synonymous with 概要.

【课文】不过为了表示诚意，就谈一谈大概吧。

【补充】他谈的只是大概，你要了解详情必须做进一步的调查。(What he talked about was just general information. If you want to know the details, you must investigate it further.)

肯定……作用　　*affirm the effectiveness/function of*

The object can also be 成绩 (merit or achievement).

【课文】在报纸上写文章，肯定蓝色风暴的作用。

【补充】董事会肯定了总经理的成绩，但是也指出了管理上的一些问题。

举行……仪式　　*hold a ceremony*

【课文】要举行高调正式仪式。

【补充】工厂将在近期举行开工仪式。

5. IMPORTANT IDIOMATIC PHRASES/PROVERBS

家喻户晓　　*every family and every household knows; widely known to all*

Used to describe the popularity of something.

【课文】让蓝色风暴在很短时间内成为家喻户晓的品牌。

【补充】这位美国明星在中国可以说家喻户晓，请他来做广告一定成功。

英雄所见略同

See **General Note on Business Communication II.**

有钱能使鬼推磨
See **General Note on Business Communication II.**

Class Discussion
课堂讨论

A. Answer questions directly related to the lesson.
1. 你觉得哪种形式广告的效果最好？为什么？
2. 说说你见到的最成功/最新奇的广告。
3. 说说你最喜欢的广告词。
4. 你买什么商品是因为是广告的作用？
5. 中国广告的主要对象是哪类人？美国呢？
6. 美国可口可乐/百事可乐公司为什么会成功？
7. 你觉得百胜的广告策划方案是否可行？
8. 你觉得广告的开支预算是否合理？可口可乐、百事可乐及日本公司的广告占成本的多少？
9. 你对这个方案有什么补充建议？
10. 我们怎样来推销"蓝色风暴"？说说你个人的广告思路。

B. Watch Chinese advertisements and then discuss. Please go to the *Close the Deal* companion website at www.webtech.cheng-tsui.com for information about, and links to, Chinese ads.
1. 说说你对中国电视广告的印象。
2. 这些广告介绍的是什么？
3. 你对哪个广告的印象最深？它的特点是什么？
4. 那个广告的意图和思路是什么？
5. 中国市场上已经有不少饮料广告，你的"蓝色风暴"将怎样胜过这些竞争对手？

Exercises
练习

PART ONE: FAST ORAL TRANSLATION
第一部分：快速口译

Refer to Lesson 1 for instructions for this exercise.

A. From Chinese into English
一位中国广告公司经理向美国客户作广告建议。

B. From English into Chinese

The manager of an American company is talking with the manager of the advertising department of China Central Television.

PART TWO: ROLE-PLAY (A PLAN TO ADVERTISE CHINESE CARS IN THE U.S.)
第二部分：角色表演（在美国为中国汽车做广告）

Tianjin FAW Xiali Automobile Ltd. of China hopes to sell their cars in the United States. Student A acts as the general manager of the company and consults with a project manager of Golden Bridge (acted by Student B) to gain a general understanding of automobile advertising in the United States. 中国天津夏利汽车公司想把他们的汽车卖到美国来，向金桥公司咨询在美国做汽车广告的基本情况。一个同学扮演夏利公司的经理，另一个同学扮演金桥公司的经理。

PART THREE: REPHRASING SENTENCES
第三部分：改写句子

Refer to Lesson 1 for instructions for this exercise.

1. 要让大家都熟悉这个产品的名字。
2. 这是专门为某类人生产的东西。
3. 我们的产品卖得非常快。
4. 先要计算一下可能要花的钱。
5. 生产产品所需要的全部费用。
6. 这是企业筹划和管理以外的问题。
7. 去年我们成交业务突破了三亿元人民币。

PART FOUR: COMPOSITION
第四部分：写作

The Stanley 150 is a two-seat, single-engine airplane for private use. It is highly automatic and very easy to fly. The manufacturer, Stanley Inc., wants to sell it on the Chinese market. Please write an advertising/promotion plan in Chinese.

The plan should include:

•   A Chinese name for this airplane.

•   A slogan that is easy to remember and will catch on quickly.

•   An advertising budget for the first six months.

LESSON 5: INVESTING IN REAL ESTATE
第五课：投资房地产

Background and Business Tasks
背景和任务

New residential buildings.

2008年国际奥林匹克运动会将在北京举行，这对北京的房地产将会有什么样的影响呢？美国的<u>克拉克</u>投资公司希望金桥公司帮助调查北京房地产的<u>前景</u>，对进入中国房地产市场作出**评估。**

Part One: At the New Era Real Estate Company in Beijing
第一部分：在北京新世纪房地产总公司

汪涛：　欢迎二位光临。我是新世纪的经纪人。非常高兴能为您服务。你们是不是准备在北京买房子？

艾琳：　我对上海和苏州的房地产比较了解，听说在北京外国人买房有很多限制，是吗？

汪涛：　前几年是这样，最近已经变得比较宽松了，毕竟中国加入了世界贸易组织。**中国人也好，外国人也好，都要平等对待。**

韩森：　现在的房价怎么样。

汪涛：　涨得很快，你们要是想买，最好快点儿。和去年同期比，现在的房价涨了百分之十五左右。有人说，到奥运前夕，房价至少是现在的六倍。

艾琳：　那奥运以后价格大概会回落吧？

汪涛：　这就很难说了。汉城奥运会以后，当地的房价仍然上涨，只是到金融危机的时候才跌了一些。

韩森：　那一套两居室的住房大概需要多少钱呢？

汪涛：　这个很难说，要看地点和房子的质量。在北京的三环以内，至少6000元一平米，但是五环附近的房子你3000多元就可以买到。

韩森：　我是美国来的，不太熟悉公制，两居室的房子大概有多少平方英尺？

汪涛：　英尺我**说不上来**，现在小的要80平米左右，大的有120平米左右，双厅双厕。你们老外一般都比较喜欢这样的房子。

艾琳：　那也就是说四十万左右可以买一套不错的公寓。

汪涛：　请注意，这是说现在，再过几个月你可能就买不到了。

韩森：　我在报纸上看到的广告好像比你说的便宜得多。

汪涛：　你说的肯定是毛坯房，也就是没有装修的，你买了还要请人装修，加在一起价格会更高。小伙子，放心，我是不会骗你的。你们是不是准备结婚啊？

韩森：　不是，不是……

汪涛：　小伙子别不好意思。我建议你们在金湖小区买一套公寓，那儿离市中心远点儿，可是风景好，有山有湖。**反正你们有车，远点儿不怕**，对吧？

艾琳：　我们的办公室可能要明年才搬到北京来，我现在买了房可以先出租一段时间吗？

汪涛：　可以啊，不过出租最好是在市中心或者是在<u>中关村</u>高新技术开发区附近才能租出好价钱，每个月四五千都可能。你们要是过<u>一年半载</u>才来，最好买**楼花**。

韩森：　什么叫楼花？

汪涛：　就是在<u>图纸</u>上买，买那些还没盖好的房。也叫**期房**。这有好处，一是价格比<u>现房</u>低一些，二是你可以让建筑开发商改变房间的结构，按照你自己的喜好装修。

艾琳：　我听说有的开发商给你看的图纸很漂亮，盖好一看，房子的质量很差。

汪涛：　的确有这种情况，关键看开发商的信誉，有的甚至收了你的钱，楼盖了一半就跑了！我给你介绍的肯定没错。

韩森：　外国人买房可以**贷款**吗？

汪涛：　房屋贷款叫**按揭**，南方已经做了几年了，北京**也就是**这两年开始试行，一般需要你的老板给你担保，至于外国人能不能借，我还真不清楚。不过，你们老外**有的是**钱，还用**分期付款**吗？

韩森：　在美国没有人会一次<u>付清</u>买房的钱。

艾琳：　我们买了房以后可以再卖给别人吗？卖的时候有没有价格限制？

汪涛：　当然可以卖。中国已经是市场经济了，什么都可以卖。只要有人愿意买，你**赚它个一百万**也没人管。不过当然啦，卖房是要交税的。现在北京人不太喜欢买<u>二手房</u>，而上海一般收入的人喜欢买二手房，这样可以省一些装修费。

韩森：　我能不能买一块地，盖我自己想盖的房子呢？

汪涛：　我有个意大利的客户，就是自己在北京郊区盖的房子。地道的<u>米兰</u>风格，**酷得要命**。不过您得知道，在中国土地都是国家的，不能买，只能买土地的使用权，而且最多只能买五十年的使用权。

艾琳：　其实我们对大型的商业建筑更感兴趣。

汪涛：　看不出来小姐这么年轻就已经是**大腕儿**了。佩服，佩服。现在还真有一个**上好**的机会。北京郊区<u>密云</u>的云海饭店正准备<u>拍卖</u>呢。

韩森：　密云在什么地方？

汪涛：　在北京的东北，开车走高速四十多分钟就到了。

艾琳：　这个饭店是什么规模？

汪涛：　有三百多个客房，三个餐厅，是密云最现代化的旅馆之一。它建在密云水库的边上，风景相当好，是北京旅游<u>度假</u>的黄金地段。一到周末外国人可多了！

韩森：　那它为什么要被拍卖呢？

汪涛：　这里边有很多**内幕**。最开始的时候这是一家军队盖的宾馆，后来中央指示军队不能经商，就转给地方经营。饭店的总经理兼董事长是一个**手眼通天**的人物，一上任就**大张旗鼓**搞装修，还做了好多广告，可没多久被查出有经济问题，**这小子**就带着公司的钱跑到南美洲躲起来了。饭店重新装修的时候跟银行借了很多钱，现在没有办法还，所以就被银行**没收**了。银行不能自己经营饭店，只好用拍卖的办法想把饭店处理掉。

艾琳：　你知道不知道拍卖的底价是多少，准备竞标的多不多？

汪涛：　我听说银行的底价是两千万，真值啊！这个旅馆的价值少说也得五千万，**一水**的德国设备，就是北京城里也找不出几个。至于有多少竞争对手现在还不太清楚，你们要是真感兴趣，我可以调查了解一下，不过我不能白忙啊，起码得给我点儿服务费吧？

艾琳：　竞**标**书出来没有？

汪涛：　拍卖的日期、办法，还有饭店的详细介绍都在这儿，八十块钱一本，要吗？

艾琳：　当然要，我们看了以后会尽快告诉您是否需要您帮我们了解竞争对手。

韩森：　这种拍卖在北京多不多？

汪涛：　公开拍卖房产也就是最近这一两年才开始的。

艾琳：　最后的结果一般怎么样，会比底价高出多少？

汪涛：　去年我记得有两次竞标，来的人**寥寥无几**，中标的价格比底价高不出多少，但是今年可就不一样了，四月拍了一个**写字楼**，让一家香港的公司买走了，出价比底价高了不止一倍。这拍卖可是一门学问，您需要的话我也可以**效劳**。

韩森：　汪先生真会做生意。希望有机会合作。

汪涛：　**好说，好说**，今天能跟二位**结识**，也是**有缘**。**这样吧**，这本竞标手册算我白送了，交个朋友。

Part Two: The Yunhai Hotel Auction Manual for Bidders
第二部分：云海饭店拍卖竞标手册

一. 饭店简介

　　云海饭店是一家现代化四星级宾馆，**建于**1985**年**，并于1999年重新装修，现有客房336套，其中包括28个<u>套间</u>和两套总统套房，还设有中、西、日餐厅各一个，大型会议室一个，小型会议室三个，总建筑面积16832平米。饭店采用的建筑材料<u>上乘</u>，结构<u>坚固</u>，据专家测算可抗八级以上<u>地震</u>。室内装修材料大多为日本和美国产品，其中<u>卫生</u>设备采用美国<u>标准</u>产品，空调等电器设备为德国生产。饭店**坐落于著名的密云水库旁**，<u>景色秀丽</u>，附近有大型<u>水上乐园</u>一个，18洞高尔夫球场两个。饭店的<u>拥有</u>者现为中国建设银行。
（饭店的照片和详图**从略**）

二. 竞标资格

　　此次拍卖面向世界各国的公司或个人，必须在拍卖前的50日内向拍卖组织机构出示不低于一亿美元的可支配财产证明。中标者必须在拍卖当天支付相当于中标金额10%的现款，并于30日内**交清全部<u>款项</u>**。

三. 拍卖时间、地点

2002年4月24日上午11时在北京前门饭店会议厅举行。

四. 拍卖<u>细则</u>

　　第一，拍卖的组织人**由中国建设银行委托的北京三甲拍卖公司担任**，主任拍卖师为王云九。
　　第二，拍卖的底价保密。如最高竞拍价低于中国建设银行<u>预设</u>的底价，将<u>另行</u>组织拍卖会。
　　第三，价格以人民币计算。
　　第四，拍卖分书面竞标和公开叫卖两个阶段。所有参加竞标的单位或个人都必须在入场时<u>呈交</u>书面竞标价格，出价最低的两个竞标者将被<u>淘汰</u>，无资格参加第二阶段的竞标。
　　第五，公开叫卖阶段的起价为最高书面竞标价格，叫价的最低<u>升幅</u>为50万元人民币。

五. 关于拍卖<u>程序</u>等技术性问题，可以同三甲公司<u>接洽</u>询问，电话：65057828，65057829。**<u>谢绝</u>**上门咨询。

Vocabulary List

克拉克		*Kèlākè*	*Clark, name of a company*
房地产	房地產	fángdìchǎn	real estate
前景		qiánjǐng	foreground, prospects
汪涛	汪濤	*Wāng Tāo*	*name of a person*
经纪人	經紀人	jīngjìrén	broker
汉城	漢城	Hànchéng	Seoul
金融危机	金融危機	jīnróng wēijī	financial crisis
三环	三環	*Sānhuán*	*The Third Ring Road*
平米		píngmǐ	square meter
五环	五環	*Wǔhuán*	*The Fifth Ring Road*
公制		gōngzhì	metric system
两居室		liǎngjūshì	two-bedroom apartment
平方英尺		píngfāng yīngchǐ	square foot
双厅双厕	雙廳雙廁	shuāngtīng shuāngcè	two living rooms and two bathrooms
公寓		gōngyù	apartment
毛坯房		máopīfáng	building with an unfinished interior
装修		zhuāngxiū	decorate; interior finishing
金湖小区	金湖小區	Jīnhú Xiǎoqū	name of a community
中关村	中關村	*Zhōngguāncūn*	*name of a place*
一年半载	一年半載	yìniánbànzǎi	about a year
楼花	樓花	lóuhuā	house on blueprint (before construction)
图纸	圖紙	túzhǐ	blueprint
期房		qīfáng	house to be built
现房	現房	xiànfáng	house available now
信誉	信譽	xìnyù	fame; reputation
贷款	貸款	dàikuǎn	v. take out or provide a loan; n. loan
按揭		ànjiē	mortgage
分期付款		fēnqī fùkuǎn	pay in installments
付清		fùqīng	pay in full

交税		jiāoshuì	pay tax
二手		èrshǒu	second-hand
米兰	米蘭	Mǐlán	Milan
酷		kù	cool
大腕儿	大腕兒	dàwànr	[cl.] VIP, celebrity
上好		shànghǎo	top-rated
密云	密雲	*Mìyún*	*name of a place*
拍卖	拍賣	pāimài	n./v. auction
度假		dùjià	v./n. vacation
内幕		nèimù	insider information
手眼通天		shǒuyǎntōngtiān	have a close relationship with the authorities
大张旗鼓		dàzhāngqígǔ	on a grand scale; in a big way
小子	小子	xiǎozi	[cl. derogatory] guy, rogue
没收		mòshōu	be confiscated; confiscate
一水		yìshuǐ	[cl.] pure
寥寥无几	寥寥無幾	liáoliáowújǐ	very few; scarce
中标	中標	zhòngbiāo	win the bid
写字楼	寫字樓	xiězìlóu	office building
效劳	效勞	xiàoláo	provide service
结识	結識	jiéshí	make someone's acquaintance
有缘	有緣	yǒuyuán	have an affinity (by fate or good fortune)
套间	套間	tàojiān	suite
上乘		shàngchéng	high quality
坚固	堅固	jiāngù	firm; sturdy
抗		kàng	resist
地震		dìzhèn	earthquake
卫生	衛生	wèishēng	sanitation
美国标准	美國標準	Měiguó Biāozhǔn	American Standard
坐落		zuòluò	be located
景色秀丽	景色秀麗	jǐnsè xiùlì	scenic
水上乐园	水上樂園	shuǐshàng lèyuán	water park
高尔夫	高爾夫	gāo'ěrfū	golf
拥有	擁有	yōngyǒu	possess
从略	從略	cónglüè	omitted

款项	款項	kuǎnxiàng	items of payments
细则	細則	xìzé	detailed rules
预设	預設	yùshè	predetermined
另行		lìngxíng	at some other time
入场	入場	rùchǎng	enter (an auction, game, show, etc.)
呈交		chéngjiāo	submit; turn in
淘汰		táotài	eliminate
升幅		shēngfú	amount of increase
程序		chéngxù	procedure
接洽		jiēqià	contact
谢绝	謝絕	xièjué	decline to accept/admit
上门	上門	shàngmén	visit in person

Notes and Explanations

1. BUSINESS AND OTHER PROFESSIONAL TERMS

评估　　*assessment*
　　【课文】对进入中国房地产市场作出评估。
　　【补充】在决定是否收购一个企业之前，详细的资产评估是非常重要的。

楼花／期房　　*pre-construction real estate*
楼花 is informal while 期房 is formal.
　　【课文】最好买楼花。
　　【课文】（楼花）也叫期房。
　　【补充】最近上海的期房市场价格上扬。（上扬＝上涨）
Related word: 期货 (futures, forward).

贷款　　*loan; take out a loan; provide a loan*
As the English translation shows, this word may mean the loan itself, or it may mean to take out or to provide a loan.
　　【课文】外国人买房可以贷款吗？ (to take out a loan)
　　【补充】中国银行最近向这家饭店贷款八千万。 (to provide a loan)

按揭　　*mortgage*
Originally used in Hong Kong, now it is widely used in the Chinese real estate market. In Cantonese, 按 means to hold a pledge, and 揭 means to take out a loan.
　　【课文】房屋贷款叫按揭。
　　【补充】现在大部分人买房子都会采用按揭的方式来付款。

分期付款　　*pay in installments*
　　【课文】你们老外有的是钱，还用分期付款吗？
　　【补充】中国人购买家用电器很少分期付款。

写字楼　　*office building*
In the past, office buildings were called 办公楼. Since the economic reform, 写字楼, a Hong Kong expression, has become a more popular term for an office building.

【课文】四月拍了一个写字楼。

【补充】因为很多跨国公司在上海开设办事处，上海的写字楼五年内增加了百分之三百。

标　　*bidding*

Many words used in auction/bidding contain this element. For example, 竞标 means to bid, and 中标 means to win the bid.

【课文】竞标资格

【课文】中标者必须在拍卖当天支付相当于中标金额10%的现款，……

Related words:

招标 invite public bidding (on a project)

投标 tender for; bid for

标底＝招标的底价

2. FORMAL EXPRESSIONS

建于……年　　*built in the year...*

The same as 是在……年建成的.

【课文】云海饭店……建于1985年

【补充】这座著名的博物馆建于上个世纪中期。

坐落于 + *place*　　*be located at...*

【课文】坐落于著名的密云水库旁……

【补充】北京大学坐落于北京西郊。

从略　　*be omitted*

The reason for the omission is often to make a presentation simple and not too technical.

【课文】饭店的照片和详图从略。

【补充】我们的结论是，黄金的价格将以每年百分之三的幅度增长。

（推导公式从略）Our conclusion is that the price of gold will increase three percent per year continuously. (The calculation formula is omitted here.)

谢绝　　*close one's doors; decline; refuse*

If followed by an object, the object must be of two or more syllables.

【课文】谢绝上门咨询。

【补充】本公司谢绝媒体采访。

3. COLLOQUIAL EXPRESSIONS

A 也好，B 也好，都……   *whether...or...(no exception)*
> 【课文】中国人也好，外国人也好，都要平等对待。
> 【补充】住宅楼也好，写字楼也好，最近价格都涨了不少。

说不上来   *cannot give a clear answer/definition*
> 【课文】英尺我说不上来，你们老外一般都比较喜欢这样的房子。
> 【补充】现在北京的私家车越来越多，但是具体有多少我说不上来。

反正……不怕   *anyway...don't fear / is not a problem*
> 【课文】反正你们有车，远点儿不怕，对吧？
> 【补充】反正不是你自己掏腰包，贵点儿不怕。

也就是＝只是   *[cl.] just, merely, no more than*

This colloquial usage of 也就是 should be differentiated from its standard meaning of "is also…" When 也就是 is used in the colloquial sense, it means "just, merely, is no more than,"and the stress falls on 就. But when used in the standard way, 也就是 has no special stress.
> 【课文】南方已经做了几年了，北京也就是这两年开始试行。
> 【补充】这种车不贵，也就是两万多块钱。

Compare with 也就是 used in its standard way:
> 期房，也就是在房屋还没有盖好的时候购买的房屋，现在越来越受到人们
> 的欢迎。

有的是   *have plenty of; be plentiful*

This phrase is sometimes followed by an object. If followed by an object, the pattern is A 有的是 B and the phrase means "what A has plenty of is B." If not followed by an object, the phrase can also be written 多的是, which means "be plentiful."
> 【课文】你们老外有的是钱，还用分期付款吗？
> 【补充】想进城打工的农民有的是 / 多的是，每小时五块钱的工作也有人
> 愿意干。

V 它/他个

Used in a bombastic statement to show that one wants to do something without reservation or to one's heart's content.

【课文】只要有人愿意买，你赚它个一百万也没人管。
【补充】写这篇论文太累了，写完以后我得睡它个三天三夜。

Popular Terms Borrowed from Foreign Languages

In recent years, many foreign terms, especially English ones, have become part of spoken Chinese. Their written forms vary, with some in characters and some in foreign letters.
【课文】酷得要命。
【补充】昨天的那个演唱会很 high。

大腕儿   *VIP; big shot*

This is a very informal word. 腕儿＝ important person. 大腕儿＝ very important person. Often refers to people in business, performing arts, or organized crime.
【课文】看不出来小姐这么年轻就已经是大腕儿了。佩服，佩服。
【补充】这个年轻人是IT产业的大腕儿。
A related word is 大款（儿）, which means "one who is very rich."
【补充】来这里吃饭的主要是一些大腕儿和大款儿。

上好   *top-rated; best*

This adjective is mainly used as a modifier.
【课文】现在还真有一个上好的机会。
【补充】老外很少喝绿茶，你把这些上好的龙井送给他们纯粹是浪费。
　　　　（龙井 is one of the best brands of green tea.）

这小子   *this guy/rogue*

A derogatory term for a man. Also 那小子.
【课文】这小子就带着公司的钱跑到南美洲躲起来了。
【补充】那小子只知道赚钱，一点儿商业道德都不讲。

一水   *pure*

Used mainly by Beijingers.
【课文】一水的德国设备，就是北京城里也找不出几个。
【补充】那个城市的出租车相当高级，一水的日本丰田。(Toyota)

好说，好说   *"easy to talk through"*

Describes something that can be easily settled through discussion. Used in answering a request. It is quite positive but does not constitute a full promise.

【课文】好说，好说，今天能跟二位结识，也是有缘。
【补充】"您能帮我了解一些上海的市场行情吗？""好说，好说。"

这样吧　　*how about this*

Used when searching for a resolution (or way out) or when making a concession.
【课文】这样吧，这本竞标手册算我白送了，交个朋友。
【补充】你的钱没带够？这样吧，你先交一半钱，余下的明天交清。

4. OTHER PATTERNS AND WORD COLLOCATIONS

交清全部款项　　*make a full payment (of all money owed)*

交 is also written as 缴.
【课文】于三十日止内交清所有款项。
【补充】如果不能在月底缴清所有款项，你们的饭店将被银行没收。

由......担任　　*(a responsibility or role) assumed by...*

【课文】拍卖的组织人由中国建设银行委托的北京三甲拍卖公司担任
【课文】合资公司的总经理由美方人员担任。

5. IMPORTANT IDIOMATIC PHRASES/PROVERBS

手眼通天　　*have a close relationship with the authorities*

Literally, "hands and eyes connect with Heaven." It is used to describe people who have great connections in the business world as well as in government.
【课文】饭店的董事长兼总经理是个手眼通天的人物。
【补充】这个人手眼通天，如果他能为我们工作就太好了。

大张旗鼓　　*on a grand scale; in a big way*

Literally, "raise all the banners and beat all the drums." Often used as an adverb.
【课文】一上任就大张旗鼓搞装修。
【补充】为了尽快占领中国市场，蓝色风暴正在报纸和电视上大张旗鼓地作宣传。

寥寥无几　　*very few or scarce*

Often used as a predicate or modifier.

【课文】来的人寥寥无几。
【课文】您看，这么多红的数字、红的线条，绿色的寥寥无几。(L6)

Class Discussion
课堂讨论

1. 你觉得现在是不是在北京购买房地产的良好时机？
2. 如果你想在北京买一套公寓，你会选择什么地方？
3. 根据课文提供的信息，在北京买房以后出租是不是有效的投资？
4. 在北京盖房是否可行？
5. 你觉得云海饭店是否值得竞标？还应该了解哪些信息？
6. 你觉得汪涛这个人怎么样？你会请他帮你竞标吗？
7. 书面竞标的价格应该是多少？
8. 你的最高叫价是多少？

Exercises
练习

PART ONE: FAST ORAL TRANSLATION
第一部分：快速口译

Refer to Lesson 1 for instructions for this exercise.

A. From Chinese into English
一位中国房地产经纪人介绍最近中国房地产市场的变化。

B. From English into Chinese
An American real estate buyer is telling a Chinese broker what kind of real estate he is interested in.

PART TWO: ROLE-PLAY (YUNHAI HOTEL AUCTION)
第二部分：角色表演（模拟拍卖会, 云海饭店）

One student acts as the auctioneer and all the other students act as bidders.
一个同学扮演拍卖员，其他同学扮演竞标人。

PART THREE: REPHRASING SENTENCES
第三部分：改写句子

Refer to Lesson 1 for instructions for this exercise.

1. 来参观博览会的人非常少。
2. 不少中国人不太习惯借钱来买房子，然后每个月还一部分钱。
3. 但是房子那么贵，不大可能一次把所有的钱全都交了。
4. 关于广告管理，我知道一些大概的规定，小的、具体的内容我现在说不清楚。
5. 想租房子的人非常多，你不用担心没有人租你的房子。
6. 这家饭店盖在上海的西边，周围有很多好玩儿的地方。

PART FOUR: COMPOSITION
第四部分：写作

The May Flower Hotel in downtown Boston will be auctioned off and many Chinese businesspeople are very interested in it. Please write a brief introduction to the hotel in Chinese. (This hotel is fictional, so just use your imagination to design the introduction.)

LESSON 6: INVESTING IN STOCKS
第六课：股市投资

Background and Business Tasks
背景和任务

美国<u>雅特</u>公司有着几十年的历史，该公司**以生产乳制品起家**，并逐步投资食品工业的其他方面以及<u>餐饮业</u>，具有雄厚的实力。但是近几年来，它在美国和南美的投资回报不是非常理想。看到中国经济的迅速发展，雅特非常希望能在中国投资。他们想通过金桥公司了解投资的<u>途径</u>和风险。艾琳和韩森先后<u>走访</u>了上海证券交易所和沪星国际投资<u>顾问</u>公司。

Part One: A Brief Introduction to the Shanghai Stock Exchange (SSE)
第一部分：上海证券交易所简介

上海证券交易所（上证）成立于1990年26日，同年12月19日正式开张营业。它的性质是非**盈**利性的**事业**法人。会员大会是交易所最高权力机构，**理事会**为日常事务决策机构，总经理为法人代表，主持交易所日常工作。上海证券交易所主要业务是**提供交易场所**、接受**上市申请**、**监督**证券交易等。上证所上市的证券包括各级政府**发行的政府债券**、各地企业公开发行的企业债券、股份有限公司公开发行的人民币股票（A股）以及人民币特种股票（B股）。上海证券交易所1998年**迁至**浦东新址，市场交易**采用电子竞价交易方式**，它是世界上具有一流设施的交易所之一。

Part Two: At the SSE
第二部分：在上海证券交易所

艾琳：　您好！请问顾**理事长**在吗？

秘书：　顾理事长正在电话上，他马上就好。

顾：　（挂上电话）二位请进。让你们**久等**了，真不好意思。

艾琳：　您太客气了。理事长**日理万机**，还专门接受我们的访谈，真是非常感谢。我叫艾琳。

顾：　**久仰久仰**！

韩森：　您好，顾理事长，敝人韩森，来自哈佛大学。

顾：　韩先生**年轻有为**，中文也说得如此流利，难得难得！

艾琳：　我们一直非常**关注中国的股市情况**，但亲身来到中国的交易所还是头一次。

顾：　好啊，既然你们来了，我想与其在办公室**纸上谈兵**，不如到实地看看，二位**意下如何**？

艾琳、
韩森：　好啊！

（三人来到股票交易所大厅）

韩森：　这交易所的大厅简直可以和纽约华尔街**媲美**了！

顾： 是啊，这楼是新建的，从外观到功能都不错。一层有<u>显示</u>股票指数的大屏幕，二楼三楼还有一些小的工作室，供一些**大户**在电脑上作分析研究。你们看，今天<u>开**盘**</u>后的数字已经显示出来了。

韩森： 看来今天股票的情况很不妙。

顾： 这两天有很多利好消息，股市应当**上扬**，韩先生**何出此言**？

韩森： 您看，这么多红的数字、红的线条，绿色的寥寥无几。

顾： **难怪**。看来你们的确需要来中国的交易所走走。在中国，包括香港等地在内，都是用红色标志股市上升，而用绿色或者黑色表示股市下降，正好跟你们美国相反。如果你看到报纸上说"红透半边天"，那就等于是说股市的行情再好不过了。

韩森： 那我差点儿误会了。您刚才说的"利好消息"一定是指公司盈利的好消息，那不好的消息是不是叫"利坏消息"。

顾： 和"利好消息"相反的叫"利空消息"。

韩森： 对了，中国人说的"熊市"和"牛市"，是不是也跟美国的相反？

顾： 这倒不是。"牛市"和"熊市"的说法实际上是从美国来的。你们想不想去一个小的股票营业所，看看普通**股民**是怎么**炒股**的？

韩森、
艾琳： 好！

（营业所中股民对话）：

股民A： 你看，很多人在买这种股票，咱们得赶快<u>跟进</u>！

股民B： 小心点儿，你在这种时候买进，是会被**套牢**的。

艾琳： 他们在说"套牢"，"套牢"是什么意思？

顾： "套牢"就是当你预计证券价格会大涨时，你买了进来，但没想到买进后价格却反而很快跌下去了，使你买的证券难以<u>脱手</u>。你要是非脱手不可，就只好亏了本钱把它卖了。

韩森： 我想我父母在美国也被套牢了。

股民C： 昨天我**算**抢到帽子了，可是今天全赔了。

股民D： 没关系，先别<u>清仓</u>，也许明天会有<u>转机</u>。

韩森： 为什么他们要抢买"帽子"股票呢？是不是中国人现在比以前喜欢戴帽子了？

顾： 这个帽子不是真的帽子。"抢帽子"也是股市上人们常常说的一个词。它的意思是，当天先低价买进股票，然后再高价卖出相同种类、相同数量的股票；或者当天先卖出股票，然后再低价买进相同种类、相同数量的股票，来赚取其中的差价。"抢帽子"是一种<u>投机</u>性特别大的交易行为，跟<u>赌博</u>差不多，需要运气，当然也需要经验和智慧。

韩森：　那么，"清仓"是不是把手里的某种股票都抛出去？

　顾：　对，就是这个意思。

韩森：　中国为什么要把股票分成AB两种呢？

　顾：　中国政府一方面希望外国投资人投资中国，但是另一方面又不希望外国的投机者在中国的市场上操盘，也就是控制股票的走向。所以A股外国人是不能买的。B股是我国一些股份公司发行的，它是用人民币标明股票面值，专门为境外投资者提供用外汇折合成人民币进行买卖的特种股票。这种股票向外国公民或投资机构发行，现在也开始向持有外币的本国公民和投资机构发行。也正因为如此，中国股市的行情常常和欧美不一样，甚至和香港也不一样。2000年全球的股市都有不同程度的下跌，可是中国股市却涨了将近50%。

艾琳：　该是吃午饭的时候了，咱们一起去外面吃个简单的工作午餐吧。我来作东。

　顾：　你们是客人，哪儿有客人作东的道理？每天中午，我们交易所给职工提供免费盒饭，咱们回交易所吃吧，顺便也可以跟我们的职工聊聊。

韩森：　我觉得这主意不错。艾琳，你说呢？

艾琳：　好啊，**恭敬不如从命**。

Part Three: At Shanghai Star International Investment Advisory Group
第三部分：在沪星国际投资顾问公司

艾琳：　您好，马先生，我们终于见面了。

　马：　真是不好意思。其实你们很早就跟我约好了，好像是两个星期前吧？可是那天上级临时通知我们开会，我就身不由己了。

韩森：　马先生，今天我们来贵公司想作一些咨询。您是资深的投资经理……

　马：　您客气，"资深"不敢当。

艾琳：　一家美国公司想在中国投资，不久前我们刚刚走访了上证，您觉得购买B股是不是最佳投资途径？

　马：　购买B股是一种投资途径，但是，简单地用这个办法来投资的外国人不多。你们仔细看看上证和深交的B股日成交金额，就不难发现B股的交易规模小得可怜。注意，现在持有外币的中国人也可以买B股。可以这样说，这不是大部分境外投资者的选择。

韩森：　那这是为什么呢？是不是因为股市的风险太大呢？

马： 既然是股市，就总有机会，也充满了风险。由于中国股市相对独立
于国际股市，所以预测分析特别困难，有一些特别的风险。

韩森： 我觉得中国经济最近几年的发展既快又稳，股市应该<u>节节上升</u>才对。

马： 但事实上中国股票市场长期在<u>低迷</u>状态<u>徘徊</u>，很难看出它的起落和
中国经济的发展有什么直接的关系。

艾琳： 这到底是怎么回事呢？

马： 一方面是上市公司的经营状况缺乏真正的<u>透明度</u>。有些公司是经过
"包装"上市的，也就是说它们的经营不太好，甚至有很大的亏
损，但是却被说成是连年盈利的公司。这是体制性问题。中国的股
票市场还比较<u>幼稚</u>，管理不够严格。当然，你们美国也有<u>恩龙公司</u>
这样的<u>丑闻</u>。另一方面，中国股市的走向常常受到一些<u>炒股</u>大户的
操盘，<u>散户</u>，也就是普通的个人投资者的力量比较弱，只能跟着大
户走。因此这些大户就可以人为地**操控**某种股票的价格。现在有了
<u>共同基金</u>以后，这种情况**略有好转。**

艾琳： 那么外国投资者在中国还有什么投资途径呢？

马： 前几年，比较多的外国投资者愿意在中国建立合资公司。但是合资
公司中的外资不能超过49%，在经营方向、利益分配和人员管理等问
题上常常**产生纠纷**。所以，现在更多的投资者倾向于建立独资企业
或者购买现成的中国公司。

韩森： 是不是只能购买民营公司？

马： 民营和国营的公司都可以买。现在中国的不少国营企业连年亏损，
政府负担很重，所以希望把这样的公司卖出去。

韩森： 现在中国的一些网络公司已经在美国<u>挂牌</u>上市了，外国公司能不能
在中国上市呢？

马： <u>很遗憾</u>，根据现行的政策，这是不可能的，但是开始有合资公司上
市了。不过要求特别严格。要看这个公司的主要业务是不是公众感
兴趣的，公司有没有三年以上的盈利记录。我这儿有一份上市公司
的具体条件，你们可以仔细看看。

艾琳： 您个人对美国的投资人有什么建议吗？

马： 如果投资人对中国市场的了解不多，希望降低投资风险，可以投资
政府发起的大型建设项目，比如机场和高速公路的建设等等。因为
这些项目由国家支持，不太可能<u>半途而废</u>，投资的回报比较有保
证。现在我手里就有一个重庆机场的扩建项目，这是一个很好的投
资机会。

韩森、
艾琳： 谢谢，希望有机会合作。

Part Four: Listing Requirements for B Shares at the SSE
第四部分：上海证券交易所B股上市的要求

公司申请B股上市，必须 **符合下述条件：**

1 股票**经国务院证券管理部门批准。**

2 <u>发起人认购的股本总额</u>不少于公司拟发行股本总额的35%，发起人出资总额不少于1.5亿元。

3 公司成立时间必须在3年以上，最近3年连续盈利。

4 拟向社会发行的股份达公司股份总数的25%以上。

5 公司在最近3年内无重大违法行为，<u>财务会计报告无虚假记载</u>。

6 国家法律、法规规章及交易所规定的其他条件。

Vocabulary List

雅特		*Yătè*	*Yortel, name of a company*
乳制品	乳製品	rǔzhìpǐn	dairy product
餐饮业	餐飲業	cānyǐnyè	restaurants, cafes, and bars
途径	途徑	tújìng	way; channel
走访	走访	zǒufǎng	pay a visit to
证券	證券	zhèngquàn	securities
交易所		jiāoyìsuǒ	stock exchange
沪星	滬星	*Hùxīng*	*Shanghai Star, name of a company*
顾问	顧問	gùwèn	advisor
事业	事業	shìyè	state-run non-profit (institution)
盈利		yínglì	profit; gain
理事会	理事會	lǐshìhuì	board of directors
日常事务	日常事務	rìcháng shìwù	daily work/ routine
场所	場所	chǎngsuǒ	place; arena
监督	監督	jiāndū	supervise; superintend
发行	發行	fāxíng	issue
债券	债券	zhàiquàn	bond
迁至	遷至	qiānzhì	move to
浦东	浦東	*Pǔdōng*	name of a place
竞价	競價	jìngjià	bidding
理事长	理事長	lǐshìzhǎng	board chairman
日理万机	日理萬機	rìlǐwànjī	attend to numerous affairs every day
年轻有为	年輕有為	niánqīngyǒuwéi	young and promising
纸上谈兵	紙上談兵	zhǐshàngtánbīng	strategize on paper (not realistic)
华尔街	華爾街	*Huá'ěrjiē*	Wall Street
媲美		pìměi	compare favorably with; rival
显示	顯示	xiǎnshì	show; display
指数	指數	zhǐshù	index number
屏幕		píngmù	screen
开盘	開盤	kāi pán	opening quotation (on the stock exchange)
标志	標誌	biāozhì	n./v. indicator; mark; symbolize

熊市		xióngshì	bear market
牛市		niúshì	bull market
跟进	跟進	gēnjìn	follow
套牢		tàoláo	be hitched to a losing investment
脱手		tuōshǒu	get (something) off one's hands
清仓	清倉	qīngcāng	sell off (all of one's shares)
转机	轉機	zhuǎnjī	a favorable turn; a turn for the better
投机	投機	tóujī	opportunistic; speculative
赌博	賭博	dǔbó	gamble
操盘	操盤	cāopán	control or manipulate the market
走向		zǒuxiàng	trend; direction
面值		miànzhí	face value
作东	作東	zuòdōng	be the host
恭敬		gōngjìng	respect; politeness
从命	從命	cóngmìng	obedience
临时	臨時	línshí	on short notice; temporary
身不由己		shēnbùyóujǐ	unable to do as one wishes
资深	資深	zīshēn	very experienced and qualified
深交		Shēnjiāo	abbreviation of 深圳证券交易所
节节上升	節節上升	jiéjiéshàngshēng	grow continuously
低迷		dīmí	low
徘徊		páihuái	pace back and forth
透明度		tòumíngdù	transparency
幼稚		yòuzhì	immature
恩龙	恩龍	Ēnlóng	Enron
丑闻	醜聞	chǒuwén	scandal
炒股		chǎogǔ	speculate on stocks
散户		sǎnhù	individual stock holder
共同基金		gòngtóngjījīn	mutual fund
纠纷	糾紛	jiūfēn	dispute; conflict
挂牌		guàpái	to list
遗憾	遺憾	yíhàn	sorry; regret
半途而废	半途而廢	bàntú'érfèi	give up at the halfway point
国务院	國務院	Guówùyuàn	the State Council
发起人	發起人	fāqǐrén	founding member

认购	認購	rèngòu	subscribe
股本总额	股本總額	gǔběn zǒng'é	shareholder's equity
财务会计	財務會計	cáiwù kuàijì	financial accounting
虚假		xūjiǎ	falsehood; phoniness
记载	記載	jìzǎi	put down in writing; record

Notes and Explanations

1. BUSINESS AND OTHER PROFESSIONAL TERMS

事业

This word has no real parallel in English. We call an organization a 事业 if it has the following characteristics: First, it must be owned by the state. Second, it is not for profit. It may collect fees from those who have received its services but its existence does not rely on those fees but on governmental support. Sometimes it even lacks an accounting department. Third, it provides services to the public but does not manufacture commodities. The 事业单位 typically include public schools, public health services, state research institutes, public libraries, public utilities, etc. In China, 事业 is contrasted with 企业, which is for-profit. Since the Reform, some of the 事业单位 have turned into 企业 or for-profit enterprises.

上市申请   *application for listing (on the stock market)*

Note: 上市 has two meanings:

1) a new product appears on the market
2) a company is listed on the stock market

盘

In the business world, 盘 is the display board of the stock exchange. Thus, much of the stock market jargon contains this word element.

开盘 the stock trade starts; the day's trading begins

操盘 control the trend of stock prices

操盘手 professional stock trader who can control the rise or fall of stocks

大盘 larger stocks; composite stock index

小盘 smaller stocks

崩盘 a stock price falls dramatically

大户   *big traders*

Related word: 散户 small traders.

股民   *stock investors*

This term refers to all those who invest in stocks, especially the small but very active traders.

炒股   *buy and sell stocks*

The meaning of this VO phrase is to buy and sell stocks. 炒 means "stir-fry." Since the traders buy and sell tirelessly, it is similar to making a stir-fry dish.

折合   *convert to; amounts to*

Used for converting one currency to another currency or calculating the cash value of goods.
　　【课文】专门为境外投资者提供用外汇折合成人民币进行买卖的特种股票。
　　【课文】那种机器折合人民币要八万左右。 (L1)

日成交金额   *daily trade volume*

In economic writings, the word "every day" as a modifier is often rendered simply as 日, not 每天 or 每日, as is 月 for every month and 年 for every year.

操控   *manipulate and control*
＝操纵 manipulate ＋ 控制 control

2. FORMAL EXPRESSIONS

迁至   *move to*
The same as 搬到.
　　【课文】上海证券交易所1998年迁至浦东新址。
　　【补充】许多美国公司把生产基地迁至国外。

久等   *wait for a long time*
The same as 等了很长时间.
　　【课文】让你们久等了，真不好意思。
　　【补充】对不起，让您久等了。

久仰久仰   *I have long been looking forward to meeting you.*
Literally, "I have admired you for a long time (before meeting you today)."
See General Notes on Business Communication I.

意下如何　　*What do you think about it?*

Used to ask for an opinion of the speaker's proposal.
　　【课文】二位意下如何？
　　【补充】我们的报价想必您已经研究过了，不知意下如何？(想必
　　　　　　=presumably, most probably)

媲美　　*rival; be on a par with*

A frequently used pattern is 和／与 something 媲美.
　　【课文】这交易所的大厅简直可以和纽约华尔街媲美了！
　　【补充】该产品可与世界名牌媲美。

Direction + Verb

In standard spoken Chinese, a directional word is often placed after a verb as a complement, forming a verb + complement compound. For example, 石油的价格降下来了. In formal speech or writing, a directional word is often placed before a verb as an adverb, forming a directional adverb + verb compound.
　　【课文】股市应当上扬。
　　【补充】最近网络股票连续下挫。（下挫＝go low）
　　【补充】金利公司的丑闻引起股市震荡，国家证券监督委员会决定派出工
　　　　　　作组入住该公司进行全面调查。(The scandal of Jinli Company shocked
　　　　　　the stock market, and the CSRC has decided to station a team in that company to
　　　　　　conduct a full investigation. 入住＝住进去, CSRC=China Securities Regulation
　　　　　　Commission)

何出此言　　*Why have you made such a remark?*

Used to express surprise at a remark made by the other person.
　　【课文】韩先生何出此言？
　　【补充】这家工厂生意一直不错，王经理何出此言？（听到王经理说这家
　　　　　　工厂效益不好）

略有好转　　*has improved a little bit*

略有＝有一点儿. The word that follows this phrase must be a two-syllable word.
　　【课文】情况略有好转。
　　【补充】他的中文水平略有进步。

经……批准   *approved by...*

经 is a preposition meaning "after/through."
　　【课文】股票经国务院证券管理部门批准……
　　【补充】他经人介绍来金桥公司应聘。

3. COLLOQUIAL EXPRESSIONS

难怪   *no wonder*

Can be followed by a clause or stand on its own.
　　【课文】难怪。看来你们的确需要来中国的交易所走走。
　　【补充】原来他的爸爸正在上海开公司，难怪他对中国经济的情况那么
　　　　　　清楚。

算＝总算   *at long last*
　　【课文】昨天我算抢到帽子了，可是今天全赔了。
　　【补充】今天我算认识你这个人了。 (Implies anger toward the addressee, who was
　　　　　　considered a good friend in the past.)

4. OTHER PATTERNS AND WORD COLLOCATIONS

以……起家   *build up a fortune by...*
　　【课文】该公司以生产乳制品起家……
　　【补充】据说韩国的大宇汽车公司是以修理自行车起家的。（大宇＝
　　　　　　Daewoo）

提供……场所   *provide a venue for...*

提供 can take various objects such as 条件, 设备, 方便, etc.
　　【课文】上海证券交易所主要业务是提供交易场所，接受上市申请，监督
　　　　　　证券交易等。
　　【补充】中国政府愿意为外资进入中国市场提供良好的条件。
　　【补充】美方将提供生产这种变压器所需要的设备。

发行……债券   *issue a bond of*
　　【课文】上证所上市的证券包括各级政府发行的政府债券。
　　【补充】为了给研制新产品筹集资金，巨星公司决定发行三亿元企业债券。

采用……方式	*adopt the mode/method of…; by means of…*

采用 can take various objects such as 方法，技术，手段，策略，etc.

【课文】市场交易采用电子竞价交易方式。

【补充】这种微型电脑采用了最先进的节能技术。

【补充】该公司采用非法手段来和我们竞争。

关注……情况	*pay attention to / be concerned about the situation of…*

The object can also be 发展, 趋势, etc.

【课文】我们一直非常关注中国的股市情况。

【补充】世界都在关注中国经济的发展。

产生……纠纷	*create…conflicts*

产生 can take various objects such as 矛盾 (contradiction), 误解, etc.

【课文】在经营方向、利益分配和人员管理等问题上常常产生纠纷。

【补充】这两家公司原来是很好的合作伙伴，但是最近却因为发展方向等问题产生了难以解决的矛盾。

符合……条件	*meet the requirement(s) of…*

【课文】公司申请B股上市，必须符合下述条件

【补充】这位申请人虽然经验不少，但是在学历和外语水平等方面明显不符合外资公司经理的条件。

5. IMPORTANT IDIOMATIC PHRASES/PROVERBS

日理万机

See **General Notes on Business Communication I.**

年轻有为	*young and talented*

Often used as a predicate.

【课文】韩先生年轻有为。

【补充】这位应聘者年轻有为，是总经理的出色人选。

纸上谈兵　　　*mere paper talk*

Literally, "Talk military affairs on paper."
　　【课文】我想与其在办公室纸上谈兵，不如到实地看看。
　　【补充】那个年轻人只会纸上谈兵，完全没有实际经验。

恭敬不如从命

See **General Notes on Business Communication II.**

Class Discussion
课堂讨论

　　1. 中国的证券交易和美国的证券交易比，有哪些主要的差别？
　　2. 中国政府为什么要把股票分成A股和B股？
　　3. 课文提到的美国公司应该投资什么项目？

Exercises
练习

 PART ONE: FAST ORAL TRANSLATION
第一部分：快速口译

Refer to Lesson 1 for instructions for this exercise.

　　A. From Chinese into English
　　一位中国政府负责证券管理的官员向外商介绍中国的B股市场。

　　B. From English into Chinese
　　An American manager of a mutual fund company is talking about his business goals for China.

PART TWO: ROLE-PLAY (INVESTMENT IN THE U.S. MARKET)
第二部分：角色表演（投资美国）

Student A acts as a very wealthy Chinese person who wants to invest in the American market. Student B acts as a personal financial advisor and answers questions on investment strategy raised by A.
一位有钱的中国人想来美国投资，正在向一位财产管理公司的经理咨询投资的策略。一个同学扮演这位中国大款，另一个同学扮演那位经理。

PART THREE: TRUE/FALSE
第三部分：根据课文判断对错

Judge the statements below as true or false in accordance with the information given in the textbook.

1. ___ B股上市只要经过上海或深圳的证券管理部门批准。
2. ___ 上市公司应当做到：公司成立时间必须在5年以上，最近3年连续盈利。
3. ___ 凡B股上市公司都应该在最近3年内无重大违法行为，财务会计报告无假帐。
4. ___ 合资公司中的外资股份不能超过51%。
5. ___ 目前外国公司还不可以在中国上市。
6. ___ 只要有人民币，中国人外国人都能买中国股票。
7. ___ 外国人可以购买中国民营和国营的公司。

PART FOUR: COMPOSITION
第四部分：写作

Follow the indices of the SSE for three consecutive days and write a report in Chinese. The report should address the following: Are the fluctuations of stocks listed on the SSE related to the Dow Jones/Nasdaq? What are the factors behind these fluctuations? If you were an investor, which stock(s) would you be willing to buy?

Lesson 7: E-commerce
第七课：电子商务

Background and Business Tasks
背景和任务

韩森和艾琳某日突发奇想，要成立一家"姣姣少女"服饰电子商务公司。正好艾琳的上海朋友高明晖对电子商务实务相当熟悉，也很感兴趣，因而三人会面洽谈，讨论如何启动。

Part One: At the Jiangzhe Restaurant in the Shanghai Hilton Hotel

第一部分：在上海喜来登大饭店江浙厅

艾琳：　来！来！来！你们两位大概还不认识，我来介绍一下！这位是韩森先生，哈佛的MBA，目前在金桥公司实习，是我的**搭档**。这位是高明晖先生，现在在一家电脑**软体**公司上班。

韩森：　久仰大名！早听艾琳提起过您。听她说您**对因特网技术相当内行**。

高明晖：　哪里！哪里！您过奖了！上个星期艾琳给我打电话提到你们的**构想**，我觉得这个想法很有**魄力**，前途**不可限量**，所以就问她可以不可以**加入你们的行列**，我个人在电脑技术方面总算还有个**一知半解**，希望能帮上一点儿忙。

艾琳：　都是自己人，不必太客气了！从上个世纪末以来，**旋风席卷全球**。虽然最近网络**泡沫破灭**了不少，但是我觉得电子商务前景**看好**。这种永不关门，三百六十五天为全球客户服务的**虚拟**商场，**不必**租用店面，而且**仓储成本低廉**，实在是很好的投资方向。所谓"**秀才不出门，能知天下事**"。

韩森：　应该说是："顾客不出门，能购全球物"了！我觉得我们的构想还太**模糊**，太不具体，我们只是觉得少女喜欢买衣服，同时现代少女又特别喜欢上网，这样一定存在着商机。究竟应该怎么做，还说不清楚。高先生是**圈内人**，相信您一定有很多高见了。我觉得**当务之急**是要考虑把我们的电子商务网络办成什么**类型**？B2B、B2C、C2B还是C2C？这些说法的中文大概是……

高明晖：　我听得懂。现在这些词中国也常说，网络上的术语有不少半英半中的东西。B是企业，C是消费者，2是英文的"to"，也就是中文的"对"。不过艾琳，大陆和台湾的说法有时候不太一样，你刚才说的"软体"我们叫"软件"；你说的"网路"我们叫"网络"。

艾琳：　是啊，其实我在这儿应该用大陆的说法，不过习惯的东西改起来有点儿难。我想，一般电子商务差不多都属于"企业对消费者"的类型。有很多专业的网路商场，像美国的**亚马逊**，台湾的蕃薯藤；也有不少的**实体**公司开辟网路店面，你们大概都知道，像沃尔玛这样的零售巨人也开始了网路销售。我们的电子商务公司经营服装，当然要直接为消费者服务了。

高明晖： 但是我想必须考虑网络销售是不是**符合中国人的消费习惯**，尤其是B2C。中国人习惯现买现取货，你让他先付钱然后等着送货上门，他总觉得心里不**踏实**。要是行销能采取让消费者在网上定货后自己到指定地点取货的方式，也许更能创造一些商机，而且送货费也省了。

艾琳： 不过这就需要店面了，而且你不可能在全国各地都建立取货处。当然了，我觉得可以在大城市建立取货处，其他地区的消费者还是要通过邮局或**货运公司**送货上门。但是在初创阶段，我们大概没有资金来建立太多的取货中心。要让网站有影响力，必须从商品质量上下功夫。我们的销售对象是少女，**我想占领这块市场**的关键是款式。

高明晖： 没错，现在的中国女孩最喜欢**赶时髦**。价钱再贵她们也**不在乎**。如果我们真能把巴黎和纽约最时髦的东西介绍给她们，那这个网站一定很**火**。从服装销售的角度看，尺寸合适非常重要，不然一定会有大量的退货，让你手忙脚乱。所以必须采用会员制，每位会员的身材尺寸都要详细登录，这样每次交易就会比较简单，你只要挑选样式和颜色就行了。我们还可以设计一种叫"网上试衣室"的特殊的软件，让会员免费下载，安装后，她们可以在电脑上看到自己试穿想要订购的服装的效果。现在的电脑图像技术越来越发达，设计这样的软件应该不成问题。

艾琳： 真是个绝妙的主意！有了这个发明，别人就很难跟我们竞争了。也许我们应该把市场扩大到全世界才对。我现在担心的是一些商业程序上的问题。第一，电子商务是不是可以不受海关监管？第二，我们的服装虽然是美国或者法国的样子，但是一定得在中国加工才能降低成本，获得可观的利润。我们对这些中国厂家了解不多，跟厂家订合同以往都是当面签订，现在听说有网上合同，网上合同的风险是不是很大？

高明晖： 我知道中国有个商品交易中心，是一个专门为企业提供商品交易中介服务的经济组织，也许我们可以上上他们的网站查一下信息。在我看来，我们不要去组织加工生产服装，只是向跟我们合作的厂家提供最时髦的设计，再帮助他们在网上打开市场。除了向厂家收取服务费以外，再从每件零售交易中**提成**。这样我们既可赚厂家的钱，又可赚消费者的钱。更重要的是我们的经营风险和经营成本都降低了。

艾琳： 高先生不愧是网路奇才！现在我们的方向比较明确了，我们的网路应该办成包括B2B和B2C两种功能的服务性网路。

韩森： 高先生的设计对我有很大的启发。我原来最担心的就是那些生产服装的<u>乡镇企业</u>不讲<u>信用</u>，消费者跟我们定货，我们不能及时**发货**。现在，我们作为中间人，可以从制度上控制他们。消费者付款后，我们先把钱拿在自己手里。等到消费者<u>确认</u>收到合格的货物以后，我们再跟企业<u>结算</u>，这样他们就不敢**乱来**了。

艾琳： 好主意！看来我们的构想越来越成熟了。我们得积极**采取行动**，要不然等韩森回美国以后，联络就不方便了。

高明晖： 这倒不用担心！我们可以用电脑在网上传递信息，传递图像，还可以面对面通话。有了互联网，中国和美国之间就没有什么距离了。对了！我觉得网上的广告收入也是个重要的东西。你们想想，那些服装生产厂一定会宣传自己的产品，而且我们还可以吸引生产<u>首饰</u>、化妆品的厂家。

韩森： 利用广告收视次数可以查出广告页面被访问的次数，<u>点击率</u>可以很精确地查出网络广告对买主的吸引力的高低。我想，网络广告收费低于传统的广告，很容易吸引商家。

艾琳： 对，网上的广告不但收费低，而且效率高。只要进入我们的网页，具有动画形式的广告就会跳出来，给消费者的印象一定很深。

高明晖： 不过，这就需要消费者的电脑有比较先进的功能，还得用<u>宽带电缆</u>，要是用电话线就太慢了。哎！上菜了，我们先吃饭吧！

韩森： 糟糕，我突然间发现我们的计划有一个**致命缺陷**。

艾琳： 先别说，不然我们就没有吃饭的<u>胃口</u>了。不过，小韩你放心，中国有句老话："**山重水复疑无路，柳暗花明又一村**。"我们一定可以找到<u>对策</u>。大家吃饭吧。为我们的合作，干杯！

Part Two: An Invitation to Join Jiaojiao.com
第二部分："姣姣少女服饰"网络招商启事

"姣姣少女服饰"是一个面向十三至二十一岁女性消费群体的全球性网络，是消费者和服装生产企业之间的桥梁。网络已有英文、日文、西班牙文等多种版本。自2001年创立以来，已经在北美、欧洲、亚洲等地接收了登录个人会员五百万名，企业会员三百多家，网上日销售额目前已经超过七十万美元。为了扩大业务，适应中国网络经济急速发展的需求，现特增设中文版网络。我们向企业会员提供下列服务：

一.建立企业的销售窗口，您可以直接接受全世界消费者的定货，生产她们需要的服饰，不必再为推销和产品**积压**担忧。（您的产品将同时在英、日、西、中四个版本中出现。）

二.公布巴黎、纽约等国际服装中心的最新款式和流行色。每周至少更新一次。

三.为您设计和刊登网上广告，包括动画广告。

本网对企业会员的基本要求是：

第一，信誉至上，必须保证产品的质量和交货日期。

第二，**一旦参加本网，不得**同时参加类似其他网站或电子商务服务。

第三，必须**持有地方工商部门的合法经营证明**。

企业会员收费标准（中国大陆地区特别优惠价格）：

每年人民币两万五千元（如需第三项服务收费另计）

本网将从每件成交的商品中**抽取百分之十的服务费**。运送费用由企业自行承担，本网可以帮助企业联络有关的专业送货公司。

详情请**垂询**：info@jiaojiao.com.cn

或电10-88437592（北京办事处）

Vocabulary List

电子商务	電子商務	diànzǐ shāngwù	e-commerce
突发奇想	突發奇想	tūfā qíxiǎng	suddenly have a fantastic idea
姣姣少女		*Jiāojiāo Shàonǚ*	*Beautiful Girls, name of a business*
服饰	服飾	fúshì	clothing; apparel
高明晖	高明暉	*Gāo Mínghuì*	*name of a person*
实务	實務	shíwù	business reality
启动	啟動	qǐdòng	start
喜来登		Xǐláidēng	Hilton
江浙		*Jiāng Zhè*	*Jiangsu and Zhejiang Provinces*
搭档	搭檔	dādàng	[cl.] coworker
软体 / 软件	軟體 / 軟件	ruǎntǐ/ruǎnjiàn	software
因特网	因特網	yīntèwǎng	internet
内行		nèiháng	insider; expert
构想	構想	gòuxiǎng	idea; conceptualization
魄力		pòlì	guts; courage
不可限量		bùkě xiànliàng	boundless; unlimited
行列		hángliè	rank; row; column
一知半解		yìzhībànjiě	have superficial knowledge of
旋风	旋風	xuànfēng	whirlwind
泡沫		pàomò	bubble
破灭	破滅	pòmiè	fall through; evaporate
虚拟	虛擬	xūnǐ	physical nonexistence
仓储	倉儲	cāngchǔ	storage; warehousing
低廉		dīlián	cheap; low-cost
秀才		xiùcái	scholar
模糊		móhú	vague
圈内人		quānnèirén	insider
当务之急	當務之急	dāngwùzhījí	urgent matter
类型	類型	lèixíng	type
亚马逊	亞馬遜	Yàmǎxùn	www.amazon.com
蕃薯藤		Fānshǔténg	www.yam.com

实体	實體	shítǐ	real (vs. 虚拟)
沃尔玛	沃爾瑪	Wò'ěrmǎ	Wal-Mart
零售		língshòu	retail
行销	行銷	xíngxiāo	sell; marketing
初创	初創	chūchuàng	first establish
阶段	階段	jiēduàn	stage; phase
关键	關鍵	guānjiàn	key; crux
款式		kuǎnshì	style
赶时髦	趕時髦	gǎn shímáo	[cl.] follow fashion trends; be fashionable
尺寸		chǐcùn	measurements; size
退货	退貨	tuìhuò	return merchandise
登录	登錄	dēnglù	register; record
下载	下載	xiàzǎi	download
安装	安裝	ānzhuāng	install
绝妙	絕妙	juémiào	extremely clever; ingenious
可观	可觀	kěguān	sizable
提成		tíchéng	deduct a percentage; draw a percentage
不愧		búkuì	be worthy of; deserve to be called
奇才		qícái	genius
乡镇企业	鄉鎮企業	xiāngzhèng qǐyè	township and village enterprise
信用		xìnyòng	trustworthiness
发货	發貨	fāhuò	send out goods
确认	確認	quèrèn	confirm
结算	結算	jiésuàn	settle accounts
首饰	首飾	shǒushì	jewelry
点击率	點擊率	diǎnjīlù	click rate
精确	精確	jīngquè	exact, precise
动画	動畫	dònghuà	animation
宽带电缆	寬帶電纜	kuāndài diànlǎn	broadband cable
致命		zhìmìng	fatal
缺陷		quēxiàn	flaw; defect
胃口		wèikǒu	appetite
山重水复	山重水複	shānchóngshuǐfù	so many hills and brooks lie ahead (i.e., many obstacles)

柳暗花明		lǐuànhuāmíng	dense willow trees and bright flowers (i.e., beautiful scene opens up, obstacles are overcome)
对策	對策	duìcè	countermeasure or plan
招商		zhāoshāng	attract business
积压	積壓	jīyā	overstock
工商部门	工商部門	gōngshāng bùmén	Administration of Industry and Commerce
垂询	垂詢	chuíxún	inquiry

Notes and Explanations

1. BUSINESS AND OTHER PROFESSIONAL TERMS

洽谈　　*contact/meet and talk*

The topics of discussion should be business and other serious matters. Not used for everyday conversation.

【课文】因而三人会面洽谈。

【课文】欢迎五大洲的朋友前来洽谈订货。(L3)

实务　　*(business) reality or practice*

This word is used to describe day-to-day reality in contrast to pure theory.

【课文】高明晖对电子商务实务相当熟悉。

【补充】我们公司需要的是懂得实务的专家，我们不需要只会纸上谈兵的理论家。

启动　　*start a project; start working*

【课文】讨论如何启动。

【补充】这个项目的启动资金无论如何不能少于五千万人民币。

货运公司　　*shipping company*

Related term: 快递公司 express shipping/delivery company (e.g. FedEx, UPS, DHL, etc.).

提成   *deduct/draw a percentage (as income/commission)*
> 【课文】从每件零售交易中提成。
> 【补充】如果你能为公司拉到百万元以上的广告，就可以从中提成百分之
> 十五。广告费越高，提成越多。

发货   *deliver goods; consignment*
Compound words: 发货人 dispatcher; 发货单 shipping list.

积压   *overstock; supply exceeds demand*
> 【课文】不必再为推销和产品积压担忧。
> 【课文】库存也在合理范围之内，并没有大量积压。(L13)

成交   *clinch a deal*
Related word: 成交额 volume of business transactions.
> 【课文】本网将从每件成交的商品中抽取百分之十的服务费。
> 【补充】这次订货会的成交额只有三百多万美元。

2. Formal Expressions

看好   *look forward to good prospects; very promising*
Often used as a predicate but may also be used as a transitive verb, especially in news headlines.
> 【课文】我觉得电子商务前景看好。
> 【补充】外商看好上海经济……(news headlines)

不必 *(vs. 未必)*   *no need to*
> 【课文】这种虚拟商场不必租用店面。
> 【补充】您不必客气，有什么话请开门见山。

Note: Do not confuse 不必 with 未必, which means "not certain that..." or "not necessarily."
Compare:
> 这次会议他不必参加。He does not need to take part in this meeting.
> 这次会议他未必参加。He may or may not take part in this meeting.

一旦……不得……   *once...cannot...*
一旦 once, in case, now that; 不得＝不可以.

一旦 can be placed before or after the subject, while 不得 must be placed after the subject if there is one.

【课文】一旦参加本网，不得同时参加类似其他网站或电子商务服务。

【补充】合同一旦签订 / 一旦合同签订，双方不得作任何修改。

垂询   *inquiry*

垂 (droop; hang down) simply makes the term more polite. 询＝问.

3. COLLOQUIAL EXPRESSIONS

踏实   *feel relieved; free from anxiety*

【课文】让他先付钱然后等送货上门，他总觉得心里不踏实。

【补充】只有等着笔生意成交了我才会觉得踏实。

This word may also mean "dependable" or "steady and sure."

【补充】他工作很踏实。 He is steadfast in his work.

赶时髦   *follow the trends of fashion (blindly or irrationally)*

【课文】现在中国的女孩最喜欢赶时髦。

【补充】其实他根本不懂电脑，但是为了赶时髦也买了一台。

不在乎   *don't care*

【课文】价钱再贵她们也不在乎。

【补充】我不在乎那俩钱儿，我只是觉得拍广告很有意思。

火   *hot; very popular*

Often used as a predicate.

【课文】这个网站一定很火。

【补充】他的那家书店火得要命。

乱来   *act foolishly or recklessly*

【课文】等到消费者确认收到合格的货物以后，我们在跟企业结算，这样他们就不敢乱来了。

【补充】你现在不是个体户了，你管理的是一个上千人的大企业，这可不能乱来。

4. OTHER PATTERNS AND WORD COLLOCATIONS

对......相当内   *be an expert at/in...*
   【课文】听她说您对网络技术相当内行。
   【补充】虽然他的专业是摄影，但是他对房地产市场也相当内行。

加入......的行列   *join the ranks of...; be a member of...*
   【课文】可以不可以加入你们的行列......
   【补充】越来越多的上海人加入了股民的行列。

符合......的习惯   *in accordance with the customs of...*
   【课文】必须考虑网络销售是不是符合中国人的消费习惯。
   【补充】借钱买房不太符合中国消费者的习惯。

占领市场   *hold a (considerable) share of the market*
   【课文】我想占领这块市场的关键是款式。
   【补充】他认为公司应该向西部发展，占领农村市场。

采取行动   *take action*
   【课文】我们得积极采取行动。
   【补充】我们必须研究对手可能采取的一切行动。

致命缺陷   *fatal flaw*
   【课文】我们的计划有一个致命缺陷。
   【补充】这种电脑的致命缺陷是只能在有空调的房间使用。

持有证明／证件   *hold a certificate/identification*
   【课文】必须持有地方工商部门的合法经营证明。
   【补充】应聘者前来面谈时应持有学历证明和身份证件。

地方   *local*

We all know that 地方 means "place." In formal language, however, 地方 may be used as a modifier meaning "local."

【课文】地方工商部门
【补充】中国出了京剧以外，还有很多地方戏。(local operas)

抽取……费   *charge a fee of...*
【课文】本网将从每件成交的商品中抽取百分之十的服务费。
【补充】这家饭店的老板从服务员得到的小费中抽取百分之三十的管理费。

5. Important Idiomatic Phrases/Proverbs

一知半解   *have a superficial knowledge of*

Often used with the preposition 对.
【课文】我个人在电脑技术方面总算还有个一知半解。
【补充】这个人对销售只有一知半解，怎么能当销售部的总监呢？

当务之急   *urgent matter; pressing matter*
【课文】我觉得当务之急是要考虑把我们的电子商务网络办成什么类型？
【补充】不要花那么多钱去做广告，提高产品质量才是当务之急。

秀才不出門，能知天下事。
See **General Notes on Business Communication II.**

山重水复疑无路，柳暗花明又一村。
See **General Notes on Business Communication II.**

Class Discussion
课堂讨论

1. 电子商务和传统的商业比较，有哪些主要的不同？
2. 电子商务有哪几种类型？
3. 谈谈你自己的网上购物经验？
4. 根据你的了解，中国电子商务的发展情况如何？
5. 猜一猜韩森所说的"致命缺陷"是什么？
6. 你觉得他们的网站会成功吗？

7. 如果你是一个服装生产商，会参加这个网站吗？

8. 谈谈你对电子商务前景的看法。

Exercises
练习

PART ONE: FAST ORAL TRANSLATION
第一部分：快速口译

Refer to Lesson 1 for instructions for this exercise.

A. From Chinese into English
一位中国专家谈中国网络市场现状。

B. From English into Chinese
An American investor is asking questions about the internet and e-commerce in China.

PART TWO: ROLE-PLAY (A DISCUSSION ABOUT SELLING MERCHANDISE ONLINE)
第二部分：角色表演（商议网上销售。）

The general manager of a clothing factory comes to the headquarters of Jiaojiao.com to discuss some important issues relating to selling merchandise online. Student A acts as the manager and student B acts as a representative for Jiaojiao.com.
一个服装厂的总经理来询问参加姣姣少女网的一些问题。一个同学扮演这位经理，另一个同学扮演网络的代表。

PART THREE: FILL IN THE BLANKS
第三部分：填空练习

1. 我可以在网上免费____我所喜欢的电脑软件。
   A. 拿　　B. 下来　　C. 下载　　D. 载

2. ____的次数越多，说明人们对这种产品关心的程度越高。
   A. 点击　　B. 拍　　C. 打　　D. 上门

3. 消费者关心的是服装的____。
   A. 图像　　B. 利润　　C. 成本　　D. 款式

4. 从服装销售的____看，质量非常重要。
   A. 态度　　B. 角度　　C. 难度　　D. 广度

5. 我们可以从每件衣服的零售交易中____。
   A. 提款　　B. 提出　　C. 提成　　D. 提取

6. 为了扩展业务，本部门拟____外语版网络。
   A. 增速　　B. 增设　　C. 增派　　D. 加大

7. 一旦产品积压，责任均由本公司____。
   A. 承担   B. 承认   C. 接受   D. 优惠

PART FOUR: COMPOSITION
第四部分：写作

Write a proposal for a new e-business. Your proposal should include a discussion of major products and/or services, target customers, and characteristics of the business.

LESSON 8: SEEKING APPROVAL FROM ENVIRONMENTAL PROTECTION AUTHORITIES
第八课：环保审批

Background and Business Tasks
背景和任务

美国泰能新技术公司研制了一种新型的生物化学电池，虽然电力性能比硷性电池略差，但是却可以减低对环境的污染，因为它的主要材料是大豆蛋白。泰能公司和中国山东的一个乡镇企业商定，在山东建设一家工厂，专门生产这种新型电池。建设项目审批报告交给当地政府以后，三个月没有听到回音。现在，泰能公司委托金桥公司设法疏通渠道，使工厂能够早日开工。

Part One: At the Foreign Enterprise Office of the Shandong Provincial Government

第一部分：在山东省外资企业办公室

韩森： 您好，我们是为泰能电池厂的事情而来，请问他们的报告现在是不是已经批下来了？

齐如玉： 要是批下来，你们就会接到通知了，要是还没批下来当然不会接到通知。

韩森： 可是**立项**申请书已经交了三个多月了！

齐如玉： 那不**新鲜**。过去一个申请要盖一百四十多个**公章**，没有一年半载根本别想拿到，现在只需要三十六个公章了，你还不知足？

艾琳： 您能不能查一下，在哪个**环节**出了问题。

齐如玉： 对不起，**无可奉告**。下一个。

（韩森和艾琳**无奈**地走出了办公室。）

韩森： 办公室的这个小姑娘怎么这么厉害？

艾琳： 政府部门嘛，总是别人求她。哎，我认识一位副省长，给他打个电话试试。（掏出手机。）喂，请找李副省长听电话。

秘书： 请问您是哪一位？

艾琳： 我是上海金桥公司艾琳。

秘书： 请稍候。

李副省长： 喂，是艾琳小姐吗？

艾琳： 正是，省长您好，最近还是那么忙吧？

李副省长： 还好。

艾琳： 前两天我刚接到小文从洛杉矶打来的电话，看来她对美国已经非常适应了，正在考驾照呢。

李副省长： 小文这孩子**多亏**你帮忙。你是从上海打来的吗？

艾琳： 不是，我就在**济南**办事，怕您太忙，不敢**登门造访**，用电话跟您打个招呼。

李副省长： 事办得顺利吗？有问题尽管说。

艾琳： 还真出了点儿麻烦。我们想了解泰能电池厂的审批情况，结果被外企办的人挡了出来，什么都没了解到。

李副省长： 真不像话！我立刻给他们挂电话，看他们还敢不敢官僚**主义**！你直接去找他们的黄主任。哎，晚上我给你**接风**，时间和地点一会儿我让秘书通知你。

艾琳： 您太客气了。好，再见。

（韩森和艾琳回到办公室）

齐如玉： 你们两个怎么又回来了，**有完没完**？都像你们这样我们还怎么工作了？

（黄主任从楼上<u>匆匆</u>下来。）

黄主任： 小齐，怎么能用这种态度对待外商？对不起，对不起，二位请跟我来。

（黄主任办公室）

黄主任： 实在对不起，这个小齐是新来的，**不知天高地厚**。

艾琳： 没关系，黄主任，我们就是想了解一下泰能电池厂项目的审批结果。

黄主任： 哦，我想起来了，是青岛西边的那个项目。对这个项目嘛，省领导是非常支持的，因为是高新技术嘛，而且还利用了山东的农产品资源。现在工商局、国土局等主管单位都批准了，但是在环保**局遇到了一些阻力。**

韩森： 环保局？泰能生产的可正是对环境保护有好处的电池啊！

黄主任： 他们对报告的一些细节有疑问，具体的情况我就不太了解了。

艾琳： 难道环保局可以不听省领导的话吗？

黄主任： **从业务上说，省环保局的上级领导是国家环保局**。如果他们不批准这个项目，省领导也**无能为力**。我建议你们直接找环保局的负责人谈一谈，也许可以找到解决问题的办法。

艾琳： **谢谢您的指教。**

Part Two: In the Director's Office at the Bureau of Environmental Protection
第二部分：在环保局局长办公室

张局长： 刚才黄主任给我打了招呼，我知道你们是为电池厂的事来的。我想告诉你们，由于这是一个非常特殊的项目，所以需要比较长的时间来审批，请你们转告泰能公司，让他们耐心等待。

韩森： 可是，我们查了有关法规，你们必须在两个月内对申请作出答复。现在已经超过三个月了！

张局长： 好啊，如果你一定要我今天答复，那我只能给你一个否定的答复。

艾琳： 对不起，小韩的意思是想知道，你们对这个项目有什么疑问。这种生物电池已经通过了美国政府有关部门的安全审查。

张局长： 能通过美国的审查不等于就能通过中国的审查。而且，电池本身安全并不等于生产电池的过程也是安全的。我们的专家在审查时发现，生产这种电池的关键技术是利用三种不同的细菌，如果这些细菌到处传播，对环境一定会造成影响。

韩森： 自然界本身就存在着大量的细菌，只有少量对人会造成威胁。这种生物电池所用的细菌是安全的，不然在美国是不会审查通过的。

张局长： 有时候，一种生物技术的有害影响要过很多年才能发现。我觉得这个电池厂应该建在中国西北的沙漠中，这样有了问题也不会造成灾难。山东这个地方嘛，你们一定知道，是中国的农业基地，北京人上海人吃的无公害蔬菜，都是我们这儿种的。我们不希望这里的环境发生任何变化。还有，厂址和青岛啤酒厂太近，**万一电池中的细菌影响了啤酒的酵母菌，那损失可就太大了。**

艾琳： 您说得很有道理，但是泰能新技术的确是安全的。

张局长： 对不起，我还有个会要参加，而且该说的都说了，**二位请回吧，恕不远送**。

艾琳： **感谢您在百忙之中抽出时间来见我们**。不过我还想再**耽误**您一两分钟的时间。您对中国环保的负责精神十分**令人钦佩**，但是如果这种新型环保产品能投入生产，将会**造福**于整个人类，这可是**功德无量**的事情啊！

韩森： 对呀，中国现在已经是世界电池第一消费大国，现在的普通电池和碱性电池都会对环境造成不同程度的危害，如果您还不放心这种新型电池的话，泰能愿意邀请您率领两三位专家去美国考察，一切费用都由他们出。

张局长：　我很欣赏他们的合作态度，我也很想去美国看看，特别是想参观一下加州，听说他们在环保方面很有成就。不过，我还要和其他领导研究一下，再答复你们。

韩　森：　您想参观加州一点问题也没有，泰能公司的研究所就设在旧金山附近，而且**巧得很**，我就是加州人，到时候我可以作您的翻译和导游。请您尽快给我们回话，好订飞机票。对了，您能不能给我们一张名片？

张局长：　当然可以。请代我**转达对泰能公司董事长和总经理的问候**，上次他们来山东的时候，我正在北京出差，没有见到。

艾　琳：　那这回好了，你们可以在旧金山见面了。那么，这个项目的审批是不是就可以……？

张局长：　请你们不要误解我的意思，现在我们还没有决定是否**赴**美考察，即使同意了，这也绝不意味着我们会**以原则作交易**，用通过审批来换取一次免费旅游。我们是去工作，不是去旅游，而且泰能**理应**邀请我们去。

韩　森：　那您的意思是泰能应该给您更多的东西？比如回扣之类？

张局长：　我想你对中国的国情并不真正了解。改革开放初期，确实出现了很多接受申请人<u>贿赂</u>等丑恶行为，但<u>贪官</u>总是少数。现在中国正在大力加强<u>廉政</u>建设，如果我接受外商<u>行贿</u>，头上这顶**乌纱帽**还能戴得住吗？告诉你们，我在这个岗位上干了将近五年了，也有不少申请人想用不正当的办法来影响我们的决定，但是一次都没有成功！环保是关系到子孙万代的大事，我绝不会因为<u>区区小利</u>而做违背原则的事情。

艾　琳：　请您<u>息怒</u>，小韩刚才可能<u>冒犯</u>了您，我们非常佩服您<u>廉洁奉公</u>的精神。

张局长：　没什么。我们当然希望引进更多的外资和先进技术，但是在环保问题上我们不得不**慎之又慎**。

韩　森：　可是……

张局长：　好了，以目前的材料看，你们说多少话也没有用，如果真想加快审批，就赶快让泰能提供更多更有说服力的材料。再见。

Part Three: Environmental Protection Regulations for New Projects and Expansion Projects (Abridged)
第三部分：国务院建设项目环境保护管理条例（节选）

（1998年11月18日国务院第1次常务会议通过，中华人民共和国国务院令第1号）

第一章　　**总则**

第一条　　为了防止建设项目产生新的污染、破坏生态环境，制定本条例。

第二条　　在中华人民共和国领域和中华人民共和国管辖的其他海域内建设对环境有影响的建设项目，适用本条例。

第三条　　建设产生污染的建设项目，必须遵守污染物排放的国家标准和地方标准；在实施重点污染物排放总量控制的区域内，还必须符合重点污染物排放总量控制的要求。

第四条　　工业建设项目应当采用能耗物耗小、污染物产生量少的清洁生产**工艺**，合理利用自然资源，防止环境污染和生态破坏。

第五条　　改建、扩建项目和技术改造项目必须采取措施，治理与该项目有关的原有环境污染和生态破坏。

第二章　　环境影响评价

第六条　　国家实行建设项目环境影响评价制度。建设项目的环境影响评价工作，由取得相应资格证书的单位承担。

第七条　　国家根据建设项目对环境的影响程度，按照下列规定对建设项目的环境保护实行分类管理：

（一）建设项目对环境可能造成重大影响的，应当编制环境影响报告书，对建设项目产生的污染和对环境的影响进行全面、详细的评价；

（二）建设项目对环境可能造成轻度影响的，应当编制环境影响报告表，对建设项目产生的污染和对环境的影响进行分析或者专项评价；

（三）建设项目对环境影响很小，不需要进行环境影响评价的，应当填报环境影响登记表。

第八条　　建设项目环境影响报告书，应当包括下列内容：

（一）建设项目概况；

（二）建设项目周围环境现状；

（三）建设项目对环境可能造成影响的分析和预测；

（四）环境保护措施及其经济、技术论证；

（五）环境影响经济损益分析；

（六）对建设项目实施环境监测的建议；

（七）环境影响评价结论。

第十条　　　　建设项目环境影响报告书、环境影响报告表或者环境影响登记表，由建设单位报有审批权的环境保护行政主管部门审批；建设项目有<u>行业主管</u>部门的，其环境影响报告书或者环境影响报告表应当经行业主管部门预审后，报有审批权的环境保护行政主管部门审批。环境保护行政主管部门应当自收到建设项目环境影响报告书之日起60日内、收到环境影响报告表之日起30日内、收到环境影响登记表之日起15日内，分别作出审批决定并书面通知建设单位。建设项目造成跨行政区域环境影响，有关环境保护行政主管部门对环境影响评价结论有争议的，其环境影响报告书或者环境影响报告表由共同上一级环境保护行政主管部门审批。

第十五条　　　建设单位编制环境影响报告书，<u>应当</u>依照有关法律规定，征求建设项目所在地有关单位和居民的意见。

第三十四条　本条例自<u>发布</u>之日起<u>施行</u>。

Vocabulary List

环保	環保	huánbǎo	environmental protection
审批	審批	shěnpī	examine and approve
泰能		*Tàinéng*	*name of a company*
电力性能	電力性能	diànlì xìngnéng	electric capacity
硷性电池	鹼性電池	jiǎnxìng diànchí	alkaline battery
略差		lüèchà	a notch under
大豆蛋白		dàdòu dànbái	soy protein
设法	設法	shèfǎ	devise a way to
疏通渠道	疏通渠道	shūtōng qúdào	remove obstacles to keep channels open
立项	立項	lìxiàng	initiate a project
盖	蓋	gài	stamp
公章		gōngzhāng	governmental seals
环节	環節	huánjié	segment; link
无可奉告	無可奉告	wúkěfènggào	no comment; have nothing to report
无奈	無奈	wúnài	helplessly; cannot help but
济南	濟南	Jǐnán	capital of Shandong Province
登门造访	登門造訪	dēngmén zàofǎng	visit in person
挡	擋	dǎng	ward off
官僚主义	官僚主義	guānliáo zhǔyì	bureaucratization
接风	接風	jiēfēng	hold a banquet to welcome
匆匆		cōngcōng	hurry
不知天高地厚		bùzhī tiāngāodìhòu	do not know the complexity of things
指教		zhǐjiào	instruction
耐心		nàixīn	patience
答复	答覆	dáfù	answer; reply
细菌	細菌	xìjūn	bacteria
传播	傳播	chuánbō	spread
沙漠		shāmò	desert
基地		jīdì	base
公害		gōnghài	pollution

蔬菜		shūcài	vegetable
酵母菌		jiàomǔjūn	yeast
恕不远送	恕不遠送	shùbùyuǎnsòng	pardon me for not seeing you out/off
耽误	耽誤	dānwù	waste (your time)
造福		zàofú	benefit
功德无量	功德無量	gōngdé wúliàng	boundless beneficence
考察		kǎochá	observe and study
赴		fù	go to
贿赂	賄賂	huìlù	bribe
贪官	貪官	tānguān	corrupt officials
廉政		liánzhèng	clean/honest government
行贿	行賄	xínghuì	offer a bribe
乌纱帽	烏紗帽	wūshāmào	black gauze cap, a symbol of an official post
区区小利	區區小利	qūqū xiǎolì	tiny profit
息怒		xīnù	cease to be angry
冒犯		màofàn	offend
廉洁奉公		liánjiéfènggōng	have integrity and always work for the public interest
慎之又慎		shènzhīyòushèn	very cautious
常务会议	常務會議	chángwù huìyì	regular meeting of the Standing Committee
总则	總則	zǒngzé	general principle
生态	生態	shēngtài	ecology
领域	領域	lǐngyù	territory
管辖	管轄	guǎnxiá	administration
海域		hǎiyù	maritime space
排放		páifàng	drain off; omit
能耗		nénghào	energy consumption
物耗		wùhào	material consumption
工艺	工藝	gōngyì	technology
概况	概況	gàikuàng	general situation
行业	行業	hángyè	profession
主管		zhǔguǎn	in charge; superintend
依照		yīzhào	follow; observe
发布	發佈	fābù	issue
施行		shīxíng	implement

Notes and Explanations

1. BUSINESS AND OTHER PROFESSIONAL TERMS

立项   *initiate a project*

This term means "to initiate a project" with considerable funds/investment.

【课文】可是立项申请书已经交了三个多月了！

【补充】看了你们的立项说明以后，很多专家表示了不同意见。

公章   *public/institutional seal*

A 章, or "seal," is very important in business activities in China. 公章 means "an official or institutional seal," commonly a big round seal, different from 私章（私人图章）or "personal seal" that is often a smaller square seal. The verb for stamping a seal is commonly 盖.

从业务上说，省环保局的上级领导是国家环保局

Although the Bureau of Environmental Protection is part of the provincial government, it operates largely independently from the provincial governor. Instead, its operations are directly guided by the National Bureau of Environmental Protection.

管理条例   *supervisory regulations*

In China, 管理条例, or "regulations for a special industry or profession," are commonly issued by the State Council.

总则   *general rules*

Stated in the beginning of formal documents such as laws and regulations.

工艺   *technology / process of manufacturing*

This word has two meanings: "technology" or "the process of making a product or handicraft." In the context of this lesson, it means the former.

2. FORMAL EXPRESSIONS

造福（于）   *bring benefit to*

Since this is a VO structure, 于 should be added before the noun. Now, however, 于 is usually dropped in writing and even in speech.

【课文】将会造福于整个人类。
【补充】保护环境是造福万代的事情。

赴　　*go to*
　【课文】现在我们还没有决定是否赴美考察。
　【补充】中国经贸代表团将于下月赴欧参加中欧双边贸易会谈。

理应　　*ought to*
　【课文】泰能理应邀请我们去。
　【课文】出售价值三亿美元的先进设备后，美方理应为我们培训操作人员。

3. Colloquial Expressions

新鲜　　*rare*

Here this word means "rare." It may also mean "fresh" in other contexts.
　【课文】那不新鲜。
　【补充】在股市上一天赚几百万一点儿都不新鲜。

多亏　　*thanks to...(otherwise things would have turned out badly)*

Used to express thanks.
　【课文】小文这孩子多亏你帮忙。
　【补充】没想到天津的街道这么复杂，多亏你给我们带路。

有完没完？　　*Lit. "Is there an end or not?"*

This phrase expresses the speaker's impatience.

万一......那...... 就......　　*if by any chance..., then...*
　【课文】万一电池中的细菌影响了啤酒的酵母菌，那损失可就太大了。
　【补充】万一你受贿的事儿让他知道了，那麻烦就来了。

Adj. 得很　　*very adj.*
　【课文】而且巧得很，我就是加州人......
　【补充】那个商店的东西贵得很。

乌纱帽　　*official post*

In ancient China (Ming dynasty and earlier), officials wore black gauze caps. Thus, the black gauze cap is used as a symbol of an official post.

【课文】头上这顶乌纱帽还能戴得住吗？

【补充】你别忘了，你头上的乌纱帽是谁给的！

4. OTHER PATTERNS AND WORD COLLOCATIONS

遇到阻力　　*face resistance; encounter obstacles*

【课文】但是在环保局遇到了一些阻力……

【补充】中国开始经济改革的时候曾经遇到了很大的阻力。

谢谢您的指教　　*lit. "thanks for your advice"*

See **General Notes on Business Communication I.**

二位请回吧，恕不远送。

See **General Notes on Business Communication VI.**

感谢您在百忙之中抽出时间来见我们

See **General Notes on Business Communication I.**

耽误时间　　*waste your time, take up your time*

【课文】不过我还想再耽误您一两分钟的时间。

【补充】他不会帮忙的，你给他打多少电话也没用，别耽误时间了。

令人钦佩　　*admirable*

【课文】您对中国环保的负责精神十分令人钦佩。

【补充】你们在三年内就完成了这项具有世界水平的研究，真是令人钦佩。

转达（……）对……的问候　　*give my regards to...*

【课文】请代我转达对泰能公司董事长和总经理的问候……

【补充】你回到微软公司以后请转达我对盖茨先生的问候。

以/拿/用原则作交易　　*throw away principles; barter away principles*

【课文】这也绝不意味着我们会以原则作交易......

【补充】他给你三十万你就同意他们建这个会造成污染的工厂了？这不是拿原则作交易吗？

5. Important Idiomatic Phrases/Proverbs

无可奉告　　*no comment; have no information to provide*

See **General Notes on Business Communication VI.**

登门造访　　*pay a visit in person*

This phrase is often used to show respect to the person to be visited. Note: In classical Chinese, 造 means "to go to."

【课文】怕您太忙，不敢登门造访。

【补充】您是这方面的专家，我们理应登门造访，现在麻烦您到我们这儿来，真是不好意思。

不知天高地厚　　*lit. "not know the immensity of heaven and earth"*

This phrase is often used to criticize a young or inexperienced person who overestimated himself or underestimated the power/immensity/complexity of someone or something.

【课文】这个小齐是新来的，不知天高地厚。

【课文】他赚了几百万就以为可以钱可以随便乱花，真是不知天高地厚。

无能为力　　*unable to help despite one's willingness*

【课文】省领导也无能为力。

【补充】我们知道你花三万块钱买个电脑不容易，但是保修期过了，我们实在无能为力。

功德无量　　*boundless beneficence*

Originally a Buddhist term meaning "a benevolent action that will bring endless good karma."

【课文】这可是功德无量的事情啊！

【补充】投资西部山区的基础教育可以说是功德无量。

区区小利　　*tiny profit*

区区 means "trivial, tiny." Another frequently used phrase is 区区小事.

【课文】我绝不会因为区区小利而做违背原则的事情。
【课文】为了这区区小利，他把乌纱帽丢了。

慎之又慎　　*extremely cautious*
【课文】在环保问题上我们不得不慎之又慎。
【补充】来申请贷款的有不少是骗子，你要慎之又慎。

Class Discussion
课堂讨论

1. 为什么齐如玉没有告诉艾琳和韩森审批的结果？
2. 在中国兴建工厂要经过哪些政府部门的审批？
3. 在谈话过程中环保局长的态度有没有变化？
4. 你觉得这个项目最后会得到环保局的批准吗？
5. 根据中国的法规，这个项目是应该用环境报告书还是环境报告表？

Exercises
练习

 PART ONE: FAST ORAL TRANSLATION
第一部分：快速口译

Refer to Lesson 1 for instructions for this exercise.

A. From Chinese into English
一名中国政府的官员正在跟一位外商讨论环境污染问题。

B. From English into Chinese
An American buyer is talking about buying Chinese organic food.

PART TWO: ROLE-PLAY (TALK IT OVER AGAIN WITH DIRECTOR ZHANG)
第二部分：角色表演（和张局长再谈一次）

Obviously, Hansen's interaction with Director Zhang was not very appropriate or effective. If he had a chance to do it over again, what should he say? Student A acts as Director Zhang; student B acts as Hansen, and student C acts as Aileen.

很显然，韩森和张局长的谈话不太成功。如果能再来一次，他应该怎样说呢？一个同学扮演张局长，另一个同学扮演韩森，第三个同学扮演艾琳。

Part Three: Rephrasing Sentences
第三部分：改写句子

Refer to Lesson 1 for instructions for this exercise.

1. 为了欢迎你们到我们城市来作客，今天晚上我请你们吃饭。
2. 很对不起，你刚才问的问题我完全不可以回答。
3. 您这么忙，还跟我们见面，我很感动。
4. 现在政府官员做事情非常小心，你想给他们钱让他们替你服务，这不可能成功。

Part Four: Composition
第四部分：写作

Write a letter from Aileen to the vice governor to express thanks for his support and to ask him to exert influence so that the proposed project is approved as soon as possible.

LESSON 9: RESOLVING CONTRACT DISPUTES
第九课：合同纠纷

Background and Business Tasks
背景和任务

1994年9月18美国桑德蓝公司与台湾美达鞋业公司签订合同，桑德蓝向美达提供080系列男鞋的设计图纸和生产技术，美达成为生产这一系列男鞋的唯一厂家，在产品投资生产六年内支付销售这种男鞋的利润的20%，六年期满后，未经双方同意，**不得**将设计和技术转让给第三者。但据初步调查，台湾美达鞋业公司于1998年10月17日与广东腾云制鞋厂签订合同，由**后者**生产080系列男鞋的鞋底。从2000年开始，后者生产了一种在080系列基础上改进的新款皮鞋，销往欧洲市场。桑德蓝公司委托金桥公司查证情况，以便采取进一步的措施。韩森和艾琳奉命对此事进行调查。

Part One: In the Conference Room at Meida Shoe Works of Taiwan

第一部分：台湾美达鞋业公司会议厅

刘副总： 哎呀！艾琳小姐！感谢光临。我们是自己人，希望这件事能够<u>妥善</u>解决。

艾琳： 这也是我的愿望。这位就是我在电话里跟您提到的韩森先生。

韩森： 刘副总，您好！因为事关紧急，我想我们就进入主题吧！据我们所获得的资料，贵公司将"080"系列男鞋的设计和技术非法转让给广东的"腾云"，这明显违背了你们和桑德蓝签订的合同。

刘副总： 没有这样的事情啦。不错，我们是和广东"腾云"签订了合同，但是并没有转让技术，只是让他们为我们生产鞋底。一个工厂不可能样样东西都生产嘛，在外面有些加工点是正常的。你们不会不知道，大陆的生产成本很低，特别是前两年，这样我们才能有钱赚，桑德蓝也才因此得到了<u>更丰厚</u>的利润。我不明白，他们为什么不喜欢赚多一些钱呢？

韩森： 桑德蓝当然知道大陆加工的成本低廉，正是因为他们要遵守和你们签订的合同，才没有在大陆另找工厂合作。

艾琳： 而且桑德蓝认为鞋底是他们总体设计的一个重要部分，这种鞋底轻而<u>耐磨</u>，材料和加工方法都有美国的<u>专利</u>。你们不和人家商量就让广东生产，这样新技术就<u>泄露</u>出去了。你看，现在腾云生产的皮鞋就是利用了桑德蓝的技术，你们对此难道没有责任吗？

刘副总： 大陆的鞋厂专门<u>仿制</u>欧美名牌，这是他们的问题，不是我们的问题。而且据我们了解，你们说的那种鞋子并没有采用080的鞋底设计，和080相似的地方只是<u>鞋面</u>，所以这和我们让他们生产鞋底没有任何关系。

韩森： 恕我直言，你们和腾云合作以后，腾云就生产了仿制品，任何一个按照<u>常识</u>推断的人都会怀疑**这里面有文章**。

刘副总： 事情到了这个<u>地步</u>，**我就跟你们实说了吧**。这件事都是让<u>李金旺</u>搞坏的。

艾琳： 李金旺是谁？

刘副总： 他是香港人，十年前我们请他来做<u>技师</u>，他的手艺的确不错，脑子也很灵活。去广东加工鞋底就是他的主意。当时腾云鞋厂的产品卖不出去，已经快<u>倒闭</u>了。我们就让他们加工鞋底，价格压得很低，他们也同意了。我们派了李金旺去监督指导他们的生产。没想到**这**

家伙后来被腾云<u>收</u>买了，从我们公司辞职，变成了腾云的总设计师。你们知道，他是很了解080的全部生产工艺的。我们甚至怀疑，080的设计图纸也被他<u>影</u>印带走了。

韩森： 你们为什么不向警方报告？

刘副总： 我们没有任何证据啊！而且我们的警察怎么管得了他们那边的事情？

艾琳： 看来这件事情比我们想象的更复杂。我们得专门去一趟广东调查了！不过，无论如何贵公司要承担一定的法律责任。第一，是你们**用人不当泄露了机密**；第二，你们和腾云签订的合同没有经过桑德蓝的同意。请给一份你们的合同的影印件，我们要仔细研究。

Part Two: In the Director's Office at Tengyun Shoe Works of Zhongshan County, Guangdong Province
第二部分：广东中山腾云鞋厂厂长办公室

黄厂长： 二位远道而来，**不知有何赐教**？

韩森： 实不相瞒，我们是为贵厂非法仿制080系列男鞋来进行调查的。

黄厂长： 本厂一贯遵守法律，**不知"非法"二字从何说起**？

韩森： **您这是明知故问**。你们的总设计师是不是李金旺先生？

黄厂长： 李先生原来确实是我厂设计师，但是他已经在半年前辞职，听说去厦门自己开了一家鞋厂。如果你们想找他的地址和电话，我可以让<u>属下</u>给予协助。

艾琳： 谢谢，我们想知道你们厂的畅销产品腾云系列鞋是不是李金旺设计的？

黄厂长： 这款鞋是我们集体设计的，李先生当然也包括在内。

韩森： 那他是不是提供了080系列的设计图纸？

黄厂长： 绝无此事。你们怀疑我们的腾云和080有什么特别的关系，但是如果你们到市场上去看看，就会发现很多鞋厂的产品样子都差不多。

艾琳： 但是你们同美达签的合同明确要求不得使用080的技术来生产与080无关的皮鞋，所以你们的<u>违约</u>行为是十分清楚的。

黄厂长： 合同中的确说不得使用080的技术，但是如果你仔细阅读合同书的全文，就不难发现，合同中的技术限于鞋底的制造技术。我们的新款皮鞋的鞋底同080完全不同，这是**有目共睹**的。

韩森： 这只是您个人的解释，在合同中，如果没有直接标明，技术应该包括所有技术。

黄厂长：　　韩森先生恐怕忽略了一个基本的事实，我们同美达签订的合同就是
　　　　　　生产鞋底的合同。我想，对此大概不需要作更多的解释了。如果没
　　　　　　有别的事的话，我还有一些重要的公务需要处理。恕不远送。

A typical contract.

Part Three: A Technology Transfer Contract between Sunderland of the U.S.A. and Meida of Taiwan

第三部分：美国桑德蓝公司与台湾美达鞋业公司技术转让合同

鉴于：

本合同签约各方就本合同书中描述项目的研究开发、成果属权、收益分配、风险责任与之相关的技术和法律问题，经过平等协商，在真实、充分地表达各自意愿的基础上，达成如下协议，由签约双方共同**恪守**。

第一条签约方

甲方　（委托方）：美国桑德蓝公司
法人代表：罗莎海曼（总经理）
乙方　（受托方）：台湾美达鞋业公司
法人代表：陆惠明（总经理）

第二条合同性质

本合同属于开发与技术转让合同。

第三条签约时间和地点

本合同由上述签约方于1994年9月18日在台湾彰化签订。

第四条项目名称

桑德蓝公司向美达公司有条件转让080系列男鞋生产设计和技术。

第五条技术内容

技术主要组成部份：080系列男鞋鞋业鞋模、设计图纸和材料的选配说明。

第六条技术转让条件

甲方将上述技术内容**有偿转让**给乙方。乙方可根据此项技术在从即日起的六年中生产080系列男鞋。六年以后是否继续合作以及合作形式由双方另行商定。甲方保证，乙方在此期间将是唯一获得此项技术和设计的公司。乙方保证，不将此项技术在此六年中或者以后转让给任何第三者，也不利用此项技术开发生产其他系列的靴鞋。甲方不限制乙方在六年中的产量，乙方必须如实将产量呈报甲方，并交付费用（详见第十一条）。

第七条保密要求

保密范围：全项内容。

第八条权利保障
签约方保证本合同涉及的全部技术内容具有自主性和真实性，并不因本合同的履行而**侵犯他人的合法权益**。

第九条风险承担
在本合同的履行过程中，除因甲方的设计和技术不合理造成的损失之外，所有风险责任均由乙方单方面承担。

第十条费用及支付方法

乙方在合同开始履行的**当日**付给甲方技术转让费50万美元，并在以后的六年中向甲方交付生产080系列的利润的百分之二十。每三个月结算付款一次。
支付方式：**银行汇款**。

第十一条合同的变更

签约方确认，在履行合同过程中，对于具体内容需要变更的，由签约各方另行协商并**书面约定**，作为本合同的变更文本。

第十二条争议解决方式

签约各方因履行合同发生争议，应协商解决。协商解决不成，签约方同意采用向有管辖权的司法机构起诉。

第十三条合同生效

本合同一式两份，经签约各方签字盖章后生效，到2000年9月17日止。

甲方：美国桑德蓝公司(签章)
地址：美国纽约曼哈顿帝国大厦1050
乙方：台湾美达鞋业公司(签章)
地址：台湾彰化市工业区中工三路888号

Part Four: A Manufacturing Contract between Meida Shoe Works of Taiwan and Tengyun Shoe Works of Guangdong

第四部分：台湾彰化美达鞋业公司委托广东中山腾云鞋厂加工生产合同

第一条　签约方

甲方：台湾彰化达美鞋业公司
法人代表：陆惠明总经理
乙方：广东中山腾云鞋厂
法人代表：黄万全厂长

第二条　加工项目说明

甲方委托乙方在合同履行之日起的两年内为甲方生产080系列男鞋鞋底200万双。

第三条　材料与设计

所有材料与设计均由甲方提供，乙方**不得挪用**材料或利用技术以生产合同之外的其他产品，也不得将生产技术泄露给第三方。

第四条　质量监督指导

甲方将在合同期内向乙方派遣技师一名以监督指导生产质量。乙方必须听从指导，并为**其**提供免费住宿。

第五条　交货期限与办法

乙方从合同履行后的第四个月开始，每月的最后一个工作日向甲方提供合格鞋底10万双。交货地点为乙方工厂，公路与海路运输由甲方负责。

第六条　加工生产费用

加工生产费用为每双鞋底0.8港币。甲方在合同履行之日向乙方交付定金五万港币。余款将在合同履行后的第九个月、第十五个月和最后一个月分三次付清。

第七条　合同的修改

双方在执行合同过程中如发现问题，应该通过认真协商对合同进行修改。合同的任何修改都必须经过双方同意。

第八条　合同生效日期

合同从签订之日起生效。

签约人：
甲方：刘玉山（副总经理）
地址：台湾彰化市工业区中工三路888号
乙方：黄炳光（厂长）
地址：广东中山石桥镇新开路22号

Vocabulary List

桑德蓝	桑德藍	*Sāngdélán*	*Sunderland, name of a company*
系列		xìliè	series; (product) line
期满	期滿	qīmǎn	expire; run out
腾云	騰雲	*Téngyún*	*Mount the Clouds, name of a company*
鞋底		xiédǐ	sole of a shoe
新款		xīnkuǎn	latest style
查证	查證	cházhèng	investigate and verify
奉命		fèngmìng	be tasked to; (do something) according to an order
妥善		tuǒshàn	well arranged
丰厚	豐厚	fēnghòu	rich and generous
耐磨		nàimó	wear-proof; durable
专利	專利	zhuānlì	patent
泄露	洩露	xièlù	leak out
仿制	仿製	fǎngzhì	copy; be modeled on; counterfeit
鞋面		xiémiàn	instep; vamp
常识	常識	chángshí	common sense
推断	推斷	tuīduàn	infer; deduce
地步		dìbù	extent; stage
李金旺		*Lǐ Jīnwàng*	*name of a person*
技师	技師	jìshī	technician
倒闭	倒閉	dǎobì	close down; go bankrupt
收买	收買	shōumǎi	buy in; buy over
影印		yǐnyìn	photocopy
警方		jǐngfāng	police
用人不当	用人不當	yòngrén búdàng	choose the wrong person for the job
机密	機密	jīmì	secret; classified information
赐教	賜教	cìjiào	grant instruction
一贯	一貫	yíguàn	consistently; always
属下	屬下	shǔxià	subordinate
给予	給予	gěiyǔ	give; provide
协助	協助	xiézhù	assist; help

违约	違約	wéiyuē	breach a contract
有目共睹		yǒumùgòngdǔ	be obvious to all
鉴于	鑒于	jiànyú	in view of; seeing that
属权	屬權	shǔquán	ownership
收益		shōuyì	income; profit
协商	協商	xiéshāng	negotiate; talk things over
恪守		kèshǒu	scrupulously abide by
罗莎海曼	羅莎海曼	*Lúoshā Hǎimàn*	*Rosa Hyman*
陆惠明	陸惠明	*Lù Huìmíng*	*name of a person*
彰化		*Zhānghuà*	*name of a place*
鞋模		xiémó	shoe pattern
选配	選配	xuǎnpèi	select and match
靴鞋		xuēxié	shoes
如实	如實	rúshí	strictly according to the facts
呈报	呈報	chéngbào	submit; present
保障		bǎozhàng	ensure; guarantee
履行		lǚxíng	perform; carry out
侵犯		qīnfàn	violate
承担	承擔	chéngdān	bear; undertake
银行汇款	銀行匯款	yínháng huìkuǎn	remit money by bank transfer
变更	變更	biàngēng	change; alter
文本		běnwén	text
管辖权	管轄權	guǎnxiáquán	jurisdiction
司法机构	司法機構	sīfǎ jīgòu	judicial organ
起诉	起訴	qǐsù	sue
曼哈顿	曼哈頓	*Mànhādùn*	*Manhattan*
挪用		nuóyòng	divert; misappropriate
派遣		pàiqiǎn	dispatch; delegate

Notes and Explanations

1. BUSINESS AND OTHER PROFESSIONAL TERMS

合同　*contract*

合同 is also called 约. The most common usages of this term are as follows:

    签订合同 sign a contract （签约）
    履行合同 fulfill the obligations of a contract （履约）
    终止合同 terminate a contract
    违背 / 违反合同 breach a contract （违约）
    合同草案 a contract draft

甲方 / 乙方　*side A / side B*

Frequently used in contracts. 甲方 is 委托方 or the entrusting party, while 乙方 is 收托方 / 受托方 or the party entrusted to do something.

有偿 / 无偿　*with payment / gratis*

有偿 means "with payment or compensation" while 无偿 means "gratis" or "without compensation."

转让　*transfer*

Commonly used objects of this verb are 技术, 设备 or other forms of property.

银行汇款　*bank transfer*

The original meaning of 汇款 is "to remit money" or "to pay by money order," transactions which are traditionally issued by the post office in China.

书面约定 / 口头约定　*written agreement / oral agreement*

For important issues such as changing the contents of a contract, a written agreement should always be signed by both parties.

挪用　*divert; appropriate; embezzle*

The meaning of this word is always negative. The most common object of this verb is 资金, or "funds."

【课文】乙方不得挪用材料或利用技术以生产合同之外的其他产品。

【补充】他因为挪用科研经费购买私人住房被撤职了。(He was dismissed because he diverted funds for research to buy a personal residence.)

2. FORMAL EXPRESSIONS

不得   *may not*

Note: pronounced as bùdé, not bùděi.

【课文】不得将设计和技术转让给第三者。

【课文】根据美国的法律，不得向未满二十一岁者出售含酒精饮料。

后者   *the latter*

Related word: 前者 the former.

【课文】由后者生产080系列男鞋的鞋底。

【补充】鸿兴公司和金龙公司的合作值得重视，因为前者是中国南方最大的健身器材公司，后者则是中国北方健身器材市场的领导者。

不知（……）从何说起   *I don't know where (the accusation) comes from; I don't know where to begin (talking about it).*

【课文】不知非法二字从何说起……

See **General Notes on Business Communication VI.**

恪守   *strictly adhere to (the contract, promise, etc.)*

【课文】由签约双方共同恪守。

【课文】我们希望贵方能恪守当初的承诺。

当日   *the same day (something happens/takes effect); that very day*

【课文】乙方在合同开始履行的当日付给甲方技术转让费50万美元。

【补充】公司负责人在事故发生的当日辞职。

其   *it, him, her, them, its, his, their*

This third person pronoun cannot be used as a subject.

【课文】为其提供免费住宿。

【课文】将其培养成合家乐的主要市场……(L15)

3. COLLOQUIAL EXPRESSIONS

这家伙　　*this guy*
【课文】没想到这家伙后来被腾云收买了。
【补充】这家伙把公司的技术秘密卖给外国人了。

我就跟你们实说了吧　　*to tell you the truth*
The same as 我就跟你们说实话吧。

4. OTHER PATTERNS AND WORD COLLOCATIONS

用人不当　　*to have put the wrong person in charge*
【课文】是你们用人不当泄漏了机密。
【补充】那个公司因为用人不当遭受了巨大的经济损失。

泄露机密　　*divulge confidential information*
【课文】是你们用人不当泄露了机密。
【补充】千万不要向我们的对手泄漏这个商业机密。

不知有何赐教　　*Lit. "I don't know what advice you will offer me."*
See **General Notes on Business Communication VI.**

侵犯权益　　*violate the rights (of...)*
【课文】并不因本合同的履行而侵犯他人的合法权益。
【补充】你们公司拒绝退换不合格产品，这侵犯了消费者的合法权益。

5. IMPORTANT IDIOMATIC PHRASES/PROVERBS

这里面有文章　　*there are hidden secrets / untold reasons*
This phrase is used to stress that the real situation beyond the surface is complicated and subtle so we have to study the situation to discover the truth.
【课文】任何一个按照常识推断的人都会怀疑这里面有文章。
【补充】他们公司突然停止生产那种非常赚钱的产品，我看这里面一定有文章。

明知故问   *pretend not to know a fact one actually knows very well*

This is a straightforward criticism.

【课文】您这是明知故问。

【补充】这件事你何必明知故问？

有目共睹   *very clear to all people*

Lit. "All those who have eyes can see it."

【课文】我们的新款皮鞋的鞋底同080完全不同，这是有目共睹的。

【补充】中国改革开放以来的经济成就是有目共睹的。

Class Discussion
课堂讨论

1. 你认为美达公司是否违背了同桑德蓝签订的合同？
2. 你认为腾云鞋厂是否违背了同美达公司签订的合同？
3. 你觉得这两份合同本身有没有缺陷？
4. 你认为李金旺的行为是否构成犯罪？
5. 你觉得还应该调查哪些情况？
6. 你建议桑德蓝公司采取什么方法来解决纠纷？

Exercises
练习

PART ONE: FAST ORAL TRANSLATION
第一部分：快速口译

Refer to Lesson 1 for instructions for this exercise.

A. From Chinese into English
中方要求更改合同条款，同美方商议.

B. From English into Chinese
An American manager is asking his Chinese counterpart to review the draft of a contract.

Part Two: Role-play (Questioning Li Jinwang)
第二部分：角色表演（询问李金旺）

If Hansen and Aileen track down Li Jinwang, what should they ask him? Student A acts as Li Jinwang, student B acts as Hansen, and student C acts as Aileen. Pay attention to question and answer tactics.

如果韩森和艾琳找到了李金旺，他们应该问他什么问题？
（请注意提问的策略。）

Part Three: Rephrasing Sentences
第三部分：改写句子

Refer to Lesson 1 for instructions for this exercise.

1. 对不起，我还有很多事情要做，请你们离开这里。
2. 你们没有按照我们的合同办事，因为你们把一些不应该告诉别人的技术告诉别人了。
3. 我们公司各方面的情况都不错，我真不明白你为什么要说我们用了不该用的人呢？

Part Four: Composition
第四部分：写作

Sunderland has designed a new model of shoes and they are in discussions with East Sea Shoe Works about outsourcing manufacturing of the shoes to East Sea. Please draft a contract for them.

LESSON 10: INTELLECTUAL PROPERTY RIGHTS
第十课：知识产权

Background and Business Tasks
背景和任务

Entrance to a court building.

康福德是美国阿灵顿制药公司2001年开始批量生产的一种降压药，2002年5月开始在中国市场销售。但是2002年10月在中国市场上出现了一种叫"降压康福"的中药，是中国南海制药厂生产的。根据阿灵顿试验室的检测，这种药品的有效成份是T3物质，和康福德完全相同。阿灵顿公司认为，南海制药厂有明显的侵权行为，所以委托金桥公司了解中国有关知识产权的法律，并寻找得力的律师准备起诉。

Part One: At Limin Drugstore
第一部分：在利民药店

Buying traditional Chinese medicine.

售货员：　小姐您想买什么药？我们刚刚进了一批<u>青春养颜冲剂</u>，经常<u>服用</u>可
　　　　　以使您青春<u>永驻</u>，不来点儿试试？今天**八折**优惠。

艾琳：　谢谢。我是来给我舅舅买降压药的，需要医生的<u>处方</u>吗？

售货员：　不用不用，我们这儿方便，什么药都不需要处方。您舅舅是**自费还**
　　　　　是公费？

韩森：　自费和公费有什么不一样？

售货员：　嘿！现在会说中文的老外越来越多了。要是公费，我就向您推荐
　　　　　美国的康福德，贵是贵了点儿，反正你能**报销**，怕什么？要是自费
　　　　　呢，您买降压康福就行了，一瓶才十八块钱，不到美国药的五分
　　　　　之一。

艾琳：　那效果怎么样？

售货员：　其实差不多，都挺有效的。

韩森：　你能肯定不是**假冒伪劣**？

售货员：　连假冒伪劣你都懂？**真有你的**。我们可是<u>正经</u>的国营药店，不是走
　　　　　<u>街串巷</u>的<u>药贩子</u>，我要是卖给你假药，把病人吃死了，我能负得起
　　　　　这责任吗？

艾琳：　他的意思是这种药是不是仿制品？

售货员：　仿制怕什么？有效又便宜**不就行了吗**？街上那么多DVD<u>光盘</u>，有多少
　　　　　是真的？能看就行了。这药也许是仿制的，可是便宜啊！**谁让你们**
　　　　　美国药贵得离谱儿啊！哎，你是美国人还是俄国人？

艾琳：　那就给我一瓶降压康福吧。

售货员：　这位先生不想试试我们中国的"老大哥"？这种中药可比你们
　　　　　的"<u>伟哥</u>"还有效呢！

A pharmacy that sells both Western and Chinese medicine.

Part Two: At the Xiongfei Law Firm of Shanghai
第二部分：在上海雄飞律师事务所

陈雄飞：	嘿，艾琳，**哪阵风把你吹来了**？
艾琳：	我是**无事不登三宝殿**。有一笔大生意，又给你送上门来了。
陈：	谢谢，谢谢。这位是……
艾琳：	我忘了介绍了，他是我的新搭档，叫韩森，是哈佛商学院的。这位是陈大律师，<u>复旦</u>和<u>耶鲁</u>的<u>双料</u>法学博士。
韩森：	幸会幸会。
陈：	什么样的案子，还是合同纠纷吗？
艾琳：	是知识产权方面的。美国的阿灵顿公司准备起诉南海制药厂。
陈：	什么？这次我恐怕帮不上忙了。
艾琳：	为什么？
陈：	实不相瞒，我两个星期前同意作南海制药厂的代理人，今天早上刚刚把<u>诉讼书</u>递上去。
韩森：	他们告谁？
陈：	当然是告美国阿灵顿了。
韩森：	这真是"**恶人先告状**"。
艾琳：	到底是怎么回事？

陈： 严格地说，作为南海的代理人，在开庭之前，我不应该泄露诉讼内容。但是咱们是老朋友，我更希望庭外和解。

韩森： 明明是南海仿制了阿灵顿的药，他们……

陈： 老弟，事情不像你想的那么简单。而且你们老美有一种不正常的心态，老觉得别人在仿冒你们的产品。根据我了解的情况，是阿灵顿侵犯了南海的权利。

韩森： 这不可能！

艾琳： 小韩，你让老陈把话说完。

陈： 我要问问你们，康福德是什么时候开始开发的？

艾琳： 我们的材料显示，1991年美国卡森大学的研究人员首次发现T3物质有调节血压的作用，1995年阿灵顿公司购买了他们的研究专利，经过三年的开发和两年的临床试验，最后在2001年由美国食品药品管理局批准出售康福德。

陈： 这就是问题了。根据我的材料，T3物质的调节血压的作用是由中国的南方大学首先发现的，他们的论文发表日期是1987年，比卡森大学的研究整整早了四年。

艾琳： 在什么杂志上发表的？

陈： 《南方大学学报》。

韩森： 我从来没听说过这本杂志。

陈： 的确不太有名，但是论文的提要在权威性的《中国医学信息索引》中可以查到。更重要的是，从1990年开始，南方大学生物系就和南海制药厂合作**先后**生产了降压一号，降压二号和降压三号中药，其中的主要成份是**富含**T3物质的草药鹅掌藤。现在的降压康福就是在降压三号的基础上改进的产品。所以，南海药厂认为，美国的有关方面侵害了他们的发明权。

艾琳： 但是美国的康福德并不是中药啊！

陈： 根据南海的调查，卡森大学从事有关研究的人员中，有两名是中国的留学生，其中**一人**正是来自南方大学生物系。由此看来，美国的研究成果很可能是借鉴了中国的研究。不管是来自草药的天然T3还是用化学合成的人造T3，反正都是T3，你能说没有关系吗？

韩森： 陈律师所说的情况我们需要核查。但是有一件事情非常清楚，这就是阿灵顿公司先在中国市场上推出了康福德，过了将近半年时间南海的降压康福才出现。你为什么要把所谓的降压三号变成降压康福呢？非常明显，南海是利用康福德的声誉来赚钱。换句话说，南海侵犯了阿灵顿公司的**注册商标**。我提醒陈律师，康福德这个商标可是经过中国官方批准的。

陈： 小韩，我们现在可不是在法庭上打官司，你别着急。我承认，你说得很有道理。但是根据我掌握的情况，在中国有一家生产轮椅和拐杖等用品的工厂，在十年前就注册了康富德商标。虽然福字和富字是两个字，但声音相似，除声调稍有不同外，汉语拼音完全一样。而且康富德虽然不是药品却是在医药商店出售的商品，这家工厂已经要求中国商标局和医药管理局收回成命，撤销阿灵顿的康福德商标。看来政府部门的管理出了一些纰漏。如果康福德商标本身就有侵权的问题，那还有什么资格告别的公司侵权呢？

艾琳： 你们这些律师真会颠倒黑白。

陈： 艾琳，律师就要为**当事人**的利益考虑，这也是身不由己。不过，根据我的经验，如果打起官司来，阿灵顿胜诉的可能性非常小。我真的希望两家庭外和解。

韩森： 怎么和解？

陈： 很简单，我的当事人提出了两个条件。第一，阿灵顿一次性付给南方大学和南海制药厂赔偿费人民币三千万元。第二，康福德退出中国和亚洲市场。南海可以保证他们的降压康福不进入欧美市场。

韩森： **笑话**，这等于投降。阿灵顿绝对不能接受。

陈： 那我们就只有在法庭上见了。当然不是和你们，而是你们找的律师。 要不要我给你们介绍几家同行？

艾琳： 谢谢，还是我们自己找吧。

陈： **看在朋友的面上**，我奉劝你们，这件事最好别插手，不然对你们的自己的咨询公司的生意也不利。至于阿灵顿嘛，他们的损失就不是三千万人民币而是三亿美元了。请转告他们，不要**敬酒不吃吃罚酒**。艾琳你是知道的，我经手了十几起经济大案，从来没有败诉过。

Part Three: A Civil Action Suit
第三部分：民事诉讼状

原告：吴运全，男，中国南海制药厂法人代表，家住中国广东省东山县祥光街26号

委托代理人：陈雄飞，男，上海雄飞律师事务所律师，上海浦东新开路208号531室

被告：美国阿灵顿制药公司上海办事处，上海浦东区光明大厦1748-1756号

请求事项：

1. 停止被告的侵权行为；
2. 赔偿原告的经济损失3亿美元。

事实与理由：

原告根据合作人中国南方大学生物系1987年4月发表的科研成果，从1990年开始在市场上推出了以T3物质为主要成份的治疗高血压病系列药品：降压一号、降压二号、降压三号和降压康福。被告在2001年推出并于2002年开始在中国市场以"康福德"为药名销售的降压药与原告开发的药品的作用机制完全相同，显然是利用了原告的开发成果，但是却从来没有向原告购买发明权，更没有经过原告的同意，构成严重的侵权行为，极大地损害了原告的商业利益。据估算，被告的药品在世界范围已经销售七百余万瓶，获取了大量利润。而由于被告的侵权行为，导致原告在市场上的销售份额急剧下降，直接经济损失已经高达四千万元，间接经济损失难以计数。

　　鉴于被告的侵权行为的严重性，根据民事有关法律规定，诉请贵院，依法准如所请。

原告代理人：陈雄飞2002年12月28日

此致上海市中级人民法院

Vocabulary List

知识产权	知識產權	zhīshí chǎnquán	intellectual property rights
康福德		*Kāngfúdé*	*name of a product*
阿灵顿	阿靈頓	*Ālíngdùn*	*Arlington, name of a company*
制药	製藥	zhìyào	pharmaceutical
降压药	降壓藥	jiàngyāyào	medicine that lowers high blood pressure
检测	檢測	jiǎncè	examine and test
有效成份		yǒuxiào chéngfèn	active ingredient; effective component
得力		délì	capable
青春养颜	青春養顏	qīnchūn yǎngyán	stay young-looking; age-defying
冲剂	沖劑	chōngjì	medicine to be taken after dissolving in hot water
服用		fúyòng	take (medicine)
永驻	永駐	yǒngzhù	forever in place
处方	處方	chǔfāng	prescription
自费	自費	zìfèi	at one's own expense
公费	公費	gōngfèi	at public expense; paid by the government
推荐	推薦	tuījiàn	recommend
报销	報銷	bàoxiāo	v. reimburse; n. reimbursement
假冒伪劣	假冒偽劣	jiǎmào wěiliè	counterfeit and low quality goods
正经	正經	zhèngjǐng	[cl.] standard; respectable
走街串巷		zǒujiēchuànxiàng	walk through streets and lanes
药贩子	藥販子	yàofànzi	[cl.] medicine peddler
光盘	光盤	guāngpán	CD; DVD
离谱儿	離譜兒	lípǔ	[cl.] unreasonable; far-fetched
伟哥	偉哥	*Wěigē*	*Viagra*
律师事务所	律師事務所	lùshī shìwùsuǒ	law firm
三宝殿	三寶殿	sānbǎodiàn	The main hall of a Buddhist monastery; your esteemed place
复旦	復旦	Fùdàn	name of a premier university in Shanghai
耶鲁	耶鲁	Yēlǔ	Yale University
双料	雙料	shuāngliào	[cl.] double
诉讼书	訴訟書	sùsòngshū	suit; formal written complaint

递	遞	dì	deliver
告状	告狀	gàozhuàng	bring suit; lodge a complaint
庭外和解		tíngwài héjiě	settle out of court
调节	調節	tiáojié	adjust
临床	臨床	línchuáng	clinical
提要		tíyào	abstract
索引		suǒyǐn	index
富含		fùhán	rich; be rich in
鹅掌藤	鵝掌藤	ézhǎngténg	goose foot ivy
借鉴	借鑒	jièjiàn	use as reference; draw from others' experience or knowledge
天然		tiānrán	natural
化学合成	化學合成	huàxué héchéng	chemical synthesis
人造		rénzào	artificial; man-made
核查		héchá	investigation; verify
声誉	聲譽	shēngyù	fame; reputation
注册商标	注冊商標	zhùcèshāngbiāo	registered trademark
轮椅	輪椅	lúnyǐ	wheelchair
拐杖		guǎizhàng	walking stick
成命		chéngmìng	order already issued
撤销	撤銷	chèxiāo	repeal; countermand
纰漏	紕漏	pīlòu	loose hole; careless mistake; slip-up
颠倒黑白	顛倒黑白	diāndǎohēibái	confuse truth and falsehood
当事人	當事人	dāngshìrén	party in a dispute; legal client
胜诉	勝訴	shèngsù	win a suit
赔偿	賠償	péicháng	compensate
投降		tóuxiáng	surrender
同行		tóngháng	person of the same profession
奉劝	奉勸	fèngquàn	advise (a polite way of warning)
插手		chāshǒu	get involved
敬酒		jìngjiǔ	proposed toast
罚酒	罰酒	fájiǔ	penalty drink (that a loser is obliged to drink)
经手	經手	jīngshǒu	undertake
起		qǐ	a measure word for case, instance
败诉	敗訴	bàisù	lose a lawsuit

民事		mínshì	civil (suit) (vs. 刑事 or criminal suit)
事项	事項	shìxiàng	matter
机制	機制	jīzhì	mechanism
难以计数	難以計數	nányǐjìshǔ	immeasurable

Notes and Explanations

1. BUSINESS AND OTHER PROFESSIONAL TERMS

起诉　　*bring a suit against somebody*

诉 means "suit or sue." An original meaning of 诉 is "to tell," but the choice of this word for the modern "lawsuit" may be attributed partially to translation. There are many legal terms with this word element:

胜诉 win a law suit
败诉 lose a law suit
诉讼书 lawsuit (formal written complaint)
公诉人 public prosecutor

折

An important word for "discount." In China, a discount is calculated as a percentage of the original price, contrary to the common practice in the United States where a discount is calculated as a percentage off the original price. Thus, 八折 is 80% of the original price or 20% off; 四折 is 40% of the original price or 60% off; 九五折 is 95% of the original price or 5% off.

【课文】今天八折优惠。
【补充】这些光盘我可以给你打六折。

自费 / 公费

The former means "at one's own expense" while the latter's meaning is somewhat ambiguous. In a narrow sense, it means "at public expense." In a broader sense, it may include expenses reimbursed by a company even if the company is privately owned.

报销　　*reimburse*

This verb can mean both "to apply for reimbursement" and "to reimburse an expense incurred by an individual."

【课文】反正你能报销，……
【补充】今天我请客不是我自己花钱，单位报销。

假冒伪劣　　*fake and low quality goods*

假＝fake; 冒＝counterfeit; 伪＝fake; 劣＝quality lower than the minimum standard. Put together, this phrase means "very low quality counterfeit (goods)."

注册商标　　*to register a trademark; registered trademark*
【课文】在十年前就注册了康富德商标。
【补充】"白山"是我们产品的注册商标。

当事人

In this lesson, it means "the client represented by an attorney." In a broader sense, it may also mean the "parties directly involved."

2. FORMAL EXPRESSIONS

先后　　*one after another; in succession*
【课文】先后生产了降压一号、降压二号和降压三号中药。
【补充】来美后他先后访问了哈佛、耶鲁和哥伦比亚等著名大学。

富含　　*be rich in*
【课文】主要成分是富含T3物质的鹅掌藤。
【补充】番茄富含维生素C。

一人

Characteristics of literary Chinese often appear in formal writing or speech. An example is the dropping of the measure word in certain contexts.
【课文】其中一人正是来自南方大学生物系。
【补充】图书馆之东有一圆形建筑。

鉴于　　*in light of..., given the fact that...*
【课文】鉴于被告的侵权行为的严重性，......
【补充】鉴于这种电脑在市场上的良好反应，公司决定扩大生产规模。

3. COLLOQUIAL EXPRESSIONS

真有你的   *you are really something*

Used for expressing surprise. Sometimes may be sarcastic.

【课文】连假冒伪劣都懂？真有你的。

【补充】五万美元一个星期就花完了？真有你的。

不就行了吗？

This rhetorical phrase is used to imply the problem is not very complicated and/or serious, and could be solved easily.

【课文】有效又便宜不就行了吗？

【补充】机器坏了没什么关系，找人来修修不就行了吗？

谁让...啊／呢   *Lit. "Who made...?" How could there be any alternative...?*

【课文】谁让你们美国药贵得离谱儿啊！

【补充】又来借钱了？拿去吧。谁让我是你哥哥呢！

离谱儿   *far from the norm; extreme*

【课文】谁让你们美国药贵得离谱儿啊！

【补充】他刚十八岁你就让他当总经理，这也太离谱儿了！

笑话

Used to imply that the suggestion/proposal mentioned is completely unacceptable and ridiculous.

【课文】笑话，这等于投降。

【补充】"你这台电脑三百块卖给我怎么样？""笑话，三千块我也不卖！"

4. OTHER PATTERNS AND WORD COLLOCATIONS

看在朋友的面上

Used to make concessions as a favor to the other party.

【课文】看在朋友的面上，我奉劝你们，这件事最好别插手。

【补充】看在朋友的面上，这笔钱我再多给你三天时间还。三天以后我就不客气了。

5. IMPORTANT IDIOMATIC PHRASES/PROVERBS

哪阵风把你给吹来了

See **General Notes on Business Communication I.**

无事不登三宝殿

Lit. "Would not come to the temple for no good reason." I wouldn't have come bother you if I didn't have a favor to ask of you. See **General Notes on Business Communication II.**

恶人先告状   *the wrongdoer (criminal) sues the victim first*

Used to describe a situation in which the offender files a preemptive complaint before the victim can.

敬酒不吃吃罚酒

Lit. "Refusing to accept a drink respectfully offered will result in having to drink as a punishment." This phrase is used to warn that if one turns down a good offer, one will have to accept a bad one.

【课文】请转告他们，不要敬酒不吃吃罚酒……

【补充】两个月前人家出三万块要买你这个小店你不卖，现在市场行情越来越差，只能把商店免费送给人家，你真是敬酒不吃吃罚酒。

Class Discussion
课堂讨论

1. 谈谈你对这起侵权案的看法。
2. 如果你是阿灵顿公司的负责人，你会考虑庭外和解吗？
3. 你觉得案子的关键在什么地方？
4. 你觉得还有哪些问题需要调查？

Exercises
练习

PART ONE: FAST ORAL TRANSLATION
第一部分：快速口译

Refer to Lesson 1 for instructions for this exercise.

    A. From Chinese into English
    中国政府官员谈保护知识产权问题。

    B. From English into Chinese
    In court, an American lawyer for the plaintiff states his views to the judge.

PART TWO: ROLE-PLAY (A COURT ARGUMENT)
第二部分：角色表演（模拟法庭抗诉）

Student A acts as Mr. Chen Xiongfei; student B acts as the lawyer for Arlington; student C acts as the judge.
一位同学扮演陈律师，一位同学扮演阿灵顿公司聘请的律师，另一位同学扮演法官。

PART THREE: REPHRASING SENTENCES (PARAGRAPH IMPROVEMENT)
第三部分：改写下面这段话

Refer to Lesson 1 for instructions for this exercise.

今天我接到了一个电话，是一家律师的公司打的，说有一家英国公司要告我们。他们说我们商店里卖的英国产品是假的。他们还说要是我们赔给他们三百万块钱，就可以不去法院告我们了。我跟他说这个条件不行。他劝我同意他们的条件，说要是我们不答应我们就会有更大的损失。

PART FOUR: COMPOSITION
第四部分：写作

Write a lawsuit for Arlington.

LESSON 11: ADDED INVESTMENT
第十一课：追加投资

Background and Business Tasks
背景和任务

美国<u>休斯</u>公司和中国<u>广厦</u>建筑开发集团公司在1999年合作建立了合资企业<u>鹰神涂料厂</u>，生产目前中国市场上最先进的<u>油漆涂料</u>。在**一期**工程中，双方各投资四千万人民币，目前项目已经完成，并开始生产鹰神牌<u>外墙涂料</u>。按照双方当初**达成的共识**，应该在2002年底进行追加投资，扩建厂房，生产内墙涂料。但是，不久前，休斯公司接到广厦**来函**，要求<u>暂缓</u>追加投资。现在，休斯公司委托金桥公司进行公关工作，说服广厦按原定计划追加投资。

Part One: In the Taxi
第一部分：在出租汽车上

韩森：　我真不明白中国人谈生意为什么总喜欢在饭桌上边吃边谈。

艾琳：　这就是中国的商业文化，我前两天看了一篇文章，说光是北京市，
一年的**商务餐**要吃掉5个亿。如果一顿商务餐需要500块钱，那难道这
些北京的商人一年一共吃了一百万次商务餐吗？

司机：　大姐，这您就**外行**了。哪有500元一顿的商务餐啊？500块就连一个人
也不够啊！

韩森：　可是我自己在街上一顿饭二三十块钱吃得很好啊！

司机：　不能这么比，我中午一个盒饭才五块钱。在北京这种地方，你**不舍
得**花钱请客，什么生意都做不成。哎，绿村酒家到了，**信不信由你**，
今天晚上这顿商务餐没有三万块钱**下不来**。

韩森：　我们这几个人真能吃那么多东西？

司机：　看来我真得给你上一课了。商务餐吃的是气氛，餐厅的装潢、音
乐、餐具都是钱，也许这三万块钱还吃不饱呢，你回家还得再冲包
方便面。

艾琳：　谢谢，这是四十块，剩下的不用找了，就算是您的讲课费吧。

Part Two: In the Special Banquet Room at Green Villa
第二部分：绿村酒家雅座

韩金刚：　我来介绍一下，这是广厦集团公司的总经理陈军先生，这是我们的
总会计师龙在天先生，这是公司办公室副主任朱安娜小姐，这是公
关部的龚小梅小姐，这位呢，是外事办公室主任许杰先生。本人韩
金刚。大家随便坐吧，我们今天不分宾主上下。

朱：　韩先生，艾琳女士，这是今天的菜单，**请过目**。

艾琳：　**客随主便**。

朱：　小姐，请上菜吧。

韩金刚：　我提议，为表示对两位远道而来的客人的敬意，先干一杯。

韩森：　对不起，我不会喝酒，而且我看我们还是先谈工作吧。

陈：　没关系，这是长白山的野葡萄酒，度数很低，风味独特，韩先生可
以试试。

艾琳： 今天**承蒙广厦的主要领导专门设宴款待**，十分过意不去。由于贵公司和休斯公司的**精诚合作**，鹰神厂**取得了辉煌的业绩**。我提议，大家<u>举杯</u>，祝愿双方的合作能够<u>更上一层楼</u>。

韩金刚： 艾琳小姐说得对，大家再干一杯！

韩森： 可是**在工厂急需扩建这个紧要关头**，你们却建议<u>暂缓</u>二期投资，这实在是**釜底抽薪**啊！

朱： 菜来了，大家先吃吧，边吃边谈。

艾琳： 我的这位同事<u>心直口快</u>，**还望韩董事长海涵**。

韩金刚： 没关系，没关系，我年轻时也是这样。老陈啊，你就把我们的困难跟两位**交个底**吧。

陈： 目前广厦在<u>资金运作</u>上确实遇到了一些困难，有几个投资项目的资金没有能够及时收回，更重要的是，我们准备<u>承包</u>和2008年奥运相关的两个重大工程，只能先把手头的资金全部投进去。我们向二位保证，一旦**资金到位**，对鹰神厂的二次投入我们一分也不会少。

韩森： 如果我没记错的话，贵国著名的《<u>孙子兵法</u>》上有一句话："**兵贵神速**"。现在鹰神的外墙涂料在市场上有口皆碑，如果及时进行二期投资，在一年内生产出高质量的内墙涂料，那它的市场占有率就有可能突破百分之三十，成为涂料市场的**龙头**。但是如果不抓住这个机遇，让正在中国<u>筹建</u>的日本森和、荷兰麦尔在内墙涂料方面<u>占了头筹</u>，我们就恐怕连第一期投资的**本金**也收不回来了。

韩金刚： 真没想到韩先生这么年轻连孙子兵法也<u>倒背如流</u>，佩服，佩服。佩服！大家都应该敬他一杯！干！

艾琳： 我觉得韩森讲得很有道理。刚才陈总说到奥运会，我觉得现在就开始2008年才会使用的建筑是不是**为时**过早？在我看来，扩建鹰神厂倒是对奥运的更好的投资，我敢<u>肯定</u>，未来几年的内墙涂料市场会越来越火，如果我们能让鹰神成为奥运村的**指定**内墙涂料，那我们投资的回报就非常**可观**了。

韩金刚： 不错，这些问题我们也考虑过，但眼下的资金实在困难，休斯可以先投进一部分资金，我们会在不久随后跟进。

艾琳： 实不相瞒，最近美国股市的走向<u>不佳</u>，这个<u>诸位</u>不会不知道。休斯的股票两年内跌了百分之六十。当然了，企业仍然有实力，绝对不会<u>破产倒闭</u>，大家可以放心。但是现在**手头**能够动用的资金实在有限，在原来承诺的五千万以外，不可能再增加了。如果没有贵方的同时投入，扩建计划无法完成。

韩森： 我们希望贵公司也能**遵守当初的承诺**。

朱： <u>松鼠鳜鱼</u>来了，大家还是先吃吧，凉了就不好吃了。

韩森： 说句心里话，我真希望能把今天的饭钱省下来，投到鹰神厂去。听说这一顿要吃掉三万块，是真的吗？

龙在天： 韩先生**精神可嘉**，我再敬您一杯。作为广厦的总会计师，我来解释两句。其实，**以我们现在的实力**，不要说投四千万，就是八千万也**不在话下**。但是我们现在要<u>竞标</u>奥运项目能否中标，其中的一个重要条件就是手里有没有可以自由<u>支配</u>的资金。所以我们的钱真是不能动。你们大概知道，如果中标，项目费用高达几十个亿，利润嘛，至少有百分之二十五，而且更重要的是企业的形象和名气。竞标将在明年五月开始，九月<u>搞定</u>，在这之前，资金要集中起来。用毛主席的话说，这叫"**集中优势兵力打歼灭战**"。

陈： 也可以说"**鱼与熊掌不可兼得**"。韩先生，这句话你也听说过吧？

韩金刚： 就是这个情况，我们的<u>苦衷</u>还请二位向休斯的老总解释。

艾琳： 龙先生，我在苏州曾经遇到过一位龙在田先生，你们两个的名字这么像，是不是一家人？

龙在天： 对，对，在田正是<u>家兄</u>。真是巧得很啊，我们兄弟二人都有生意要请您艾琳小姐帮助。

艾琳： 那么借助于广厦的关系网络，能不能向其他的企业或者社会<u>筹借</u>一部分资金呢？

韩金刚： 你的意思是找米下锅，借鸡生蛋？

韩森： 对啊！这样鱼和熊掌就可以兼得了。

龚小梅： 真巧，说到熊掌熊掌就来了！两位尝尝，绿村的熊掌豆腐是非常有名的。

韩森： 你们怎么能吃野<u>生</u>动物呢？

朱： 韩先生误会了，这不是真的熊掌，是把豆腐做成熊掌的样子，味道也和熊掌差不多。

艾琳： 我们还是谈正事吧。韩董觉得筹借资金是不是<u>可行之计</u>？

龙在天： 董事长，我觉得可以一试。虽然涂料的利润会让别人分去一部分，但是总比白白丢给日本人好。

陈： 这个我们还要再研究研究，我们改日再谈吧。谢谢艾琳小姐给我们出主意。我敬你一杯。

（在出租车上）

韩森： 艾琳，我的头有点晕。

艾琳： 其实你的<u>酒量</u>还不错嘛。我觉得他们有点儿松动。现在需要调查核实广厦的资金<u>周转</u>到底出了哪些问题，我们得赶紧上互联网**搜索情报**。

A poor-quality construction job.

Part Three: Online Discovery

第三部分：网上发现

www.xinwen.com.cn

又一个<u>豆腐渣工程</u>

最近**国家质检总局**接到大量的群众反映，金州市乐康新村<u>住宅区</u>的新建居民楼出现严重的质量问题，其中，<u>卫生间</u>的漏水现象高达百分之八十，还有<u>天花板坠落</u>砸伤住户的事件发生。接到<u>举报</u>后，国家质检总局立即组成工作小组赴金州调查。经过初步检测，发现这批由广厦建筑开发集团公司下属三喜建筑公司**承包**兴建的楼群存在着严重的质量问题。除了已建成的居民楼的装修质量外，还发现正在兴建的十栋居民楼存在着重大的结构缺陷，因钢筋和<u>水泥</u>的质量不合格，一旦居民入住可能发生楼房坍塌的严重事故。国家质检总局已经同金州市有关方面下令停止<u>**施工**</u>，已经<u>**竣工**</u>尚未出售的三栋楼房从房地产市场收回，对三喜公司处以1500万人民币的罚款，并对问题进行进一步调查。

据报导，广厦建筑开发集团公司的副董事长黄平已经**专程**赶赴金州处理这一重大质量问题。集团公司已经作出三项决定，第一，撤销王宝光的三喜公司总经理职务，并对其他责任者进行处罚；第二，在半年内免费重新装修已经建成的居民楼，并根据损失情况发给住户赔偿金；第三，根据需要，对正在兴建的住宅楼**采取结构<u>补救措施</u>**或者彻底推倒重建。黄平对记者表示，广厦会**不惜一切代价挽回损失**，保证住户的安全。

　　另据报导，<u>纪检</u>和<u>公安</u>部门也已经开展调查，很多人怀疑，在豆腐渣工程的背后，可能有行贿、受贿等违法行为。

Part Four: A Memorandum of Intent Signed by Hughes Company of the United States and Guangsha Construction Company of China

第四部分：美国休斯公司和中国广厦建筑开发集团公司追加投资意向书

休斯公司和广厦公司经过友好协商，达成如下合作意向：

第一，在双方合作投资兴建的鹰神涂料厂一期工程完工并投入批量生产后，共同投资兴建该厂的二期工程。

第二，二期投资的**额度**暂定为：休斯公司投入5000万人民币，广厦公司投入4000万人民币。

第三，以上投资应一次到位。

第四，一期投资和二期投资的回报统一**结算**，利润双方五五分成。

第五，根据市场的需要等具体情况，双方可以通过协商对投资的细节作出修改。

第六，本意向书一式两份，每份包括中文和英文两种效力等同的文本，双方各保留一份。

签字人：
休斯公司　　广厦公司
罗斯特（总经理）　　　韩金刚（董事长）

日期：1999年10月23日

Vocabulary List

追加		zhuījiā	make an additional allocation for (investment)
休斯		*Xiūsī*	*Hughes, name of a company*
广厦	廣廈	*Guǎngshà*	*name of a company*
集团公司	集團公司	jítuán gōngsī	corporate group; conglomerate
鹰神	鷹神	*Yīngshén*	*name of a brand*
涂料	塗料	túliào	paint
油漆		yóuqī	(oil) paint
外墙	外牆	wàiqiáng	exterior wall
共识	共識	gòngshí	agreement; mutual understanding
扩建	擴建	kuòjiàn	expand; expansion
内墙	內牆	nèiqiáng	interior wall
来函		láihán	incoming letter
暂缓	暫緩	zànhuǎn	postpone
下不来		xiàbùlái	[cl.] not enough; cannot get by
气氛	氣氛	qìfēn/qìfèn	atmosphere; ambience
装潢	裝潢	zhuānghuáng	interior finishing
餐具		cānjù	dinnerware
冲	沖	chōng	pour hot water onto
方便面	方便麵	fāngbiànmiàn	instant noodle
雅座		yǎzuò	special dining room in a restaurant
过目	過目	guòmù	take a look (for approval)
客随主便	客隨主便	kèsuízhǔbiàn	a guest will follow the arrangement of a host
宾主上下	宾主上下	bīnzhǔ shàngxià	guest and host; superior and inferior
长白山	長白山	*Chángbáishān*	*name of a mountain*
野葡萄酒		yěpútáo jiǔ	wine made from wild grapes
度数	度數	dùshù	alcohol content
独特	獨特	dútè	unique
承蒙		chéngméng	be indebted to; receive the grace of
款待		kuǎndài	generous treatment
辉煌	輝煌	huīhuáng	brilliant
举杯	舉杯	jǔbēi	propose a toast

紧要关头	緊要關頭	jǐnyào guāntóu	crucial moment
暂缓	暫緩	zànhuǎn	postpone for the time being
釜底抽薪		fǔdǐchōuxīn	pull the rug out from under
心直口快		xīnzhíkǒukuài	outspoken
海涵		hǎihán	grant forgiveness/immense tolerance
交个底	交個底	jiāogedǐ	[cl.] tell the truth / give the bottom line
资金运作	資金運作	zījīn yùnzuò	capital/fund management
承包		chéngbāo	contract (with)
手头	手頭	shǒutóu	[cl.] (money) in hand
到位		dàowèi	put (money) in place
孙子兵法	孫子兵法	Sūnzǐ Bīngfǎ	*The Art of War* by Sunzi
兵贵神速	兵貴神速	bīngguìshénsù	speed is precious in war
有口皆碑		yǒukǒujiēbēi	be praised by all who know
龙头	龍頭	lóngtóu	number one (in a profession/field)
筹建	籌建	chóujiàn	plan to build
森和		*Sēnhé*	*name of a company*
荷兰	荷蘭	Hélán	Holland
麦尔	麥爾	*Mài'ěr*	*name of a company*
占了头筹	佔了頭籌	zhànle tóuchóu	receive first place
本金		běnjīn	principal
倒背如流		dàobèirúliú	recite fluently
指定		zhǐdìng	designated
佳		jiā	good
诸位	諸位	zhùwèi	you all
破产	破產	pòchǎn	go bankrupt
承诺	承諾	chéngnuò	commitment; promise
松鼠鳜鱼	松鼠鱖魚	sōngshǔ guìyú	deep-fried mandarin fish in sweet sauce
精神可嘉		jīngshén kějiā	have a fine spirit or good intentions
竞标	競標	jìngbiāo	bid
支配		zhīpèi	allocate
搞定		gǎodìng	[cl.] get the job done
歼灭战	殲滅戰	jiānmièzhàn	annihilative battle
熊掌		xióngzhǎng	bear paw
兼得		jiāndé	get both
苦衷		kǔzhōng	difficulties that one is hard put to explain

老总	老總	lǎozǒng	[cl.] top leaders
家兄		jiāxiōng	elder brother
借助		jièzhù	rely on; lean on
筹借	籌借	chóujiè	borrow (money)
找米下锅	找米下鍋	zhǎomǐxiàguō	seek rice to cook
借鸡生蛋	借雞生蛋	jièjīshēngdàn	borrow a hen to lay eggs
野生动物	野生動物	yěshēng dòngwù	wild animal
可行之计	可行之計	kěxíngzhījì	feasible plan
晕	暈	yūn	dizzy
酒量		jiǔliàng	alcohol tolerance
松动	鬆動	sōngdòng	loosen
核实	核實	héshí	investigate; verify
周转	周轉	zhōuzhuǎn	(capital) turnover; circulation
搜索		sōusuǒ	search
情报	情報	qíngbào	information
豆腐渣工程		dòufuzhā gōngchéng	poor-quality construction project
住宅区	住宅區	zhùzháiqū	residential area
居民楼	居民樓	jūmínlóu	residential building
卫生间	衛生間	wèishēngjiān	bathroom
天花板		tiānhuābǎn	ceiling
坠落	墜落	zhuìluò	falling
砸		zá	hit from above
举报	舉報	jǔbào	tip-off; file a complaint
三喜		*Sānxǐ*	*name of a company*
栋	棟	dòng	measure word for a tall building
钢筋	鋼筋	gāngjīn	steel reinforcing bar
水泥		shuǐní	cement, concrete
坍塌		tāntā	collapse
施工		shīgōng	construction
竣工		jùngōng	completed construction
尚未		shàngwèi	not yet
专程	專程	zhuānchéng	make a special trip
撤销	撤銷	chèxiāo	remove somebody from a position
赔偿金	賠償金	péichángjīn	compensation
补救	補救	bǔjiù	remedy; make up for

不惜一切代价	不惜一切代價	bùxī yíqiè dàijià	not sparing any cost; at any cost
挽回		wǎnhuí	retrieve
纪检	紀檢	jìjiǎn	abbr. for 纪律检查 disciplinary inspection
公安		gōng'ān	public security
额度	額度	édù	portion; quota
一次到位		yícì dàowèi	in one payment; in one lump sum
五五分成		wǔwǔ fēnchéng	divide 50/50; split down the middle
一式两份	一式兩份	yíshì liǎngfèn	two copies of one document
效力等同		xiàolì děngtóng	equally effective

Notes and Explanations

1. Business and Other Professional Terms

一期   *phase one*

A huge project often develops over several phases. The Chinese terms for them are 一期 (工程), 二期(工程), 三期(工程), and so on. Some may use the term 第一期工程 but that doesn't sound as good and professional as 一期工程.

商务餐   *business meals*

This term denotes all company paid meals. Basically, there are two kinds. First are free lunches/dinners provided to the managers and white-collar employees of a company. Second are dinners or banquets honoring guests from other companies or the government. 商务餐 in the latter sense are typically extravagant.

资金到位   *lit. "funds reach their place"*

This means the promised fund/investment has arrived.

本金   *capital*

A more colloquial term with the same meaning is 本钱.

指定（产品）　　*designated (product)*

When there is a big event, e.g., the Olympic Games, the organization will seek sponsorships. In exchange, the sponsors' products will be advertised with the event logos and sometimes, with higher contributions, become the exclusive supplier of certain products for the event.

豆腐渣工程　　*lit. "soybean residue construction"*

Soybean residue is a by-product of making tofu. It is a gravel-like substance and cannot form a solid shape. It is very cheap and essentially useless. Therefore, people use this term to describe construction projects of the lowest quality. They will soon collapse after completion.

国家质检总局

The full name of this government body is 国家质量监督检验检疫总局. It is in charge of the quality control and inspection of all products, including import and export commodities, except for medicine and food.

承包　　*to contract (a business or project)*

This verb can be used beyond the field of construction. 承包 usually applies to the party receiving the contract, whereas 承包给 applies to the party issuing the contract.

【课文】三喜建筑公司承包兴建的楼群存在着严重的质量问题。
【补充】老张承包了老王的汽车修理厂。
【补充】老王把汽车修理厂承包给老张了。（意思和上面的一样）

施工 / 竣工

The former means construction is in process, and the latter means construction has been completed.

【课文】负责施工的是一家合资建筑公司。
【补充】由于大家的努力，这座住宅楼提前两个月竣工。

额度　　*quota*

Typically, it refers to money. For people, use 名额.

结算　　*settle an account*

结=conclude; 算=calculation. There are many word compounds with 结算, for example:

结算报告 final accounts report
年终结算 end of year financial statement
结算货币 currency of settlement

2. FORMAL EXPRESSIONS

来函/回函
函＝信.
　　【课文】休斯公司接到广厦来函，……
　　【补充】请你为公司起草回函。

请过目＝请看一下
　　【课文】这是今天的菜单，请过目。
　　【补充】这是我为公司起草的回函，请总经理过目。

为时＝从时间上说
The word following 为时 must be a two-syllable word.
Related word: 为期 for a period of...
　　【课文】我觉得现在就开始2008年才会使用的建筑是不是为时过早？
　　【补充】根据我的研究，投资影碟制造为时已晚。
　　【补充】全体职工务必参加为期三周的培训。

可观　　*considerable, impressive*
　　【课文】那我们投资的回报就非常可观了。
　　【补充】公司成立才两个月就已经取得了可观的经济效益。

苦衷　　*difficulties that one is hard put to explain*
苦 means "hard or difficult," and 衷 means "intention or heart." This term is typically used in a situation where one is doing something that may incite criticism or misunderstanding. The person is in a bind, but for some reason is reluctant to reveal or explain the situation to someone else.
　　【课文】我们的苦衷还请二位向休斯的老总解释。
　　【补充】我把这个经营得很好的饭店卖掉是为了开始一个现在必须保密的新项目，但是在别人的眼里，我简直是个疯子。除了你以外没有人理解我的苦衷。

家兄＝我哥哥

Similarly, 家父＝我爸爸.

专程 *make a special trip*

This word is just for important business or political matters. It is seldom used in everyday life situations.

【课文】黄平已经专程赶赴金州处理这一重大质量问题。

【补充】张总经理胜利地完成了和美方谈判的任务，王董事长专程前往机场迎接他的归来。

3. COLLOQUIAL EXPRESSIONS

外行   *nonprofessional, lacking experience*

This word can be used as a noun or an adjective. Antonym: 内行.

【课文】您这就外行了……

【补充】在网络方面他完全是外行。

【课文】听她说您对网络技术相当内行。(L7)

不舍得   *not begrudge (an expense)*

The same as 舍不得 but mostly used in conditional sentences.

【课文】您不舍得花钱请客，什么生意也做不成。

【补充】不舍得投资新产品的研制，一个企业就很难在竞争中取胜。

信不信由你   *believe it or not*

Generally, what follows will be something difficult to believe.

【课文】信不信由你，这顿商务餐没有三万块钱下不来。

【补充】信不信由你，这家电脑公司不出两个星期就会关门倒闭。

下不来   *The bill will not be less than...*

【课文】信不信由你，这顿商务餐没有三万块钱下不来。

【补充】这么豪华的新车，没有六十万下不来吧？

交底   *tell the facts; give the bottom line; put all one's cards on the table*

【课文】你就把我们的困难跟两位交个底吧。

【补充】我可以给你交个底，这家饭馆没有八十万你别想买走。

龙头   *lit. "dragon head"; number one (in a profession/field)*
　　【课文】成为涂料市场的龙头
　　【补充】二十多年来长春汽车厂一直是中国汽车工业的龙头。

手头（儿）   *(money) on hand; one's financial situation*
　　【课文】现在手头能够动用的资金实在有限，......
　　【补充】我手头儿很紧，怎么能借给你八万块钱呢？

不在话下   *so easy that you don't even need to mention it*
　　【课文】不要说投四千万，就是八千万也不在话下。
　　【补充】老王是公司的总经理，解决这个问题当然不在话下。

4. OTHER PATTERNS AND WORD COLLOCATIONS

达成共识   *reach a common understanding*
　　【课文】按照双方达成的共识，......
　　【补充】经过紧张的谈判，中方和美方终于达成了共识。

承蒙款待   *receive generous treatment or hospitality*

Both 承 and 蒙 mean "to receive." Used for expressing thanks to someone.
　　【课文】今天承蒙广厦的主要领导专门设宴款待，......
　　【补充】承蒙市领导的关心和支持，我们的工程进展非常顺利。

精诚合作   *sincere cooperation*

精＝pure; 诚＝sincere.
　　【课文】由于贵公司和休斯公司的精诚合作，鹰神厂取得了辉煌的业绩。
　　【补充】面对目前的经济危机，我们两个公司必须精诚合作。

取得业绩   *achieve great success*
　　【课文】由于贵公司和休斯公司的精诚合作，鹰神厂取得了辉煌的业绩。
　　【补充】这家只有二十多员工的公司在短短的半年时间内取得了惊人的
　　　　　　业绩。

在...的紧要关头   *at the critical moment of...*
   【课文】在工厂急需扩建这个紧要关头，你们却建议暂缓二期投资，……
   【补充】在最后一轮竞标的紧要关头，鸿兴公司突然宣布退出。

还望……海涵   *hope you will forgive...in a generous way*

海 is a metaphorical way of expressing immensity, e.g., 海量 "immense capacity (for liquor)."
   【课文】我这位同事心直口快，还望韩董事长海涵。
   【补充】招待不周，还望阁下海涵。（阁下 géxià＝Your Excellency）

遵守承诺   *keep a promise; abide by a commitment*
   【课文】我们希望贵公司也能遵守当初的承诺。
   【补充】如果不遵守承诺，以后还会有谁跟你合作呢？

精神可嘉   *one's spirit/intention is praiseworthy*

This phrase often implies that the intention is good but the idea is not feasible/realistic.
   【课文】韩先生精神可嘉。
   【补充】你要去西北发展网络经济固然精神可嘉，但是那个地区有不少
          人还没有解决温饱问题，怎么能有钱买电脑呢？（温饱＝to have
          enough food and clothing, the basic necessities of life）

以……的实力   *with somebody's strength or capacity*
   【课文】以我们现在的实力，不要说投四千万，就是八千万也不在话下。
   【补充】以金龙公司的实力，半年内完成这座住宅楼肯定没有问题。

搜索情报   *search for or gather information/intelligence*

搜集 may be used instead of 搜索.
   【课文】我们得赶紧上互联网搜索情报。
   【补充】听说那个制药公司正在研制一种治疗心脏病的新药，股民们纷纷
          搜集有关情报以决定是否购买该公司的股票。

采取...措施   *take the measure of*
   【课文】对正在兴建的住宅楼采取结构补救措施或者彻底推倒重建。
   【补充】为了防止股票价格进一步下跌，公司采取了一系列措施。

不惜一切代价   *at any cost*

　　【课文】不惜一切代价挽回损失。

　　【补充】这场官司关系到公司的声誉，我们要不惜一切代价打赢。(This lawsuit is critical to our company's reputation; we must win at any cost.)

挽回损失   *recover a loss*

　　【课文】不惜一切代价挽回损失。

　　【补充】工人们连续工作了三天三夜，基本上挽回了因大雨造成的损失。

5. IMPORTANT IDIOMATIC PHRASES/PROVERBS

客随主便   *lit. "a guest should follow the host's convenience"*

This is a polite reply to a host who asks what a guest would prefer or whether an arrangement is acceptable.

釜底抽薪   *lit. "take away the firewood from under a boiling cauldron"*

This phrase has two different meanings. Traditionally, it means to be determined to solve a problem at its foundation. If the soup is already too hot, you should turn off the fire, not just add cold water to the soup. Thus, it is positive in meaning. In recent years, however, it has a new meaning of "to suddenly take away something vital from an ongoing project." This is obviously negative in meaning. In this lesson, it is used in the second way.

　　【课文】这实在是釜底抽薪啊。

　　【补充】外国高科技公司釜底抽薪，中国手机生产商面临困境。(This is the title of a news article on the internet. The story is about some foreign hi-tech companies that suddenly stopped supplying key parts to Chinese cell phone manufacturers.)

兵贵神速   *"swiftness is extremely important in war"*

神速＝"godly speed," lightning speed. This phrase is often used to urge people to make a move quickly.

集中优势兵力打歼灭战

See **General Notes on Business Communication II.**

鱼与熊掌不可兼得

See **General Notes on Business Communication II.**

Class Discussion
课堂讨论

1. 对涂料厂工程追加投资的意义是什么？
2. 不能及时追加投资可能导致什么样的后果？
3. 广厦公司延缓追加投资的原因是什么？
4. 在目前形势下，休斯公司应该采取什么对策？
5. 你认为在宴会上韩森和艾琳的表现怎么样？

Exercises
练习

PART ONE: FAST ORAL TRANSLATION
第一部分：快速口译

Refer to Lesson 1 for instructions for this exercise.

A. From Chinese into English
中方要求美方追加投资。

B. From English into Chinese
The American side tries to convince the Chinese side not to postpone the second phase of investment.

PART TWO: ROLE-PLAY (THE SECOND ROUND OF NEGOTIATIONS 10 DAYS LATER)
第二部分：角色表演（模拟十天后的第二轮谈判）

Two students act as the representatives of the Golden Bridge Consulting Group and two or three other students act respectively as the president, general manager, and CFO of the Chinese company.
两个同学扮演金桥公司的代表，另外三位同学分别扮演广厦集团公司的董事长，总经理和总会计师。

PART THREE: FILL IN THE BLANKS
第三部分：填空练习

1. 在我看来，现在就研制这种新产品为时____早。
   A. 非常   B. 有些   C. 过   D. 已

2. "下午我们想请王先生去建筑工地看看，不知您意下如何？" "____。"
   A. 还请海涵   B. 客随主便   C. 等米下锅   D. 承蒙款待

3. 既然事故已经发生了，当务之急就是如何____损失。
   A. 造成　　B. 取得　　C. 举报　　D. 挽回

4. 海尔公司是中国家用电器制造业的____。
   A. 龙头　　B. 手头　　C. 头筹　　D. 部门

5. 奥运工程会为我们带来良好的商誉，所以必须不惜____代价夺标。
   A. 所有　　B. 各种　　C. 一切　　D. 一点

PART FOUR: COMPOSITION
第四部分：写作

Write a letter on behalf of the Hughes Company requesting that the other party make allocations for additional investment immediately.

LESSON 12: MERGERS AND ACQUISITIONS
第十二课：企业并购

Background and Business Tasks
背景和任务

美国利达公司主要生产高档运动型自行车。这家公司想在中国扩大生产规模，以进一步降低生产成本。了解到有家中国国营企业**濒临**倒闭，利达想把这家公司买下来，但是不知道中国政府是否允许外国公司购买中国国营企业。受利达公司的委托，金桥公司的艾琳和韩森进行了政策调查。之后他们又代表利达公司和飞力自行车厂作了初步谈判。

Part One: Merging Is an Irresistible Trend (an Article from a Well-known Chinese Economic Periodical)
第一部分：企业兼并，**大势所趋**（摘自中国某权威性经济周刊）

中国经济的发展正**处于**一个非常关键的转型期。在这个特殊时期，处理好中国国有企业的兼并收购等问题具有十分重要的意义。根据国家最新**出台**的政策，外国公司可以购买中国的国有企业。毫无疑问，这是中国经济改革向深度发展**跨出的新的一步**。

我国国有企业的运作方式现在已经很难适应市场经济体制了。改革开放十几年来，私营、民营、合资等企业都发展得很快，但仍有不少国有企业亏损的范围和亏损金额天天在增大。一批建厂较早的老企业由于设备老化、设计过时、管理落后、资金不足等许多问题，生产的产品不能适应市场的需求，不但根本无法盈利，甚至连职工的基本工资都发不出，**拖欠**银行的贷款无法**偿还**。从政府的角度看，这类"夕阳工业"不但不能为国家创造税收，而且已经成为沉重的经济负担，被形象地形容为**填不满的无底洞**。

一般来说，企业走到这一步已经无法依靠自身的力量再生了。让外国公司收购濒临破产的中国国有企业是一条出路。外资把这些企业买下来以后，将独立负责盈亏的问题。由于外资要交纳**增值税**和**所得税**，所以国家不但得到了解脱，而且从中获得了利益。另外一条出路就是国内兼并。国有企业通过改革和重组，可以建立和发展一大批大型和超大型企业集团，使民族工业有走向世界的能力。

企业并购并不都是收购破产或者经营**欠**佳的企业。有些是因为企业组织规模偏小和行业分布过于分散需要兼并，有些是用强强联合等方式组织起来，形成**规模化**的集团。中国的经济改革要求尽快建立起一大批适应市场经济规范要求的跨地区、跨产业、跨所有制，甚至跨国的大企业。美国一些大企业几乎没有不走并购这条道路的。从19　世纪美国洛克菲勒石油公司、通用电气公司、福特汽车公司和杜邦化学公司的发展，到20世纪的微软公司和思科公司的快速成长都和并购有关。全球已经经历了四次并购浪潮，每一次都促进了经济**大幅度**增长。现在正在兴起的第五次浪潮声势更大。可以预言，企业并购将促使中国经济更健康地发展。

Part Two: A Brief Introduction to Feili Bicycle Factory
第二部分：飞利自行车厂简介

苏州市飞利自行车厂是一家大型的国有企业。工厂不仅生产专业产品，还自办医院、幼儿园、技术学校、**电大**等。这些年来，该厂生产的自行车逐渐成了**弱势产品**，加上领导班子决策**不当**，企业绩效很差，经济上亏损严重。国家调整税收额度后，使这家企业年收益降幅达2,000万元以上。目前它已处于半停产状态。

Part Three: In the Conference Room at Suzhou Bicycle Works
第三部分：苏州飞利自行车厂会议室

艾琳：　我先作个自我介绍吧。我叫艾琳，金桥公司项目经理。这位是我的同事韩森。我们和贵厂以前有过几次接触，那都是通过电话和传真。今天我们来，主要想就购买贵厂一事达成一些意向性的协议。

陈：　很高兴你们对敝厂有兴趣。对了，我也来介绍一下。我叫陈福，福气的福。我是负责生产的副厂长。这位是我们厂的工会主席。

沈招弟：　我叫沈招弟，**招商引资**的招，弟弟的弟。

艾琳：　哎，你们许厂长怎么还没来呢？

沈：　他今天上午临时有事，让我和老陈好好地接待你们。

（艾琳、韩森对视，无言。）

韩森：　陈厂长，请您谈谈你们厂的现有资产情况。

陈：　我们现有的现金**流动资产**没有多少了。但是我们有固定资产，像土地、厂房、设备等，这些价值远远高于我们的流动资产，这些也是现在我们最**能卖价**的东西。

艾琳：　你能不能跟我们说说具体的数字。

陈：　这个……我们许厂长说是商业机密，不能随便泄露。

韩森：　如果不谈具体数字，就很难作**实质性**的分析和谈判了。

陈：　利达公司想出多少钱买下我们的工厂呢？

艾琳：　根据我们得到的商业信息，贵厂已经无法偿还银行**债务**了。如果把厂房和其它的流动资金加起来，最高的出价是三千万元。

陈：　这……有点低了吧？

艾琳：　那么您觉得多少是合理的呢？

陈：　这我说不上来，**得由我们许厂长来拍板**。

沈： 你们的开价太低了。我们工厂的**无形资产**算不算？

韩森： 当然应该算，但是如果利达公司买下这个厂，大概他们不会再用你们以前用的商标、商誉或者专利权了。因为他们会考虑用目前他们已经打出的美国品牌。所以，你们以前有的这些无形资产大概也没有多大价值了。

沈： 什么？以前谁不知道"飞利"牌自行车？这几年因为买汽车的多了，加上我们没钱做广告，它才被挤出了市场。资产评估时应该包括无形资产。

韩森： 我不是说不包括，而是就它目前的市场价值来评论。

沈： 好了，好了。小伙子，别看你中文说得不错，到关键时刻，你就帮美国人了。

艾琳： 我们换个话题吧。你们能谈谈现在职工的基本情况吗？如果你们有诚意的话，就应该说得实一点，不然大家都很忙……

（陈和沈对视一下）

陈： 好吧。我们也不想跟你们**打太极拳**。我们目前工厂现有职工11511人，其中退休职工有2556人。工厂在职职工中，直接从事生产的职工只有5100人，富余人员有3000多人。

韩森： 人员严重过剩。

艾琳： 我不懂，你们为什么招那么多职工呢？

陈： 以前中国是没有人失业的。人人有工作，大家有饭吃。工厂为了安置富余人员，不得不分解工作量，**因人设岗**，所以造成了**人浮于事**。

沈： 作为**群众的父母官**，我最关心的是公司被买走以后，会不会有很多人下岗？

韩森： 这是不可避免的，不然要养一大批不干活的人，不管什么样的企业也都只有死路一条。企业和慈善机构不一样。

沈： 我承认，我们有的职工确实**跟不上趟**了。可是他们辛辛苦苦工作了一辈子，他们曾经为我们厂子**立下了汗马功劳**，我们不能**抛下他们不管**啊。

艾琳： 其实，解决这些问题的形式和渠道很多。比如，可以分流**非经营性**人员，像你们厂在医院、学校、幼儿园等**后勤部门**工作的人，可以通过集资方法，成立新的实业公司。新公司实行**独立核算**，**自负盈亏**。

韩森： 有的下岗人员可以去"再就业服务中心"接受培训，实行生产自救，或者通过**劳务输出**等方法解决生计问题。这些都是你们的《人民日报》上说的。

陈： 我们还有很多退休职工，他们的工资、医疗保险谁管？新职工住房问题怎么解决？

韩森： 工厂以前要帮助职工解决住房吗？

沈： 当然啦。国家不分配房子，老百姓住哪儿啊？

艾琳： 看来，要解决的问题真不少啊。我们今天也一时回答不了这些问题。我们也许得去别的厂看看。

陈： 慢一点儿。我给许厂长打个电话，看看他回来了没有。

（出去打电话）

许： （赶到会议室）啊呀，不好意思，不好意思。我一直没参加你们的讨论。这一上午应该有个结论了吧？

韩森： 还没有，因为关键人物才出场啊。

许： 啊呀，我们的陈厂长是专管生产线的，所以有些情况他还不太了解。你们有什么意见或建议尽管说。上面说了，我们要有个**双赢**的结局。

艾琳： 我们还希望许厂长能提供进一步的财务数据，这样我们才能对贵厂进行投资分析。比如你们目前的资产净值是多少，你们厂有没有**有价证券**或者**呆帐**、**三角债**等等。

许： 好说，好说。我们吃了饭再说。今天中午我请客。

韩森： 你们不是已经**入不敷出**了吗？别客气了。

许： 咳，不管怎么样，吃饭的开支总会有的嘛。为了表示诚意，我已经定好了本市最高级的一家饭店。吃完饭，我还要请你们**桑拿**、**按摩**，消除工作中的疲劳。

Vocabulary List

濒临	瀕臨	bīnlín	on the verge of
大势所趋	大勢所趨	dàshìsuǒqū	unstoppable trend
转型	轉型	zhuǎnxíng	transition
拖欠		tuōqiàn	owe
偿还	償還	chánghuán	to pay back
夕阳工业	夕陽工業	xīyáng gōngyè	sunset industry; a declining industry
无底洞	無底洞	wúdǐdòng	a bottomless pit
增值税	增值稅	zēngzhíshuì	value-added tax
所得税		suǒdéshuì	income tax
民族工业	民族工業	mínzú gōngyè	indigenous industries
强强联合	強強聯合	qiángqiáng liánhé	a merger of two strong companies
洛克菲勒		Luòkèfēilè	Rockefeller
通用电气	通用電氣	Tōngyòng Diànqì	General Electric
福特		Fútè	Ford
杜邦		Dùbāng	Dupont
微软	微軟	Wēiruǎn	Microsoft
思科		Sīkē	Cisco
电大	電大	diàndà	college by TV; distance learning
弱势	弱勢	ruòshì	in a weak position
绩效	績效	jìxiào	achievement and efficiency
引资	引資	yǐnzī	attract investment
流动资产	流動資產	liúdòng zīchǎn	liquid assets
实质性	實質性	shízhìxìng	substantive
拍板		pāibǎn	[cl.] to make the final decision
商誉	商譽	shāngyù	business reputation
打太极拳	打太極拳	dǎ tàijíquán	do shadow boxing (tai chi martial arts)
富余	富餘	fùyú	surplus; redundant
过剩	過剩	guòshèng	excess; surplus
分解		fēnjiě	split up; break down
因人设岗	因人設崗	yīnrén shègǎng	create positions on the basis of persons (in need of jobs)
人浮于事	人浮於事	rénfúyúshì	have more hands than needed
群众	群眾	qúnzhòng	the masses

死路一条	死路一條	sǐlùyìtiáo	there is only one way (out of a predicament)—die
慈善机构	慈善機構	císhàn jīgòu	charitable organizations
跟不上趟		gēnbùshàngtàng	[cl.] cannot keep up with the situation
一辈子	一輩子	yíbèizi	all one's life
汗马功劳	汗馬功勞	hànmǎgōngláo	(perform) deeds of valor in battle
抛		pāo	throw; discard
渠道		qúdào	channel
分流		fēnliú	bifurcation; distribution; divert
后勤	後勤	hòuqín	support services
集资	集資	jízī	raise funds
实业	實業	shíyè	industry; enterprise
核算		hésuàn	business accounting
自负盈亏	自負盈虧	zìfù yíngkuī	assume sole responsibility for its own profits or losses
劳务输出	勞務輸出	láowù shūchū	the export of labor services
生计	生計	shēngjì	means of livelihood
双赢	雙贏	shuāngyíng	win-win; victory for both sides
净值	淨值	jìngzhí	net worth; net value
有价证券	有價證券	yǒujià zhèngquàn	securities
呆帐	呆帳	dāizhàng	bad debt
三角债	三角債	sānjiǎozhài	"triangle debts"
入不敷出		rùbùfūchū	income is surpassed by expenses; running at a deficit
桑拿		sāngná	sauna
按摩		ànmó	massage

An old state-owned company.

Notes and Explanations

1. BUSINESS AND OTHER PROFESSIONAL TERMS

拖欠   *be behind on payments; be in arrears*

Its object must have at least two syllables.

【课文】拖欠银行的贷款无法偿还。

【补充】这位新任总经理非常能干，不到半年公司就还清了所有拖欠的
债务。

偿还   *pay back*

Its object must have at least two syllables.

【课文】拖欠银行的贷款无法偿还。

【补充】恕我直言，贵公司已经没有偿还债务的能力了。

夕阳工业   *sunset industries*

This term describes industrial sectors whose markets had been strong but are now diminishing.
Its antonym is 朝阳工业. 夕阳=setting sun; 朝阳=rising sun.

债务   *debt*

The verb before it should be disyllabic.

【课文】贵厂已经无法偿还银行债务了。
【补充】如果贷款制度不严格，一定会造成许多债务纠纷。

增值税　*value-added tax*

This is imposed on companies who are engaged in processing, repairing, or importing. The regular rate is 17%.

所得税　*income tax*

Currently, the income tax imposed on foreign ventures in China is 33%, but some may enjoy a reduced rate.

规模化

This term means to reach a size that is big enough for competition. Thus, the actual meaning of this term is 大规模化.
　　【课文】形成规模化的集团。
　　【补充】中国农业的效率太低，要想提高效率只能走规模化的道路。

大幅度　*large scale*

幅度＝range, scope.
　　【课文】每一次都促进了经济大幅度增长。
　　【补充】最近全球石油价格大幅度上升。

电大　abbreviation of 电视大学 *(college by TV, distance learning)*

Students are organized and managed by companies or local communities while the lectures are given via TV broadcast. They are quite informal and their quality is far below a regular college.

弱势产品　*products in a weak or disadvantaged position due to a diminishing market, low quality, or insufficient advertisement*

Its antonym is 强势产品 or 旺销产品.

流动资产　*liquid assets*

This term refers to assets that can be turned into cash in a short period of time. Its antonym is 固定资产, or fixed assets.

无形资产   *intangible assets*

The intangible assets of a company often include patents, special technologies, trademarks, and business reputation. The first three are called 可辨认无形资产, or discernible intangible assets, and the last one is called 不可辨认无形资产, or indiscernible intangible assets.

非经营性   *not directly related to business operations*

非经营性人员 employees whose activities are not directly related to business operations
非经营性开支 expenses that are not directly related to business operations

后勤部门   *support service sector*

Denotes such services as factory cafeteria, factory nursery, etc.

独立核算   *keep separate accounts; independent accounting*

核算＝business accounting

自负盈亏   *be responsible for one's own profits and losses*

自负＝自己负责; 盈＝盈利 profit; 亏＝亏损 loss

劳务输出

In a narrow sense, this term means (organized) labor exports. For example, now many Chinese workers are working for construction projects in the Middle East. In a broader sense, it may mean to channel surplus labor into another region (within China) under contract.

呆帐   *bad debt*

Repayment is long overdue and the debt is unlikely to ever be paid. Also called 坏帐.

三角债   *triangle debts*

三角 means "triangle." When Company A owes money to Company B, Company B owes money to Company C, and Company C owes money to Company A, their debt chains will form a triangle.

2. FORMAL EXPRESSIONS

濒临　　*be on the verge of*

The objects of this verb must be two-syllable nouns with very negative meanings, such as 倒闭,
破产, 崩溃 (collapse), or 灭绝 (extinction).
　　【课文】有家中国国营企业濒临倒闭。
　　【补充】由于产品严重积压，那家公司濒临破产。

处于　　*be in (a certain condition/situation)*

　　【课文】中国经济的发展正处于一个非常关键的转型期。
　　【课文】目前它已处于半停产状态。

欠 ＋ Adj.　　*not sufficiently...*

There are many word compounds with 欠. Typically, 欠 is followed by a single syllable word.
欠佳＝不够好欠妥＝不够妥当 (not proper; inappropriate)
　　【课文】企业并购并不都是收购破产或者经营欠佳的企业。
　　【补充】董事会认为总经理提出的并购方案欠妥，必须加以修改。

......不当　　*...is not proper*

The word before 不当 must be disyllabic.
　　【课文】领导班子决策不当......
　　【课文】你们因为用人不当泄漏了机密。(L9)

3. COLLOQUIAL EXPRESSIONS

能卖价（儿）　　*can be sold easily at a high price*
　　【课文】这些也是现在我们最能卖价的东西。
　　【补充】这种德国生产的老式相机很能卖价儿。

由......拍板（儿）　　*be decided by...*

The original meaning of 拍板 is "beat the clapper (in a musical performance)" or "rap the gavel."
Now it means "call the shots" or "have the final say."
　　【课文】得由我们许厂长来拍板。
　　【补充】我们公司的大事小事都由他一个人拍板儿。

打太极拳　　*be evasive*

Lit. "do tai chi boxing" (shadow boxing). Since the characteristic of tai chi is to avoid direct contact with the opponent, it is used to describe people who talk in an evasive way.

【课文】我们也不想跟你们打太极拳。

【补充】我希望你们少打太极拳，有什么事情应该开门见山。

跟不上趟（儿）　　*lag behind; be obsolete*

Often used to describe somebody who is too old to learn new things.

【课文】我们有的职工确实跟不上趟了。

【补充】张经理在管理方面可以说有丰富的经验，但是到了我们这个电脑时代他就跟不上趟儿了。

4. OTHER PATTERNS AND WORD COLLOCATIONS

出台　　*promulgate; come out*

The original meaning of this word is "to appear on stage" (of an actor/actress). In recent years, it has been extended to mean the promulgation of policies, laws, or regulations. Although the word itself is a VO structure, it functions as a verb and may take an object.

【课文】根据国家最新出台的政策，……

【补充】近年来中国出台了一系列保护知识产权的法规。（法规＝法律，规定）……

跨出……的一步　　*take a...step*

【课文】这是中国经济改革向深度发展跨出的新的一步。

【补充】中国加入世界贸易组织，这向经济全球化跨出了关键的一步。

抛下／抛开……不管　　*cast aside somebody or something and leave them helpless*

【课文】我们不能抛下他们不管啊。

【补充】他想赚大钱，就抛下父母妻儿不管，一个人去了海南岛。

5. IMPORTANT IDIOMATIC PHRASES/PROVERBS

大势所趋　　*be pushed by the general trend of events*

Used to urge people to follow the inevitable trend, not go against it.

填不满的无底洞   *a bottomless pit that can never be filled*

In business contexts, it is often used to describe a faulty investment.

因人设岗   *creating jobs for redundant staff*

A position is created to meet a personal need instead of a company's need.

人浮于事   *more personnel than work available*

This and the previous two phrases are often used to criticize the old business/governmental structure before reform.

群众的父母官

In old times government officials called themselves the fathers and mothers of the common people. This implies that government leaders had the responsibility to feed and clothe the people. Now some officials/leaders still use it to remind themselves that they must provide the basic necessities of life to the people under their leadership.

立下了汗马功劳

This phrase was originally used to praise people who fought many hard battles and achieved great distinction. Now it is just used to praise those who have made significant contributions to their company or their country.

入不敷出   *income is surpassed by expenses; running at a deficit*

Used to describe a difficult financial situation.

Class Discussion
课堂讨论

1. 你觉得企业兼并是否符合经济规律？
2. 在你看来，外国公司应该购买盈利的还是亏损的企业？
3. 飞力自行车厂是否具备了被购买的条件？
4. 许厂长为什么不参加会议而要请客吃饭？你觉得他应该怎么做？
5. 对沈招弟的说法和看法你能不能接受？

Exercises
练习

PART ONE: FAST ORAL TRANSLATION
第一部分：快速口译

Refer to Lesson 1 for instructions for this exercise.

A. From Chinese into English
一家等待兼并的工厂的厂长介绍工厂情况。

B. From English into Chinese
An American buyer of a Chinese factory is engaged in price negotiations.

PART TWO: ROLE-PLAY (SECOND ROUND OF NEGOTIATIONS)
第二部分：角色表演（模拟第二轮谈判）

Two students act as the representatives of the buying party and two other students act as the director and deputy director of Feili Bicycle Factory.
两个同学扮演买方代表，两个同学扮演飞力自行车厂的正副厂长。

PART THREE: REPHRASING SENTENCES (PARAGRAPH IMPROVEMENT)
第三部分：改写下面这段话

Refer to Lesson 1 for instructions for this exercise.

最近这两年我们公司的开支比我们的收入还要多，人太多了，要做的工作却不太多。工厂欠了太多的钱，没有办法还钱，所以现在已经差不多要破产了。你可能会建议让年纪太大的工人离开工厂。但是这些老工人有很多经验，更重要的是他们曾经为我们公司做了很多的事情。而且只有政府才能决定是不是让一个工人离开工厂。

PART FOUR: COMPOSITION
第四部分：写作

Write a letter from Aileen or Hansen to Director Xu, subtly pressuring him to agree to the price set by the American company.

LESSON 13: FINANCIAL AUDIT
第十三课：财务清查

Background and Business Tasks
背景和任务

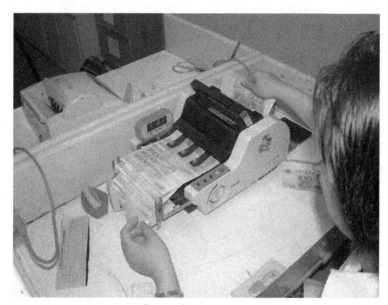

Counting money.

中美合资湖南百利发电机股份有限公司成立于1997年，虽然产品的销售不断增长，但是公司的亏损却也越来越严重。美国的投资者对这种情况非常不满，所以委托金桥公司对公司的财务问题进行调查，并且希望这家合资公司能够引进美国万亿财务公司研制的财务管理系统，使公司的财务管理科学化、透明化。

Part One: In the Conference Room at Baili Generator Ltd.
第一部分：百利发电机股份有限公司会议厅

蔡敬民： 二位作为美国股东的代表远道而来，我谨代表公司的全体员工表示
欢迎！百利当前面临已无利可图甚至亏损的惨重局面，我作为总
经理非常痛心，但是这个结果实在不是始料可及的。公司的领导层
已经尽了最大的努力，但是仍然无法挽救亏损的命运。我希望二位
能够对我们加以指导。我听说韩森先生是哈佛工商管理学院的高才
生，想必您带来了扭转乾坤的高见。

韩森： 蔡总，我听说毛泽东说过"**没有调查研究就没有发言权**。"虽然我
不是共产主义者，但是他的这句话我非常欣赏。我和艾琳首先希望
听听你们的看法。在您看来，公司亏损的主要原因是什么？

蔡总： **一言难尽**。为了和同行竞争，我们不得不压低产品的价格，采取了
赔本也要占领市场的原则。我们原来的期望是对手在我们的压力下
倒闭。事实上，也的确有两家比较大的发电机厂被我们挤垮了。但
是不知道从什么地方**冒出来**许多乡镇企业，这些新的竞争对手的价
格比我们更低，他们在销售的时候给百分之二十以上的回扣，而且
还用各种方法来逃税。我们的这个公司没有办法去做这样的事情。
难啊！

艾琳： 我相信您讲的这些乡镇企业的确是用违法手段来和百利竞争。但是
他们的产品质量根本没有办法和百利比。我看了统计资料，你们去
年一共售出发电机37万台，平均售价是4500元。我觉得这个销售量
和售价，工厂还是有利可图的，而且，**库存**的数量也在合理范围之
内，并没有大量积压，你们完全不应该亏损啊！

韩森： 恕我直言，你们的财务报表上存在着很多疑点。在员工的正常工薪
和原材料等消耗之外，有很多莫名其妙的开支。

蔡总： 韩先生，在中国经营企业不像在美国那么简单。具体的开支请王总
会计师来解释一下吧。

王德发： 是，蔡总。我们的开支有一大项叫关系网络开支。二位可能对此有
疑问。你们大概不知道，在中国，不管做什么事情，都需要关系
网。除了政府机关、税务部门这些**明摆着**的"进贡"对象外，还有
电力部门、公安部门、自来水公司、甚至电话公司等等，你要是不
给**打点**到，就可能出现意想不到的问题。

艾琳： 那怎么打点呢？

王： 主要是请客吃饭，逢年过节还要送礼。饭和礼品都必须是最高
级的。

韩森：我在报纸上看到中国正在进行廉政建设，你们不觉得做这样的事情是行贿吗？

王：只要不送钱就行。吃顿饭没什么关系。

韩森：是不是那种三万一桌的，自己公司还要出五六位**作陪**？

王：这个……

艾琳：我们**姑且不**谈所谓的关系网络开支。我觉得你们的财务报表中有一个<u>自相矛盾</u>的地方。既然公司亏损，效益不好，为什么还要发那么多的奖金？你看，你们的奖金发放总额是普通工资的四倍。蔡总和王总能不能给我们一份奖金发放的详细说明，我们想具体地知道给谁发了多少。

蔡总：我们是把奖金的发放权力下放给车间主任，所以每个员工到底谁得到了多少我们也不太清楚。

韩森：我倒是想知道蔡总和王总自己分到了多少奖金？这个数字二位大概不会忘掉吧？

王：蔡总为了厂里的工作每天工作将近二十个小时，他多拿一些奖金是应该的嘛。至于我本人，一分奖金也没有。

艾琳：那您每个月只拿三千工资没有任何别的收入吗？

王：作为总会计师我当然领取特殊**津贴**了。

艾琳：能告诉我数量吗？

王：蔡总，您看……

蔡：告诉他们。

王：每年六十万。

韩森：美国的工资**也不过如此**。

王：韩先生不要开玩笑，谁不知道美国的总会计师的年薪起码百万美元。

艾琳：那要看什么样的公司了。你们的一项重大支出是**基建费**，我真不明白，刚刚建了不到五年的厂房，还有什么需要再建的吗？

蔡：公司要为企业的骨干解决住房问题，不然人才怎么能留得住呢？

韩森：你们的建房标准一定不低吧。您所说的骨干指哪些人？

蔡：车间主任以上。

艾琳：那当然也包括二位自己了！你们的**差旅费**也花了几百万，这怎么解释？我听说中国有个说法叫做"公费旅游"，是不是公司的领导拿钱去游山玩水了？

蔡：二位说话越来越**尖刻**了，我实在不希望继续这种剑拔弩张的谈话。不去参加全国各地的**订货会议**又怎么能把产品卖出去呢？我提醒二位，根据中国的企业管理法规，必须**具有会计师资格证书的人**才有权力察看企业的**明细帐目**。我们是本着合作的态度向你们提供信息的，大家**有话好好说**嘛。

王： 听说你们带来了美国万亿财务公司的财务管理系统软件。能不能介绍一下？

韩森： 这套系统可以自动<u>监视</u>企业的收入、营业成本、库存情况等等，在发生不正常的情况的时候会发出预警。所以这套系统能在短期内改善企业经营状况，合理降低库存，提高资金周转率，提高工作效率。

王： 是给我们预警还是给董事会预警？

艾琳： 公司和董事会会同时收到预警信号。

蔡： 这个可不行。那等于我们时时刻刻都在董事会的监控之下了。

韩森： 难道总经理不应该接受董事会的监督吗？

蔡： **话是这样说**，但是你们总得给企业一些<u>灵活</u>性吧。如果我们一举一动都有人管，这个工作就没有办法做了。

艾琳： 看来我们的共同语言实在不多。我想提最后一个问题。你们的"员工<u>分红</u>"是怎么回事？

韩森： 是啊，一般员工不是<u>持股人</u>，有什么权利参加分红呢？

王： 你们美国的这一套在中国**行不通**。在我们看来，一般员工虽然不是股东，但是他们的劳动就是对企业的投资，有了员工分红制度才能<u>激励</u>员工努力工作，也是提高员工的向心力的一种好方法。

韩森： 股东投资是为了赚钱，期待着能带来回报，能有较多的分红。现在你们**倒好**，没有投资的人年底分了不少红利，投资者却分不到红利。如果都像你们这样还会有人投资吗？这简直就是<u>本末倒置</u>，不是分红而是<u>分赃</u>！

蔡： 分赃？！年轻人，要是你来管理工厂，**不出**三天工人就会全部跳槽。说句不客气的话，很多东西在你们哈佛的课堂上是学不到的。

韩森： 不错，你们这种管理的办法我们哈佛确实不教。

王： 十二点了，厂里为二位准备了工作餐，四菜一汤，绝对是合理开支，咱们边吃边谈好不好？

艾琳： 不了，我实在没有一点胃口。

Part Two: Year-end Financial Figures for 2001
第二部分：2001年财务结算总表

单位：百万元

总销售额：166.5
非销售性收入：2.3
总收入：168.8

原材料消耗：54.3   水电运输消耗：11.1
销售纳税：16.7   土地租用费：3.3
销售回扣：15.0   职工薪金：11.2
职工奖金和骨干津贴：37.5   基本建设费：22.0
差旅费：8.7   广告宣传费：10.0
关系网络费：8.1   办公费：17.5
职工培训：2.3   文化活动费：1.3
赞助地方文化教育：2.0

总支出：221.0

盈亏：-52.2

Part Three: Office Expenditures
第三部分：办公费用分类

购买机关所用<u>轿车</u>：2.2（<u>奔驰</u>400一辆，<u>丰田佳美</u>一辆，<u>桑塔纳</u>2000一辆）
购买机关所用其他车辆：2.8（<u>大宇</u>中型巴士一辆，大型巴士三辆）
车辆<u>牌照</u>、保险、维修保养费用及事故<u>赔款</u>：0.4
购买长城电脑系统：3.7
购买其他办公机器（<u>佳能</u>电传、影印、摄像、<u>投影机</u>，索尼电视、
音响、数码相机、录像机及所<u>需</u><u>附件</u>和操作人员培训维修等）：1.1
购买通讯器材及服务计划费：0.6
办公室装修费：2.3
购买办公桌椅及其他家具：2.4
其他<u>杂费</u>：2.0

Vocabulary List

透明化		tòumínghuà	make transparent
股东	股東	gǔdōng	shareholder
谨	謹	jǐn	sincerely
无利可图	無利可圖	wúlìkětú	no profit to be gained
惨重		cǎnzhòng	disastrous
始料可及		shǐliàokějí	can be predicted from the outset
高才生		gāocáishēng	an outstanding student
扭转乾坤	扭轉乾坤	niǔzhuǎnqiánkūn	turn around a situation
高见	高見	gāojiàn	your brilliant idea
发言权	發言權	fāyánquán	right to speak
一言难尽	一言難盡	yìyánnánjìn	it's a long story
赔本	賠本	péiběn	to lose one's capital; run a business at a loss
库存	庫存	kùcún	inventory
疑点	疑點	yídiǎn	doubtful point; suspicious point
消耗		xiāohào	consumption; cost
莫名其妙		mòmíngqímiào	be baffled; baffling
进贡	進貢	jìngòng	pay tribute
打点	打點	dǎdiǎn	bribe
意想不到		yìxiǎngbúdào	unexpected
自相矛盾		zìxiāngmáodùn	contradict oneself
津贴	津貼	jīntiē	allowance; subsidy
基建		jījiàn	infrastructure construction
差旅费	差旅費	chāilǚfèi	travel expense
尖刻		jiānkè	caustic
剑拔弩张	劍拔弩張	jiànbánǔzhāng	daggers drawn
明细帐目	明細帳目	míngxìzhàngmù	detailed/itemized accounts
监视	監視	jiānshì	keep watch on
灵活	靈活	línghuó	flexible; nimble
分红	分紅	fēnhóng	share dividend
持股人		chígǔrén	shareholder
激励	激勵	jīlì	encourage; urge
向心力		xiàngxīnlì	centripetal force; loyalty to the company

本末倒置		běnmòdàozhì	put the cart before the horse
分赃	分贓	fēnzāng	divide the spoils
纳税	納稅	nàshuì	pay tax
盈亏	盈虧	yíngkuī	gain/lose
轿车	轎車	jiàochē	passenger car
奔驰	奔馳	Bēnchí	Mercedes Benz
丰田	豐田	Fēngtián	Toyota
佳美		*Jiāměi*	*Camry*
桑塔纳	桑塔納	*Sāngtǎnà*	*(VW) Santana*
大宇		Dàyǔ	Daewoo
巴士		bāshì	bus
牌照		páizhào	license plate
赔款	賠款	péikuǎn	compensation
佳能		Jiānéng	Canon
投影机	投影機	tóuyǐngjī	projector
索尼		Suǒní	Sony
音响	音響	yīnxiǎng	stereo
数码	數碼	shùmǎ	digital
附件		fùjiàn	accessory
操作		cāozuò	operation
通讯器材	通訊器材	tōngxùnqìcái	telecommunications equipment
杂费	雜費	záfèi	miscellaneous fees

Notes and Explanations

1. BUSINESS AND OTHER PROFESSIONAL TERMS

库存   *inventory; stock*

库＝warehouse; 存＝storage. If commodities are overstocked, it is called 积压.

津贴   *subsidies; allowances*

【课文】作为总会计师我当然领取特殊津贴了。
【补充】出差时每天可以享受八十元的伙食津贴。

基建费   *capital construction or infrastructure construction*

An abbreviation of 基本建设费.

订货会（议）   *conferences for placing orders*

Generally, these kind of conferences are held in popular tourist areas.

具有会计师资格证书的人   *certified accountant*

资格＝qualification; 证书＝certificate.

明细帐目   *detailed/itemized accounts*

This term refers to accounts in which each item is clearly described in detail.

资金周转   *capital turnover*

Related word: 资金周转率 (capital turnover rate). It is calculated as the percentage of capital that is turned into income during a specific period.

分红   *draw (extra) dividends*

As you have learned in Lesson Five, 红 (red) in China is a symbol of profit. 分红 theoretically should be the dividends shareholders receive. In some cases (as in this lesson), however, some non-shareholders also try to obtain dividends.

2. FORMAL EXPRESSIONS

作陪   *accompany (in a banquet, reception, etc.)*
【课文】是不是那种三万一桌的，自己公司还要出五六位作陪？
【补充】刘董事长在长城酒店为美国代表团接风，公司的其他三位领导出席作陪。

姑且不......   *leave something aside for the moment*
【课文】我们姑且不谈所谓的关系网络开支。
【补充】贵厂的情况实在不妙，姑且不说拖欠的巨额债务，仅仅是目前的这种人浮于事的状况就足以使企业倒闭了。

......也不过如此   *not more than this; ...is merely this*
【课文】美国的工资也不过如此。
【补充】过去人们都说德国汽车的质量特别好，我觉得也不过如此。

3. COLLOQUIAL EXPRESSIONS

冒出来   *suddenly come out*
【课文】但是不知道从什么地方冒出来许多乡镇企业......
【补充】改革开放不到两年，大街小巷上就冒出了许许多多的商店和饭馆。

明摆着   *obvious; clearly out in the open*
【课文】除了政府机关、税务部门这些明摆着的"进贡"对象外，还有电力部门、公安部门、自来水公司、甚至电话公司等等。
【补充】他说要对领导班子进行调整，这明摆着是冲我这个总经理来的。

打点
The original meaning of this word is to make logistical preparations before a huge military force arrives. Now, it refers to various kinds of offerings (money, gifts, and other favorites) to people in a "network" outside a company in order to grease the wheel for business.
【课文】你要是不给打点到，就可能出现意想不到的问题。
【补充】我们这笔生意能不能拿到关键看环保部门的审批，你去打点打点吧。

话是这样 / 这么说　　*although it is true in theory*

The implication is that in reality, things are different.

【课文】话是这样说，但是你们总得给企业一些灵活性吧。

【补充】"不是有规定不许接受回扣吗？""话是这么说，但是拿一点点回扣没什么关系。"

行不通　　*does not work*

【课文】你们美国的这一套在中国行不通。

【补充】我认为你的这个让所有人免费上网的计划根本行不通。

……倒好

In everyday conversation, a negative remark is sometimes made in such a way that its literal meaning is positive. It is a kind of sarcasm. Thus 好 may actually mean 不好.

【课文】现在你们倒好，没有投资的人年底分了不少红利，投资者却分不到红利。

【补充】别人都在忙着干活，他倒好，一个人在屋里睡大觉。

【补充】好啊你！上班的时候给女朋友写情书！

不出……　　*within*

This word should be followed by a time word indicating duration.

【课文】不出三天工人就会全部跳槽。

【补充】如果让他当厂长，不出两个月工厂就会扭亏为盈。（扭亏为盈＝turn losses into profits）

4. OTHER PATTERNS AND WORD COLLOCATIONS

想必　　*(I think that) surely; presumably*

【课文】想必您带来了扭转乾坤的高见。

【补充】鸿兴公司破产的消息想必您已经听说了。

本着……的……　　*in line with; on the basis of*

【课文】我们是本着合作的态度向你们提供信息的……

【补充】我希望我们双方能够本着互相理解的精神来进行谈判。

5. IMPORTANT IDIOMATIC PHRASES/PROVERBS

始料可及   *can be predicted at the outset*

A related phrase is 始料不及, which means "cannot be predicted at the outset."

没有调查研究就没有发言权。

See **General Notes on Business Communication II.**

一言难尽   *it's a long story*

This phrase is often used to start a long story or to give a complicated explanation.

有话好好说   *please talk peacefully; don't fight*

Class Discussion
课堂讨论

1. 百利公司的销售情况怎么样？
2. 百利公司亏损的原因是什么？
3. 你觉得企业应该给员工盖宿舍楼吗？
4. 你觉得百利公司的工资制度是否合理？
5. 在你看来，财务报表上还有什么疑点？
6. 美国的投资者应该对这家公司采取什么措施？

Exercises
练习

PART ONE: FAST ORAL TRANSLATION
第一部分：快速口译

Refer to Lesson 1 for instructions for this exercise.

A. From Chinese into English
一家中国公司的负责人询问准备合作的美国公司的财务情况。

B. From English into Chinese
An American manager talks with Chinese government officials about business regulations.

PART TWO: ROLE-PLAY (FURTHER INVESTIGATION INTO THE CAUSE OF LOSS)
第二部分：角色表演（进一步调查亏损原因）

Student A acts as the representative of Golden Bridge Consulting Group; student B acts as the director of the factory.
一个同学扮演金桥公司的代表，另一个同学扮演厂长。

PART THREE: REPHRASING SENTENCES
第三部分：改写句子

Refer to Lesson 1 for instructions for this exercise.

1. 网络经济的泡沫破灭得这么快，这是原来很难想到的。
2. 甘肃酒泉宾馆的设备非常豪华，和北京的长城饭店差不多。
3. 这件事很难用短短的几句话说清楚。
4. 这个公司运营得不错，所以股东每年可以分到两次钱。
5. 你们的很详细的帐上有一些非常奇怪的花出去的钱。

PART FOUR: COMPOSITION
第四部分：写作

Write an email in Chinese from Golden Bridge Consulting Group to the Baili Company to tell them that if they do not change their management and accounting practices, the American shareholders will have to withdraw their investment.

LESSON 14: LIFE INSURANCE
第十四课：平安保险

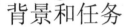

Background and Business Tasks
背景和任务

中国政府承诺：中国加入世贸五年内开放保险市场。西方保险公司纷纷想在中国建立独资或合资公司，**拓展业务**。美国安康人寿保险公司委托金桥公司了解外资保险公司在中国的机遇，特别是对人寿保险情况进行调查，对这一行业的发展前景做出评估。金桥公司准备从两方面着手了解：一，找一家保险公司的圈内人了解中国目前的保险业务状况；二，从中国报纸上查找有关的文章。

Part One: A Brief Introduction to Tai'an Life Insurance Company
第一部分：太安人寿保险有限公司简介

本公司于1996年10月在北京注册成立，是一家专门从事<u>人寿保险</u>的民营公司。公司自成立以后，业务迅速发展。去年年度保费收入人民币8098万元，完成年计划108.10%，<u>同比增长</u>超过280%，保费<u>累计</u>突破亿元。

太安人寿去年可投资性资产收益率为5.84%，并在7月经中国<u>保监会</u>批准，成为首批将基金的比例从总资产的5%提高到10%的民营保险公司。

公司现有职工572人。今年公司推出的"万代福<u>终身年金保险</u>"是全国第一个<u>帐户型</u>年金保险。产品自7月开始销售以来，保费收入累计2486万元，以<u>强劲</u>的优势占同期总保费收入的30.70%。

本公司将企业形象与公司的服务理念、行为联结为一个整体。公司一系列的前瞻性措施，保证了公司的发展步入快车道，为全国人民提供优质的保险服务。

地址：北京朝阳区东环南路1号写字楼8层
邮编：100022
电话：（010）65605237
传真：（010）65605345

Part Two: At Green Mountain Teahouse
第二部分：青山茶楼

艾琳：方总！您真准时！

方凯：艾琳，你今天请我出来喝茶，**该不是**让我再卖给你一份保险吧？这位是……

艾琳：这位是哈佛大学的韩森先生。

方凯/韩森：幸会，幸会。

艾琳：方总今天是要西湖龙井还是福建乌龙？

方凯：都行。艾琳，咱们也不是一天两天的朋友了，别**一口一个方总的**，我不过是个普普通通的经理，要是什么事情我能帮忙，你们就直说吧。

韩森：我就喜欢方先生这种性格，那我也就**明人不说暗话**了，我们今天是代表美国的安康公司来向您请教关于保险业的一些问题的。

方凯： 这恐怕不太合适吧？现在保险市场竞争激烈，我绝对不能透露我们太安公司的商业机密。

艾琳： 方总**言重了**，安康只是想了解中国保险市场的一般情况，您**大可不必**担心。

方凯： 那就好，你们想了解什么？

韩森： 贵公司主要从事人寿保险，我们想就从您熟悉的方面谈起吧。我在美国就读过中国的保险<u>年鉴</u>，看来这些年中国保险公司的效益特别好，这是什么原因呢？

方凯： 这些年，整个中国的保险业做得**如火如荼**，原因很多。但首先是大环境变了。一方面是保险业顺<u>应</u>了改革开放的需要，现在大家口袋里有钱了，不然谁会买保险？另一方面，中国人也逐渐接受了"保险"这一概念。以前中国人的生老病死都是由政府或者单位**一揽子包下来**。改革开放以后，情况有很大的改变，很多东西政府不包了。老百姓也意识到保险可以**转移现实生活中的许多风险**。

艾琳： 但是我觉得东方人<u>忌讳</u>说到"死"，这是不是会影响保险业的发展？

方凯： 的确是这样。要是一个年轻轻、<u>好端端</u>的人早早地就为自己作死后的准备，家人都会觉得奇怪，自己也认为是不吉利的事。

韩森： 这可能是价值观念的不同。美国人觉得人寿保险是个人经济生活中必不可少的一部分。在美国，三十岁左右就写好了<u>遗嘱</u>是很普遍的事，因为法律有这种要求。

方凯： 但是从有利的方面来看，中国人的家庭观念和家庭责任心很强，他们觉得人活着不仅仅是为了自己。买**寿险**不仅让自己百年之后可以放心，对家庭也是个<u>交代</u>。我国国内的寿险是从1982年开始恢复的。原来它只占全国保费比重的2%，1985年上升到16.9%，到了1993年已占36.9%，1999年寿险保费收入达到872亿元人民币，占保费总收入的62.6%。这些年来，人寿保险险种从**死亡保险**、**生存保险**、**生死合险**等为主体，又开发出七十多种。比如我们的"万代福"这个新品种就很受欢迎。

艾琳： 这样看来，在中国做寿险很容易了？

方凯： 事实上并没有那么简单。除了刚才说到的长期的政府负责**福利**的影响以外，还有其他的不利于保险业发展的想法。过去，很多中国老年人习惯于把钱藏在家里，觉得钱放在银行里还是有风险。这些年来越来越多的人，特别是年轻人，愿意把钱放到股市上博，真正考虑买保险的大多数是中上水平收入的中年人。还有，虽然中国人平常很喜欢问别人的<u>隐私</u>，但是却不太愿意把自己的经济安排清清楚楚地告诉你。你问他准备留给太太多少钱，多少钱给孩子，多少钱给母亲，说到关键的时候，他会说："现在不方便讲。"

韩森：　那么谈话只好中断了？

方凯：　是啊。

韩森：　谢谢您，方先生。我希望以后还有机会向您请教。

方凯：　不客气。安康公司真的准备在中国开设分公司吗？

艾琳：　恐怕还要有一段时间的准备，但是如果方总有意跳槽的话，我愿意向他们推荐您这位难得的人才。

方凯：　现在还没有这个考虑，咱们保持联络。

艾琳：　对了，能不能给我们一些你们的保险宣传材料？

方凯：　没问题，这是我们公司的五个主要险种的详细说明。

Part Three: The Chinese Insurance Market Has Unlimited Potential (an article from a highly respected weekly magazine on the economy)

第三部分：中国保险，商机无限（摘自某权威性经济周刊）

十几年来，让众多洋保险**锲而不舍**的动力，自然是中国潜力巨大的保险市场。中国人口多，基数大，是一个不可忽视的重要因素。目前，中国是世界上保费收入增长最快的地区。20多年来，保费收入年均增长速度超过30%，远远高于同期国内生产总值的增长速度。

据保守统计，中国保险业市场的保费潜力至少在250亿美元以上。中国2003年居民储蓄存款余额已近10万亿元，而投保金额和储蓄比较尚不足3%，如果这一比例上升到10%，则保费收入可增加几倍。因此，有外国专家**断言**，中国迟早将超过美国，成为全球最大的保险市场。

在很多人的心目中，尤其是在外资和合资工作的白领阶层的心目中，外资保险公司具有更强的经济实力、更多的投资渠道、更好的诚信度，因而会有更好的回报。目前我国已相继批准了美国友邦、日本东京海上、瑞士丰泰等几十家独资保险公司分别在上海、广州、深圳经营保险业务，并批准了美、英、日、德、法、加拿大、瑞士、澳大利亚及香港等国家和地区百余家保险机构在中国设立了近200多家代表处。其中，最引人注目的是友邦公司。1992年9月，中国人民银行批准该公司作为首家在上海开展经营性保险业务的外资保险公司分公司。在被批准的第一年，保费总收入仅为1928万元，到1995年，全年保费收入已增至4.15亿元。该公司将国际保险理念、先进的管理系统和技术引进上海市场，在中国保险业刮起了强劲的"友邦旋风"，带动了中国本土的保险企业纷纷进行行销方式的重大变革。

面对如此强大的对手，年轻的中国民族保险业的命运成了关注的焦点。当然，外资保险机构从目前来看，还没有对中国保险业造成致命的冲击，一方面是因为中国的保险市场还远未饱和，市场容量巨大，在整体市场份额上，外资保险公司只拥有中国保险市场的1%；但是，在局部市场上，外资公司已显现出非常具有竞争力和威胁性的信号。例如在上海，友邦保险公司的市场份额就占到11%。另一方面，多数外资公司还没真正掌握在中国开展业务的法宝，有些险种、价格还需要进一步调整。比如某些寿险，在一些发达国家也不是普通老百姓能够买得起的，这对于收入水平较低的大多数中国人来讲肯定是接受不了的。在可以预见的将来，一些保险公司将被兼并，一些不适合的险种将被取消，而大量新的保险产品会不断推出。

总体上讲，我国保险业仍将继续保持持续高速增长的势头。预计未来5年，我国保险业将以每年20-30%的速度增长，远高于金融行业的平均增长速度，成为我国发展最快的行业。这一趋势将延续15-20年。到2025年，商业保险保费总收入将达到5万亿元，占当年GDP的12%(其中，人寿保险保费收入将达到3万亿元，占整个GDP的6.8%)，超过英国、德国和法国。届时，商业保险将占整个社会保障体系的60%。

An insurance advertisement at the top of a tall building.

Part Four: Hansen's Proposal
第四部分：韩森的计划

鉴于中国保险市场发展迅速，前景广阔，建议由安康保险公司出资49%，寻找中国民营企业中实力雄厚准备投资保险业的公司，出资51%，成立一家合资公司，中文名称为华康公司，经营项目为人寿保险所有主要险种。公司的总部应该设立在上海，同时在北京、天津、重庆、广州等大城市设立办事处。公司的总经理应该在现存的保险公司中物色，条件除了有经验、熟悉业务以外，还应该具有现代管理意识和良好的公关能力。公司的推销人员应该从国营企业的下岗人员中招聘，采取合同制和以奖励性提成为主的工资体制。公司**可望**在运营的第二年开始获利。

Vocabulary List

拓展		tuòzhǎn	expand
人寿保险	人壽保險	rénshòu bǎoxiǎn	life insurance
同比		tóngbǐ	as compared with the same period last year
累计	累計	lěijì	accumulate
保监会	保監會	Bǎojiānhuì	Insurance Regulatory Commission
终身年金	終身年金	zhōngshēn niánjīn	annuity
帐户型	帳戶型	zhànghùxíng	saving deposit type (of insurance)
强劲	強勁	qiángjìng	powerful; strong
年鉴	年鑒	niánjiàn	yearbook; annals
如火如荼		rúhuǒrútú	like a raging fire
顺应	順應	shùnyìng	comply with; go along with the tide
一揽子	一攬子	yīlǎnzi	comprehensive
包		bāo	take care of everything; monopolize
忌讳	忌諱	jìhuì	avoid as taboo
好端端		hǎoduānduān	when everything is all right
吉利		jílì	lucky; auspicious
遗嘱	遺囑	yízhǔ	last will and testament
交代		jiāodài	handover; dispatch one's responsibility
搏		bó	risk; gamble
隐私		yǐnsī	privacy
锲而不舍	鍥而不捨	qièrbùshě	be persistent
余额	餘額	yú'é	surplus
投保		tóubǎo	take out insurance
断言	斷言	duànyán	assert; say with confidence
诚信	誠信	chéngxìn	trustworthiness
相继	相繼	xiāngjì	in succession; one after another
友邦		Yǒubāng	American International Assurance Company
东京海上	東京海上	Dōngjīnghǎishàng	Tokio Marine and Fire Insurance Company
瑞士		Ruìshì	Switzerland; Swiss
丰泰	豐泰	Fēngtài	Winterthur Swiss Insurance
旋风	旋風	xuànfēng	whirlwind
焦点	焦點	jiāodiǎn	focus

饱和	飽和	bǎohé	saturate; filled to capacity
法宝	法寶	fǎbǎo	magic weapon
势头	勢頭	shìtóu	trend; momentum
届时	屆時	jièshí	at the appointed time; by that time
社会保障	社會保障	shèhuìbǎozhàng	social security
物色		wùsè	search for; recruit

Notes and Explanations

1. BUSINESS AND OTHER PROFESSIONAL TERMS

寿险   *life insurance*

An abbreviation of 人寿保险.

死亡保险   *common term life insurance*

If the insured dies within the set period, his/her beneficiaries will be paid by the insurance company.

生存保险   *special term life insurance*

If the insured lives beyond the set period of time, he/she will be paid by the insurance company. But if the insured dies within the period, no money will be paid.

生死合险   *combined term insurance*

If the insured dies within the set period, his/her beneficiaries will be paid. If the insured lives beyond the set period, he/she will also be paid (principal plus interest).

福利   *welfare; fringe benefits*

Related term: 社会福利院, a nursing home for the aged and disabled.
　　【课文】政府负责福利……
　　【课文】这家公司的工资虽然稍微低一些，但是福利非常好，所有的医疗费都可以报销。

2. FORMAL EXPRESSIONS

言重了　*overstated*

Lit. "word is too serious." This expression can be used to show the speaker's modesty when hearing a compliment or praise.

【课文】方总言重了。

【补充】您言重了，我只是没有事情做来帮帮忙，哪里算得上"救星"呢？（救星＝savior）

大可不必　*totally unnecessary*

【课文】安康只是想了解中国保险市场的一般情况，您大可不必担心。

【课文】我不是警察，只是来你们这里了解一些情况，你大可不必紧张。

断言　*make an assertion*

【课文】有外国专家断言，中国迟早将超过美国，成为全球最大的保险市场。

【补充】这位学者认为网络经济将在二十年后成为世界经济的主体，大部分人觉得作出这样的断言未免为时过早。

可望　*be expected to; can look forward to*

【课文】公司可望在运营的第二年开始获利。

【补充】这两家公司可望在明天上午达成合并的最后协议。

3. COLLOQUIAL EXPRESSIONS

该不是 / 该不会　*I guess it is not for...*

Used when asking a question.

【课文】你今天请我出来喝茶该不是让我再卖给你一份保险吧？

【补充】这家保险公司近几年做得很好，该不会兼并我们这些小公司吧？

一口一个的　*use a word very frequently (in every sentence/clause)*

【课文】咱们也不是一天两天的朋友了，别一口一个方总的。

【补充】这点小事算不了什么，不要一口一个对不起的。

一揽子   *a whole package*

【课文】以前中国人的生老病死都是由政府或者单位一揽子包下来。
【补充】他把在上海成立分公司，招聘骨干，装修办公室等大事小事都一揽子包了下来。

4. OTHER PATTERNS AND WORD COLLOCATIONS

拓展……业务/市场   *expand [one's] business/market*

【课文】西方保险公司纷纷想在中国建立独资或合资公司拓展业务。
【补充】世界五百强已经将很大一部分注意力放到拓展中国市场上了。

转移……风险   *divert the risk of...*

【课文】老百姓也意识到保险可以转移现实生活中的许多风险。
【补充】我们这个电脑公司投资房地产是为了转移风险，现在谁也说不清网络到底有多大的希望。

5. IMPORTANT IDIOMATIC PHRASES/PROVERBS

明人不说暗话/明人不做暗事   *An honest person doesn't do shady things.*

See General Notes on Business Communication V.

如火如荼   *(spreading) vigorously*

Lit. "Like a raging fire and like the white flowers of weeds."

锲而不舍

An ancient Confucian text says that if you keep on carving, even metals can be cut through. Now people use the first half of this saying to encourage an attitude of perseverance.

Class Discussion
课堂讨论

1. 你觉得什么样的人应该买人寿保险？
2. 中国的保险市场和美国的保险市场有什么不同？

3. 中国保险业最近发展特别迅速的原因是什么？
4. 你觉得韩森的方案可行吗？

Exercises
练习

 PART ONE: FAST ORAL TRANSLATION
第一部分：快速口译

Refer to Lesson 1 for instructions for this exercise.

A. From Chinese into English
一位中国保险公司经理介绍自己的公司。

B. From English into Chinese
An American insurance manager is talking about the possibility of entering the Chinese auto insurance market.

PART TWO: ROLE-PLAY (MARKET RESEARCH)
第二部分：角色表演(调查人寿保险市场)

Student A acts as an insurance salesperson and student B acts as a potential buyer who has not yet made up his mind.
一个同学扮演合资公司的保险推销员，另一个同学扮演一位想买保险但是还没下决心的人。

PART THREE: SEARCHING FOR INFORMATION ON THE INTERNET
第三部分：寻找网上信息

上网寻找下面的信息：
1. 中国最大的保险公司是哪一家？
2. 现在中国有没有合资保险公司？
3. 外国独资公司能否在中国卖人寿保险？

PART FOUR: COMPOSITION
第四部分：写作

Revise Hansen's proposal or write a new proposal for an American insurance company to enter the Chinese market.

LESSON 15: BUSINESS STRATEGY
第十五课：企业战略

Background and Business Tasks
背景和任务

Corporate offices of an appliance company.

合家乐家电集团在改革开放以后的二十几年中由一个地区性的乡镇小企业发展成全国的龙头企业，每年以30%的速度发展。企业集团由单一生产电风扇，发展到生产电冰箱、电视机、空调、浴霸、消毒柜等产品领域。现在企业内部有人提出进一步扩大企业规模和生产领域的设想。但是也有人提出反对意见，认为这样追求大而全最终会导致全军覆没。企业到底何去何从，为此他们不惜出巨资请金桥为他们做战略咨询。

Part One: In the General Manager's Office at Hejiale Home Appliances Group

第一部分：合家乐家电集团总经理办公室

艾琳：　万总，您好！曹总，您好！

韩森：　您好！您好！

万一成：你好！你好！（分别与艾、韩握手）劳您二位大驾来敝公司面谈。路上辛苦了。

韩森：　应该，应该。

万：　二位**过五关斩六将**，在与几家著名的跨国战略咨询公司竞争中<u>夺魁</u>，真是英勇善战啊！

艾琳：　还是万总<u>胆识</u>过人。当初从100万人民币起家发展成今天全国瞩目的规模。**时下**又不惜掷千金，请咨询公司参与策划，此举令全国<u>震惊</u>。

万：　说实话，企业规模一大，我们真的感到**江郎才尽**了。是啊，请外国公司给民营企业作咨询，我们<u>开了先河</u>。

韩森：　虽然西方企业往往要花总投资的百分之几进行可行性论证，但是在中国只有您有这种<u>大手笔</u>。

万：　要拿出1000多万人民币做咨询，对我们来说是痛苦的，但我相信我们收回来的是快乐。中国企业最缺乏的是经验，我们现在走的路都是未来的路，在国内已经没有什么可借鉴的了，那就需要借助外来的帮助。如果我们能知道怎样才能顺利地到达胜利的<u>彼岸</u>，那么"快乐"就会伴随而来。

艾琳：　您的"彼岸"在哪儿呢？

万：　成为全球家电、电脑、<u>厨卫</u>产品制造商和服务商。

韩森：　我想，你们的雄心是有一定的依据的，对吗？

曹副总：创业之初，我们采取"专业化品牌策略"，用了三年时间初步**奠定了专业市场的领导地位**。之后我们顺利地发展到生产电视机、电冰箱、空调等其他家电产品。去年我们开始进行一些**核心多元化**的尝试，并率先进入整体橱柜、浴霸、消毒柜等产品领域。再下一步就是开发电脑和手机产品，不久将进入国际市场。

艾琳：　这一点我**不敢苟同**。我认为，盲目追求发展速度、盲目追求多元化经营正是很多民营企业失败的原因。

曹：　如果我们**一味**地满足过去所取得的成绩，企业哪一天才能走向全球呢？

韩森： 其实，很多公司之所以**享有国际盛名**，并不是追求大而全，而往往注重产品生产的专一性。如美国的福特汽车公司只生产汽车，<u>柯达</u>公司只生产和摄影有关的产品。

万： 但是如果我们只生产某一两种产品，一旦市场上这方面的需求下降，那企业就会面临困境。有句俗话说，鸡蛋不能放在一只篮子里，正是这个意思。

韩森： 中国有位企业家说，那要看编织那些篮子要花多少钱。如果篮子代价太高，外加资金周转不灵，企业就会**陷入停滞状态**。

曹： 照您这么说，鸡蛋还是应该考虑集中在一起是吗？

艾琳： 扩大投资领域并非<u>下策</u>。就拿合家乐来说，首先得看投资领域是不是<u>朝阳产业</u>，其次，要考虑对所投资的行业熟悉不熟悉，再次，看企业的骨干能不能发挥特长，等等。

万： 还有呢？

韩森： 为了提高抗风险能力，除了主营业务之外，企业还可持有一些债券、上市公司**股权**等。一些成功的外国公司正是通过这种方式保存公司实力的。他们利用手中的一部分资金永远**和成功者为伍**。

曹： 为什么同是电脑软件公司，不少中国公司从成功走向失败，而美国著名的微软公司则一直**立于不败之地**？

艾琳： 其实美国也有很多电脑公司倒闭了。一个公司站起来，千万个公司倒下去，商场如同战场，处处**刀光剑影**。企业成败的因素很多，但关键是战略选择。这可以从中国的<u>骏马</u>集团和美国的微软公司发展历程的比较分析中得以<u>验证</u>。他们<u>起步</u>条件十分相似，却导致了两种**截然不同**的发展结果。

韩森： 其实，微软的崛起壮大，骏马的崛起衰败原因当然是多方面的，如创新意识、管理水平、市场动作、经验等等、但关键是两者在战略选择上的差异。骏马公司从电脑一直发展到房地产、饮料、家具等等，等等，结果<u>全局失控</u>，<u>不可收拾</u>。

万： 看来，求大求全常常**潜伏着危机**。

韩森： 某些中国的民营企业在强烈的扩张意识推动下加大了企业资本的投入，资本的流动性和**变现能力**似乎被忽视得一干二净。资金使用分散，使得项目<u>专款</u>得不到保证，因此给企业带来了<u>灭顶之灾</u>。

曹： 没想到哈佛的MBA还是个中国通。真是**耳听为虚，眼见为实**啊，佩服，佩服！难怪大家要请<u>洋教头</u>呢！

艾琳： 有人说，事情是日本人干的，理论是美国人吹的。当然我们希望给贵公司设计的战略并非凭空瞎吹。希望万总为我们提供贵公司的更详细的运营数据，我们还要作深入的调研，提出一个进一步发展的可行性方案。

Part Two: A Strategic Plan for Hejiale Group
第二部分：合家乐战略计划（摘要）

拿破仑说过：中国这头雄狮一旦醒来，必将震惊世界。

经过多年的发展和积累，中国一部分民营企业已经完成了原始积累的过程，正在向更大的规模，更高的技术、更现代化的经营发展。民营企业要有所创新，必须有一个大的跨越。这种跨越包括企业组织制度的创新，经营领域的调整，经营方式的转变等。合家乐能否成为当今世界大企业中的一头雄狮，关键看企业的战略选择。

核心观点：造就中国家电市场的领导者。只有牢牢把握住中国国内的家电市场，才是正确的方向。

1 激励机制—每个员工都有固定的考核指标，并对考核指标进行量化，根据**定员定岗**、工作分析、岗位职责等自上而下地进行统一考核。只有新的薪酬制度和绩效考核体系建立健全了，才能够对员工实施更为合理的激励和培训。

2 组织构架脱离集权式管理，把主要产品的生产销售及各个**板块**的业务集中起来管理，施行**事业部制**，使经营管理重心下移，减少管理层次，简化管理程序，提高管理效率。

3 企业管理升级—业务结构、文化变革、战略规划与执行。

应该考虑这些方面：首先，未来三至五年企业发展的战略方向和目标；其次，未来五年企业发展的速度；第三，未来十年企业可支配的战略资源的多少。企业各部门应严格按照日程表，循序渐进地推进管理升级工作。

4 超前品牌定位—实行高技术含量、高价格、**高端用户**的"三高"战略。合家乐产品应该比其他产品价格高20%以上，合家乐可凭借技术的优势，实现差异化的竞争卖点，获得一个特殊的竞争平台。

5 集中专业力量—合家乐应该集中实力做家电，特别是厨卫电器，果断地从不占优势的电视机等电子音像产品等领域退出，更不适合扩张到电脑、手机等其他全新的领域。

6 集中资源—对广州、上海、武汉、北京四个一级目标市场集中资源，以优先资源将其培养成合家乐的主要市场；二级目标市场包括哈尔滨、苏州、西安、重庆等，这些市场为关注市场；三级市场则是自由发展市场。以集中资源策略，实现低成本运作，**以点带面、连面成片**，用三年时间将合家乐培养成全国主要商场销量第一的产品。

7 发展潜在销售网点。十年以后，农村将成为家电的重要市场。为此，应该投入一部分资金，在农村地区，特别是在较发达地区的农村建立销售和维修网点。

8 暂缓投资发展国外市场—外销不如内销获利多。当前，国际商业重心已转向中国这个巨大的市场，由原先的中国生产、国外销售转为中国生产、中国销售的策略。如日本、德国等汽车公司等已经不失时机地抓住了在中国市场销售的<u>契机</u>，合家乐更不应该**与国际大趋势相悖**。

总而言之，企业要以提高企业总体素质和产品质量为本，在此前提下考虑企业的规模和数量。当两者出现不一致时，应当优先保证企业总体素质，适当减少企业在规模、数量上的考虑。

Vocabulary List

家电	家電	jiādiàn	home appliances and consumer electronics
浴霸		yùbà	bathroom heating light bulb
消毒柜		xiāodúguì	sterilizing cabinet
全军覆没	全軍覆沒	quánjūnfùmò	completely annihilated
何去何从	何去何從	héqùhécóng	what course to follow
关	關	guān	pass
斩	斬	zhǎn	kill
夺魁	奪魁	duókuí	win the championship in a competition
胆识	膽識	dǎnshí	courage and insight
瞩目	矚目	zhǔmù	eye-catching; noteworthy
掷	擲	zhì	throw; cast
江郎才尽	江郎才盡	jiānglángcáijìn	have used up one's talent
开先河	開先河	kāi xiānhé	be the first; unprecedented
大手笔	大手筆	dàshǒubǐ	very skillful; do with bold strokes
彼岸		bǐ'àn	the other shore; goal
厨卫	廚衛	chúwèi	kitchen and bathroom
奠定		diàndìng	lay the foundation for
核心		héxīn	core
率先		shuàixiān	be the first to do sth.
整体橱柜	整體櫥櫃	zhěngtǐchúguì	integral counter and cabinet with appliances
不敢苟同		bùgǎngǒutóng	cannot agree
柯达	柯達	Kēdá	Kodak
停滞	停滯	tíngzhì	stagnation
下策		xiàcè	the worst plan/strategy
朝阳产业	朝陽產業	zhāoyángchǎnyè	rising industry
股权	股權	gǔquán	stock option
为伍	為伍	wéiwǔ	be allied with
刀光剑影	刀光劍影	dāoguāngjiànyǐng	the glint and flash of swords
骏马	駿馬	*Jùnmǎ*	*Fast Horse, name of a company*
验证	驗證	yànzhèng	proof
起步		qǐbù	start
截然不同		jiéránbùtóng	totally different

崛起		juéqǐ	rise
全局失控		quánjúshīkòng	lose control of the whole situation
不可收拾		bùkěshōushi	cannot restore order
变现	變現	biànxiàn	cash in
专款	專款	zhuānkuǎn	special fund for a particular purpose
灭顶之灾	滅頂之災	mièdǐngzhīzāi	disaster resulting in a total loss
洋教头	洋教頭	yáng jiàotóu	foreign coach
拿破仑	拿破崙	Nápòlún	Napoleon
雄狮	雄獅	xióngshī	male lion
原始积累	原始積累	yuánshǐjīlěi	primitive accumulation
造就		zàojiù	bring up; foster
构架	構架	gòujià	frame, structure
集权式	集權式	jíquánshì	centralized power structure/style
事业部制	事業部制	shìyèbùzhì	task force structure
日程表		rìchéngbiǎo	agenda
循序渐进	循序漸進	xúnxǔjiànjìn	process in an orderly way; step by step
超前		chāoqián	ahead of schedule
高端用户		gāoduān yònghù	high-end customers
卖点	賣點	màidiǎn	selling point; point of attraction to consumers
果断	果斷	guǒduàn	decisively
网点	网点	wǎngdiǎn	network
契机	契機	qìjī	opportunity
悖		bèi	contradictory

Notes and Explanations

1. BUSINESS AND OTHER PROFESSIONAL TERMS

核心多元化

The meaning of this term is that the company is changing from focusing on a single field to having several fields of equal importance.

变现能力 *ability to turn assets into cash*

Obviously, liquid assets have more potential and can be more readily converted into cash than fixed assets.

定员定岗 *having a fixed number of staff members/employees, each with a clear responsibility*

Antonym: 人浮于事.

板块 *part; division*

Originally a geological term meaning "plate." Now it has extended usage in many other fields, but its meaning is simply "part/division." People use these kinds of words simply to be fashionable.

事业部制 *task force structure*

In contrast to the traditional structure in which power and responsibility are centralized. A company is organized into several task forces, each of which is in charge of a project.

高端用户 *high-end consumers/customers*

Antonym: 低端用户, low-end consumers/customers.

2. FORMAL EXPRESSIONS

时下 *at present*

【课文】时下又不惜掷千金，请咨询公司参与策划，此举令全国震惊。
【补充】这是时下最流行的款式。

不敢苟同　　*I am afraid I cannot agree with you.*

Lit. "Dare not agree with you in a careless manner." It cannot have an object.

【课文】这一点我不敢苟同。

【补充】你认为石油的价格将大幅度下降，对此我实在不敢苟同。

一味　　*single-mindedly*

【课文】如果我们一味满足过去所取得的成绩，企业哪一天才能走向国际呢？

【补充】广告最重要的是效果，现在很多电视广告一味追求美感，对消费者没有多少影响。

有所……　　*have some or make some…*

The word that follows it must be a two-syllable action word.

【课文】民营企业要有所创新，必须有一个大的跨越。

【补充】他对那个公司的情况有所了解。

与……相悖　　*contradictory to*

【课文】合家乐更不应该与国际大趋势相悖。

【补充】他认为日本对农产品进口的限制与全球化的潮流相悖。

3. OTHER PATTERNS AND WORD COLLOCATIONS

奠定……地位　　*lay the foundation for one's position in…*

【课文】用了三年时间初步奠定了专业市场的领导地位。

【补充】南海制药厂通过研制有效治疗高血压的药物奠定了其在同行中的领先地位。

享有……盛名　　*enjoy great fame in…*

【课文】其实，很多公司之所以享有国际盛名，并不是追求大而全，而往往注重产品生产的专一性。

【补充】杭州生产的丝绸在亚洲和整个世界都享有盛名。

陷入……状态　　*sink into a situation of…*

This phrase is always negative.

【课文】资金周转不灵，企业就会陷入停滞状态。
【补充】那项石油和食品可以自由提价的政策公布以后，市场立刻陷入了疯狂抢购的混乱状态。（抢购＝panic buying）

和/与...... 为伍   *be allied with...*
【课文】他们利用手中的一部分资金永远和成功者为伍。
【补充】我们是一家跨国公司，绝对不能与那些不法商人为伍。

潜伏......危机   *A crisis (of...) is lurking/latent*
【课文】看来，求大求全常常潜伏着危机。
【补充】在王教授看来，股票市场的平静背后潜伏着巨大的危机。

4. IMPORTANT IDIOMATIC PHRASES/PROVERBS

何去何从   *lit. "where to go and whom to follow"*

Used when a person or an institution is at a critical life-or-death juncture, but does not know what course to take next.
【课文】企业到底何去何从，为此他们不惜出巨资请金桥为他们做战略咨询。
【补充】你们这样干下去是不可能成功的。何去何从，由你们自己选择！

过五关斩六将   *lit. "cross five passes and behead six enemy generals"*

Based on a story from *Romance of Three Kingdoms*. Guan Yu, a famous general, fought against many rivals and overcame many obstacles to reunite with his sworn brothers. Now it is simply used to describe someone overcoming many obstacles.

江郎才尽

This is another story-based idiomatic phrase. Mr. Jiang showed literary talent in his early years but was later unable to create any poems or prose. It means "to have used up one's talent" and is used to describe someone who had, at one time, many good and creative ideas but can no longer offer new ones.

立于不败之地   *always successful*
Lit. "standing in an invincible position."

耳听为虚，眼见为实
What the ear hears is unreliable, what the eye sees is true.

Class Discussion
课堂讨论

1. 合家乐公司为什么要请金桥公司进行战略咨询？
2. 你发现这套方案贯彻到公司执行后可能会有什么样的致命问题？
3. 金桥出台的方案与合家乐多年来形成的企业文化和考核标准有没有冲突？
4. 严格的考评标准会不会导致业绩积极性的减退？
5. 由个人权力式管理方式向程序化管理方式转变，会不会与公司原有的管理方式和决策管理层有根本性冲突？
6. 在中国农村市场建立商业网点，会不会得到预期的回报？

Exercises
练习

Part One: Fast Oral Translation
第一部分：快速口译

Refer to Lesson 1 for instructions for this exercise.

A. From Chinese into English
一位中国咨询公司的负责人介绍自己的公司。

B. From English into Chinese
A global manager is talking about the competitive advantage of his company.

Part Two: Role-play (Explaining a Strategic Plan)
第二部分：角色表演（解释战略计划）

Student A acts as the representative of Golden Bridge Consulting Group, and student B acts as a Chinese company's top leader.
一个同学扮演金桥公司的代表，一个同学扮演中国公司的领导。

PART THREE: FILL IN THE BLANKS
第三部分：选择填空

1. 你们的计划有一定道理，但是对中国农村市场的分析我不____苟同。
   A.相   B.能   C.会   D.敢
2. 由于用人不当，公司的经营____了困难状态。
   A.进入   B.陷入   C.投入   D.加入
3. 刘教授提出，只有让人民币变成国际通行货币，才能____中国在世界市场上的地位。
   A.奠定   B.决定   C.处于   D.立于
4. 由于东部和西部的发展非常不平衡，中国经济____着巨大的危机。
   A.处于   B.享有   C.具有   D.潜伏
5. 如果我们____强调国际市场，忽视了国内市场的潜力，我们很可能会在竞争中全军覆没。
   A.一味   B.一贯   C.一直   D. 一起

PART FOUR: COMPOSITION
第四部分：写作

Write a strategic plan for Northwest Transformer Works. (Refer to Lesson Three.)

LESSON 16: ESTABLISHING A RESTAURANT CHAIN
第十六课：餐饮连锁店

Background and Business Tasks
背景和任务

"长江火锅王"是一家**以经营火锅为主**的餐饮连锁店，它的总部设在四川重庆，**分店**遍布中国的二十余个省市以及韩国、新加坡、俄罗斯等国，生意**蒸蒸日上**。现在，公司的领导层打算把分店开到美国，为此，他们向金桥公司咨询在美国投资餐饮的可能性。

Part One: At the Shanghai Branch of the Yangtze River Hot Pot Restaurant

第一部分：在长江火锅城上海浦东分店

宋长江： 贵客光临，**有失**远迎。

艾琳： 宋总您太客气了。这位是我的同事韩森先生。

韩森： **初次见面，请多关照**。

王新平： 韩森先生以前吃过我们四川的麻辣火锅吗？

韩森： 去北京的时候吃过<u>涮羊肉</u>，四川火锅和涮羊肉差不多吗？

宋： 那是完全不一样的。好，今天我们就边吃边谈，让二位品尝一下我们四川火锅的精华。请入席。新平是我们上海分公司的总经理，就请他来介绍吧。

王： 这是麻辣海鲜火锅，这是最传统的<u>毛肚</u>火锅，这个呢，是**药膳**<u>滋补</u>火锅。本来我们中国人喜欢几个人共用一个大火锅，今天是按照你们外国的习惯，都是独用的小火锅，不要客气，随便尝尝。

韩森： 这海鲜火锅真是**绝了**！我从来没有吃过这么好吃的火锅。

艾琳： 我倒是更喜欢药膳火锅，风味满独特的。

宋： 好啊，看来我们的火锅在美国也会大受欢迎的。

韩森： 恕我直言，问题恐怕没有那么简单。我这个学中文的美国人比较特殊，不能代表一般的美国人。

王： 那你觉得哪些东西美国人不容易接受呢？

韩： 你看这个毛肚火锅，主要是动物的<u>内脏</u>，美国人一般是不吃的。

艾琳： 虽然我很喜欢药膳，但是你在美国不能宣传食品有医疗效果，美国的食品药品管理局在这方面的要求特别严格。

韩： 还有就是麻辣。现在爱吃辣的美国人不少，但是<u>花椒</u>的麻味儿太奇怪了，最好不要放。

宋： 那怎么行？我们四川火锅的最大的特点就是麻，俄罗斯人能接受，美国人真的接受不了吗？

王： 如果不放花椒，那就根本不能叫四川火锅！

艾琳： 可是你不能不考虑各种不同地区的顾客的习惯啊！比方说川菜在台湾就不能那么辣。

宋： 你可以用<u>刀叉</u>不用筷子，但是菜必须保持正宗川菜的原汁原味。我去新加坡考察的时候发现他们那儿原来的川菜根本**不对路**，花椒一点儿都不放，简直是笑话。我们在新加坡的成功也正是靠"正宗" 这两个字。我们不会用根本不是川菜的东西去欺骗消费者，我们也不能让<u>历史悠久</u>的川菜的**牌子砸在我们手里**。

韩森： 根据我的研究，您所说的正宗川菜其实只有不过百年的历史。不说别的，就说这红辣椒，十七世纪才传入中国。

王： 这怎么可能呢？我们四川人世世代代都离不开辣椒啊！

艾琳： 咱们不要研究历史了，还是讨论你们投资美国的计划吧。

宋： 对，对。我们打算先在美国的纽约、洛杉矶、芝加哥等大城市开设二十家连锁店，<u>大张旗鼓</u>，<u>造出声势</u>，然后再向中小城市扩展，就像美国的肯德基在中国一样。

韩森： 宋总勇气可嘉，但是我觉得这样做的**时机恐怕还不成熟**，最好先在一两个城市试验一下，看看是否受欢迎。

艾琳： 如果你们坚持原汁原味的正宗川菜，最好选洛杉矶或者旧金山这些华人众多的城市。现在那些地方已经有了比较正宗的台湾菜和上海菜了。

宋： 办好饭馆最重要的是人才。但是我听说很难拿到美国的签证，如果我们不能保证从经理、厨师到服务员都是从我们四川派去的，那饭菜的质量就难以保证了。

韩森： 对有特殊技能的厨师，美国可以为他们<u>办理移民手续</u>，但是需要很长的时间。至于一般的服务员，完全<u>可以</u>在美国找嘛。中国肯德基和麦当劳的服务员恐怕没有美国人吧？

艾琳： 其实，经理也完全可以在美国找。在我看来，最好的投资方法不是直接投资直接管理，而是在美国华人中征求合作伙伴，长江只要提供技术、原料以及人员培训就可以了。现在美国的中餐馆特别多，有很多老板都**苦于**没有经营特色，如果挂上长江火锅城的**金字招牌**，就会吸引更多的消费者，我想一定有不少人愿意<u>加盟</u>连锁店。

宋： 这好像是把我们的牌子出租给别人。我们不太习惯做这样的事情。

韩森： 但是美国很多的餐饮连锁店都是用这种模式，每个店必须在食品和质量上严格遵守总公司的要求，但是在具体的管理上有相对的独立性。

宋： 好，那就**烦请**二位为我们做一个计划。想不想到我们的<u>音乐茶座</u>去坐坐？

艾琳： 谢谢，今天下午我们还有个重要的会议，只能**告辞**了。

王： 欢迎二位常来。

韩森： 宋总、王经理**请留步**。**后会有期**。

Part Two: An Invitation to Join the Yangtze River Hot Pot Restaurant Chain
第二部分：加盟长江火锅城招商启示

（将刊登于《世界日报》、《星岛日报》等主要美国中文报纸。）

长江火锅城以正宗的四川麻辣火锅**驰名中外**，**享誉全球**，已经在亚洲和欧洲建立连锁店二十余家，成为跨国公司的长江集团现筹划在美国西岸发展连锁店，欢迎餐饮业**同仁**加盟。集团公司将向加盟者提供详细的技术指导和厨师培训，保证供应正宗四川调味品等原料及专用火锅餐具，还将提供饭店外观装修设计蓝图。投资少，见效快，合作条件优惠，**机会极为难得**。详情请与美国金桥国际咨询公司上海分公司联络。

联络人：艾琳、韩森
电话：011862175953383

Vocabulary List

火锅	火鍋	huǒguō	hot pot
连锁店	連鎖店	liánsuǒdiàn	chain restaurant
蒸蒸日上		zhēngzhēngrìshàng	thriving
关照	關照	guānzhào	do a favor for; look after
涮羊肉		shuàn yángròu	lamb hotpot
精华	精華	jīnghuá	essence
入席		rùxí	take one's seat at a banquet
海鲜		hǎixiān	seafood
毛肚		máodǔ	beef tripe
药膳	藥膳	yàoshàn	foods cooked with medicinal herbs
滋补	滋補	zībǔ	nourishing; imparting a medicinal effect
绝	絕	jué	unmatched; superb
内脏	內臟	nèizàng	inner organs
花椒		huājiāo	Chinese peppercorn
刀叉		dāochā	knife and fork
正宗		zhèngzōng	authentic
原汁原味		yuánzhīyuánwèi	original seasoning and taste
不对路	不對路	bú duìlù	does not meet the standard; below par
历史悠久	歷史悠久	lìshǐ yōujiǔ	time-honored
造出声势	造出聲勢	zàochū shēngshì	create an impetus
办理	辦理	bànlǐ	carry out (formalities)
苦于		kǔyú	suffer from
金字招牌		jīnzì zhāopai	gold-lettered signboard; famous brand
加盟		jiāméng	join in alliance
烦请	煩請	fánqǐng	may I trouble you to
音乐茶座	音樂茶座	yīnyuè cházuò	music teahouse
告辞	告辭	gàocí	say goodbye
请留步		qǐngliúbù	don't bother to see me out
后会有期	後會有期	hòuhuìyǒuqī	we'll meet again someday
驰名中外	馳名中外	chímíng Zhōngwài	renowned at home and abroad
享誉全球	享譽全球	xiǎngyù quánqiú	enjoy a great reputation all around the world
筹划	籌劃	chóuhuà	plan and prepare

同仁		tóngrén	colleagues in the same professional field
调味品	調味品	tiáowèipǐn	seasoning
餐具		cānjù	tableware
蓝图	藍圖	lántú	blueprint

Notes and Explanations

1. BUSINESS AND OTHER PROFESSIONAL TERMS

分店   *branch store*

This word is used only for branches of retail stores or restaurants. Otherwise, it should be 分公司.

药膳   *foods cooked with medicinal herbs*

In China, especially in south China, it is quite popular to make dishes cooked with medicinal herbs. Many believe that these dishes can make people stronger and more energetic. Various dishes are prepared to meet the needs of different age groups and to help people adjust to the different seasons. This is a combination of Chinese culinary art and Chinese medicine.

金字招牌   *golden signboard*

This expression is mainly used for brand names that are famous and have a long history.

2. FORMAL EXPRESSIONS

有失　　*have failed to*

The word following it must be disyllabic.

【课文】有失远迎。

【补充】很多人认为美国在中东支持以色列的政策有失公道。

苦于　　*suffer from*

【课文】有很多老板都苦于没有经营特色，......

【补充】大家都知道在西北地区修建高速公路极为重要，但是苦于资金短缺，很多已经设计好的公路无法施工。

烦请　　*trouble somebody (to do something)*

【课文】那就烦请二位为我们做一个计划。

【补充】我们建立电池厂的申请报告不见回音，烦请艾琳小姐为我们疏通渠道。

告辞　　*say goodbye*

【课文】只能告辞了。

【补充】我还有一些重要的公务，就先告辞了。

同仁　　*those of the same profession*

The original meaning of this term is "those who have the same will and ideals." Now it just means "those of the same profession," but with the positive connotation of camaraderie.

【课文】欢迎餐饮业同仁加盟......

【补充】我们公司的成立大会邀请了本省二百多位同仁参加。

3. COLLOQUIAL EXPRESSIONS

绝了！　　*unmatched; superb*

【课文】这海鲜火锅真是绝了！

【补充】这房子的装修真是绝了！比宫殿还要漂亮。

不对路　　　*wrong*

Lit. "on the wrong track." It is used to criticize things that are contrary to well-established (and often professional) standards.

【课文】他们那儿原来的川菜根本不对路。

【补充】我们是一家经济类的报纸，你学的是诗歌创作，到我们这儿工作恐怕有点儿专业不对路。

4. OTHER PATTERNS AND WORD COLLOCATIONS

以……为主的……　　　*with a (business) focus on...*

【课文】"长江火锅王"是一家以经营火锅为主的餐饮连锁店。

【补充】金海公司是一家以销售进口电子产品为主的零售企业。

砸……牌子　　　*destroy a brand name*

【课文】我们也不能让历史悠久的川菜的牌子砸在我们手里。

【补充】如果你们把不合格的产品也拿到市场上卖，就等于是砸自己公司的牌子。

时机（不）成熟　　　*the time is (not) ripe to; it is (not yet) time to*

【课文】我觉得这样做的时机还不太成熟。

【补充】一旦时机成熟，我们就会向国外开放农产品市场。

机会难得　　　*it is a rare opportunity*

【课文】机会极为难得。

【补充】机会难得，欲购从速。(A slogan frequently used by retail stores. 欲购从速＝要想买就要快一点，不然就买不到了。)

5. IMPORTANT IDIOMATIC PHRASES/PROVERBS

蒸蒸日上

Used to describe the fast growth of a business.

初次见面，请多关照。

See **General Notes on Business Communication I.**

请留步   *don't bother to see me out; don't bother to come any further*
This phrase is used by a guest whose host is seeing him/her out.

后会有期。
We can look forward to meeting again someday. A graceful substitute for 再见.

驰名中外，享誉全球
Lit. "Our fame gallops quickly across China and abroad, and we enjoy fame around the whole world." A frequently used phrase in advertisements.

Class Discussion
课堂讨论

1. 长江火锅城现在的生意怎么样？
2. 这家饭店在哪些国家建立了分店？分店的情况如何？
3. 四川火锅有什么特点？
4. 为什么艾琳和韩森认为普通美国人不容易接受四川火锅？
5. 你认为四川火锅在美国是否会受到欢迎？为什么？
6. 为什么要在美国的中文报纸上做广告？
7. 艾琳和韩森提出的连锁店方案会不会砸四川火锅的牌子？
8. 你对这个连锁店有什么建议？

Exercises
练习

PART ONE: FAST ORAL TRANSLATION
第一部分：快速口译

Refer to Lesson 1 for instructions for this exercise.

A. From Chinese into English
重庆火锅城总公司的代表在美国分店开业典礼上致词。

B. From English into Chinese
An American reporter is talking about Chinese food.

PART TWO: ROLE-PLAY (AN ADVERTISING PLAN)
第二部分：角色表演(广告方案)

Student A acts as a project manager for Golden Bridge. Student B acts as the general manager of the Yangtze River Hot Pot Restaurant Chain. They discuss plans to publish ads in mainstream American newspapers.
一位同学扮演金桥公司的代表，另一位同学扮演长江火锅城的总经理，商谈在美国主流媒体上刊登广告的问题。

PART THREE: REPHRASING SENTENCES WITH THE GIVEN IDIOMS
第三部分：用成语改写句子

（何去何从 / 后会有期 / 截然不同 / 全军覆没 / 循序渐进 / 蒸蒸日上）
1. 我们公司的生意很好，而且越来越好。
2. 我们以后一定有机会再见面。
3. 美国消费者和中国消费者的习惯完全不一样。
4. 连锁店要慢慢发展，不要追求快速扩张。
5. 今后公司应该向什么方向发展，我想听听大家的意见。
6. 如果我们不作调查研究就进入美国市场，很可能会彻底失败。

PART FOUR: COMPOSITION
第四部分：写作

An owner of a Chinese restaurant in Boston reads the advertisements and is very interested in the hot pot restaurant chain. Write a letter of inquiry from him asking for some details.

General Notes on Business Communication

I. Meeting for the First Time

When two businesspeople meet for the first time, they are inclined to use flattering words to address the other party and disparaging words to introduce themselves. In so doing, a number of idiomatic expressions are frequently used. The words may sound insincere, but this method of communication is a necessity among Chinese. The following are examples from this book (the idiomatic expressions are in bold):

Group One: Exalting Words

唐先生是蓝海健身俱乐部的经理，**幸会，幸会**。 *(L1)*

(Lit. "It is my great luck to meet you.")

理事长**日理万机** *(L6)*

(Lit. "You deal with ten thousand things every day.")

久仰久仰！ *(L6)*

(Lit. "I have admired you for a long time [but have not had a chance to meet you in person]".) *In most cases, the speaker has never heard of the other person.*

韩先生**年轻有为**，中文也说得如此流利，**难得难得**！ *(L6)*

(Lit. "Mr. Han, you are so successful at such a young age and speak the Chinese language so fluently. You are really a rare find.")

久仰大名！ *(L7)*

(Lit. "I have admired your great name for long time [but have not had a chance to meet you in person.]")

高先生**不愧是**网路**奇才**！ *(L7)*

(Lit. "Mr. Gao, you are no stranger to being called a rare internet talent.")

谢谢您的指教。 *(L8)*

(Lit. "Thank you for your guidance and instruction.")

感谢您在**百忙之中**抽出时间来见我们 *(L8)*

(Lit. "Thank you for taking time, in the middle of your hundred business dealings, to meet us.")

马先生，今天我们来**贵公司**想作一些咨询。您是**资深**的投资经理…… *(L6)*

(Lit. "Mr. Ma, today we come to your noble company for consultation. You are an experienced senior investment manager…")

我听说韩森先生是哈佛工商管理学院的**高才生**，想必您带来了**扭转乾坤的高见**。 *(L13)*

(Lit. "I have heard Mr. Hansen is a top student at the Harvard Business School. I am sure you have brought us excellent ideas that are so powerful as to turn the sky down and the earth up.")
When mentioning someone's educational background, always use 高才生 *or "top student" no matter what the person's real rank is.*

万总**胆识过人**。 *(L15)*

(Lit. "President Wan, you have extraordinary courage.")

GROUP TWO: DISPARAGING WORDS

敝人何飞虎，东北飞虎公司总经理，这是我的名片。 *(L1)*
敝人韩森，来自哈佛大学。 *(L6)*
很高兴你们对**敝厂**有兴趣。 *(L12)*

(敝=poor, inferior. It is the most commonly used word to introduce oneself or one's institution.)

哪里！哪里！您过奖了！ *(L7)*

(Lit. "Where? You over-praise me.") *This is a typical expression for responding to another party's words of praise.*

我个人在电脑技术方面**总算还有个一知半解**，希望能**帮上一点儿忙**。 *(L7)*

(Lit. "I myself have a very shallow understanding of computer technology [but] I hope I can make a tiny contribution to your project.") *The speaker is actually a leading expert in IT.*

您客气， "资深" **不敢当。** *(L6)*

(Lit. "You are too polite. I don't dare assume the title of 'experienced senior' [manager]".)

我们甘肃这个地方也没有什么好东西，**粗茶淡饭** *(L3)*

(Lit. "Gansu, this region of ours, really has nothing good [to eat], [what we can provide today is just] some coarse tea and tasteless food.") *The reality is just the opposite: the speaker prepared a superb meal.*

Besides using exalting words to address the other party and using disparaging words to refer to oneself, businesspeople often use formal/classical Chinese expressions when meeting for the first time. These expressions are distinctively different from those of everyday life. The purpose of speaking in an elegant and classical style is not only to show respect to the other party but also to show one's cultural and educational excellence. Even after they are well acquainted, those who are in leadership positions in a big company or a governmental institution will continue to speak in this style from time to time. The following are examples of the classical/formal expressions in this context.

A word of caution: using classical/formal expressions consistently may make the other party feel somewhat distant, which will be discussed later.

他们已等候你**多时**了 *(L2)*
＝很长时间

我相信我的实际能力会证明**物超所值** *(L2)*
＝得到的东西超过付出的价钱

欢迎二位**不远万里**来到我们这儿考察 *(L3)*
＝从很远的地方

非常感谢你们的**盛情**安排 *(L3)*
＝非常热情和好客

让你们**久等**了，真不好意思。 *(L6)*
＝等了很长时间

(Note: This expression is different from 等候多时 and is only used to apologize.)

二位**意下如何** *(L6)*
＝对我的建议有什么看法

韩先生**何出此言**？ *(L6)*
＝为什么会说出这样的话

我就**身不由己**了 *(L6)*
＝没有办法不做某件自己不想做的事情

情况**略有好转** *(L6)*
＝比过去好了一些

我觉得**当务之急**是要考虑把我们的电子商务网络办成什么类型 *(L7)*
＝现在最重要的事情

请稍候。 *(L7)*
＝请你稍微等一会儿

在环保问题上我们不得不**慎之又慎**。 *(L7)*
＝非常小心，在决定做一件事情之前要考虑很长时间

感谢**光临**。 *(L9)*
＝你到我们这儿来

还望韩董事长**海涵**。 *(L11)*
＝原谅

在市场上**有口皆碑** *(L11)*
＝所有的人都说好

最近美国股市的走向**不佳**，这个**诸位**不会不知道。 *(L11)*
＝不好／你们所有的人

主要想**就**购买贵厂**一事**达成一些意向性的协议。 *(L12)*
＝regarding/这一件事情

这个结果实在不是**始料可及**的。 *(L13)*
＝在开始的时候就能预料到

初次见面，请多关照。 *(L16)*
＝这是我们第一次见面，请你在生意上多给我一些照顾。

II. Using Proverbs, Aphorisms, and Quotations

Proverbs and aphorisms are frequently used in business conversations. They can add elegance to speech and can also make arguments more convincing. In addition to the quotations from ancient Chinese classics, there are also some frequently used quotations from famous persons of modern times or from folk adages.

中国有句老话，"**人往高处走， 水往低处流**"。 *(L2)*
People run upward while water runs downward.
A not-so-old saying mainly used to explain why a person always wants to advance to a higher position.

人贵有自知之明。 *(L2)*
It is very valuable to know oneself.
*This saying can be traced back to the **Book of Laozi**. It is used to emphasize that one should know one's own strengths and weaknesses.*

千军易得， 一将难求。 *(L2)*
It is much easier to find a thousand soldiers than a single commander.
In a business setting, this classical phrase is used to stress that leadership is the key factor of a company.

英雄所见略同。 *(L4)*

Heroes have similar ideas. (A common English equivalent might be: "Great minds think alike.")
This popular phrase is typically used when one knows that the other party shares the same idea/opinion without any previous discussion.

有钱能使鬼推磨 *(L4)*

You can make a ghost turn a mill for you as long as you pay enough money.
This is a very old folk adage.

恭敬不如从命。 *(L6)*

The best way for a guest to pay respect to a host is to follow the host's command.
This phrase is from classical Confucian teachings. It is used when the speaker originally wanted to do something respectful, but ends up deferring to the other party's wish. For example, A wants to see B off at the airport to show his respect, but finally accepts B's wish that he spare himself the trouble. In this case, A can say "恭敬不如从命。"

"秀才不出门，能知天下事"。 *(L7)*

This saying can be traced back to the **Book of Laozi**. It means that one doesn't need to travel far to become knowledgeable.

山重水复疑无路，柳暗花明又一村。 *(L7)*

From a famous Tang poem.

我是无事不登三宝殿。 *(L10)*

Without a serious problem one will not go visit the Temple of the Buddha.

这真是"恶人先告状"。 *(L10)*

The wrongdoer (criminal) sues [the victim] first.

祝愿双方的合作能够更上一层楼。 *(L11)*

"Climb one story higher." To advance further from an already high position.
This phrase is from a famous Tang poem.

贵国著名的《孙子兵法》上有一句话：**"兵贵神速"**。 *(L11)*

Swiftness is the most important factor in military action.
*This is one of the most famous sayings of the **Military Arts of Sunzi**.*

"集中优势兵力打歼灭战"。 *(L11)*

Concentrate superior forces for a war of annihilation.
This is a famous quotation from Chairman Mao.

"鱼与熊掌不可兼得"。 *(L11)*

One cannot have both fish and bear paws at the same time (two highly prized delicacies).
*This is from the **Works of Mencius.***

我听说毛泽东说过 **"没有调查研究就没有发言权。"** *(L13)*

No investigation, no right to speak.

有句俗话，**鸡蛋不能放在一只篮子里** *(L15)*

Don't put all your eggs in one basket.
This is a folk adage and its moral is that it is too risky to put all your bets on one thing.

真是**耳听为虚，眼见为实**啊 *(L15)*

What you hear is unreliable, what you see is real.
This saying is perhaps from a pre-modern novel.

III. Getting Closer

We have learned that conversations between two businesspeople often start in a formal or even a classical style. When one party really wants to close a deal, or simply wants to establish a friendlier atmosphere, he or she will purposely change the tone to an informal/colloquial style. The function of this style is to shorten the distance between the two parties.

The expressions after the "=" sign in the examples in this section do not have the same colloquial flavor as the given expressions, but they do have the same basic meaning.

我们买的一律是进口高档，不然的话会员就不来了，**人家就是冲着高级设备来的。** *(L1)*
＝会员到我们这里来就是因为我们有高级设备。

我们不必草签协议，**我说了算** *(L1)*
＝我可以作决定，不用和别人商量。

哎呀我的妈呀， 闭上眼睛听你的中文简直就跟中国人一样啊！ *(L1)*
＝真是想不到

那还用说吗！ *(L1)*
＝当然是这样

光顾着说话，您水还没喝呢。 *(L2)*
＝刚才我们的讨论很紧张，您忘了喝我们给您倒的水了。

哎呀，没关系嘛， 不值几个钱。 *(L3)*
＝没有关系，这个东西很便宜。

你这个**小伙子还挺叫真儿，** 我想十二天也许差不多。 *(L3)*
＝年轻人做事情很认真。

要是真发生了这样的事情，那**你的钱就白扔了。** *(L4)*
＝钱花了却没有任何效果。

中国自己的明星也不是**给俩钱儿就能打发**的。 *(L4)*
＝给一点儿钱他们就会很高兴地去做了

小伙子， 放心，我是不会骗你的。 *(L5)*
＝年轻人

我们是自己人 *(L9)*
＝我们是非常好的朋友，我们有共同利益。

嘿，艾琳，**哪阵风把你吹来了**？ *(L10)*
＝我没想到你会到我这儿来。

老弟，事情不像你想的那么简单。 *(L10)*
＝年轻人

咱们也不是一天两天的朋友了， 别一口一个方总的 *(L14)*
＝咱们做朋友的时间不短了，你不用这么客气地称呼我。

IV. Addressing a Businessperson

In China, it is an extremely complicated art to address different people in different ways. In the business world, there are even more rules.

GROUP ONE: 先生、女士、小姐

These are the most common ways to address someone. Family names can be added if known. If you meet someone for the first time and you don't know his/her exact business title, these are the safest forms of address.

GROUP TWO: BUSINESS TITLE, OR FAMILY NAME + BUSINESS TITLE

If you know the business title of the person you meet, and it is a fairly high position, you should address this person 王经理，刘董事长，陈主任， etc. Note: if this person is a vice president or deputy director, you should simply address him/her as president or director, dropping the 副 to show respect, especially when the president or the director is not present. This convention seems uncommon and unnecessary among Taiwanese businessmen. Sometimes you may drop the person's family name; doing so shows a closer relationship.

韩森：**厂长**，您现在是不是能告诉我你们的报价了 *(L3)*

Hansen has already talked a while with Mr. Jianmin Liu, so he uses 厂长 instead of 刘厂长.

艾琳：**省长**您好 *(L8)*

The person being greeted, Mr. Li, is actually 副省长. Aileen uses 省长 to show both respect and a closer relationship.

GROUP THREE: FAMILY NAME + SHORT FORM OF BUSINESS TITLE

If you have a very close relationship with a businessperson or you want to make him/her feel closer, you may use a shortened business title. A very common term is 总 (general). 王总 may be 王总经理 or 王总工程师 or 王总会计师 or any other leadership position. For 张局长 you may call him/her 张局; for 赵董事长 you may call him/her 赵董. This makes people feel closer because this form of address is commonly used among colleagues or within a company. You use it to show that you consider yourself a member of his/her company.

艾琳：我们还是谈正事吧。**韩董**觉得筹借资金是不是可行之计？ *(L11)*

GROUP FOUR: INFORMAL FORMS OF ADDRESS

To show an even more intimate relationship, some very informal forms of address can be used. For example, you may use 小/老 ＋ family name or you may call a young man 小伙子 or 老弟.

小韩，我们现在可不是在法庭上打官司 *(L10)*
老弟，事情不像你想的那么简单。 *(L10)*

OTHER NOTES:

If a host has two, three, or more guests, addressing them as 二位，三位，几位 is more polite than using 你们.

今天晚上，龙厂长会在苏州最有名的姑苏饭店设宴招待**二位** *(L3)*

Family name + 大 + title is used to show respect but has a strong informal tone.

这位是**陈大律师** *(L10)*

V. Getting Straight to the Point...or Evading It

Businesspeople stress efficiency and they want to close a deal as quickly as possible. Therefore, they often prefer getting straight to the point.

跟你开门见山吧 *(L1)*

请您直说吧，每千套的报价是多少？ *(L3)*

因为事关紧急，我想我们就进入主题吧！ *(L9)*

实不相瞒，我们是为贵厂非法仿制080系列男鞋来进行调查的。 *(L9)*

方：　要是什么事情我能帮忙，你们就直说吧。
韩森：我就喜欢方先生这种性格，那我也就明人不说暗话了。 *(L14)*

In some special situations, a businessperson may be evasive. One way he/she can do so is by changing the subject.

韩森：谢谢，我不会喝酒。什么时候我们可以到你们的生产车间看看呢？我们在酒泉只能停留二十小时。

张梅：那太可惜了，我本来是准备带二位游览黄河公园和灵岩寺的。韩先生，您的汉语说得太棒了！ *(L3)*

Because the production line of the factory is old and the hosts are quite reluctant to show it, they want to take more time for lunch and sightseeing. Then 张梅 quickly tries to change the subject to Hansen's excellent Chinese.

韩森：可是在工厂急需扩建这个紧要关头，你们却建议暂缓二期投资，这实在是釜底抽薪啊！

朱：　菜来了，大家先吃吧，边吃边谈。 *(L11)*

Since Hansen's criticism is difficult to respond to, the host wants to shift the topic to food.

VI. Disagreeing and Refusing

In Lesson 8, when Hansen asks if a construction plan has been approved, the reply is 无可奉告 (have nothing to say). This is a straightforward rejection and is not polite. Therefore Hansen feels quite upset.

Except for extreme situations, a businessperson will always try to avoid using rude and direct language to express disagreement or to reject a proposal.

艾琳：非常感谢您的好意，可是我们公司有纪律，不许收客户的礼物。这么贵重的礼物，我们绝对不能收。 *(L3)*

When Aileen refuses to accept a gift, she expresses her thanks first.

汪涛：这拍卖可是一门学问，您需要的话我也可以效劳。

韩森：汪先生真会做生意。希望有机会合作。 *(L5)*

Do you think Hansen will hire Mr. Wang? Not likely. "Mr. Wang really knows how to do business" contains a touch of sarcasm; and implies NOT this time. This answer is much better than 不用了.

Another frequently used method to refuse or reject a proposal is to say one does not have time to continue the discussion.

张局长：对不起，我还有个会要参加，而且该说的都说了，二位请回吧，恕不远送。 *(L8)*

我想，对此大概不需要作更多的解释了。如果没有别的事的话，我还有一些重要的公务需要处理。恕不远送。 *(L9)*

Although 恕不远送 (pardon me for not seeing you off) sounds very polite, it is really used to ask the visitors to leave immediately.

It is quite common not to say yes or no, but to say instead that one needs more time to think it over. This, in many contexts, is actually a polite refusal.

这个我们还要再研究研究，我们改日再谈吧。 *(L11)*

"We need more time to study this [proposal]. Let's discuss it another day." Who knows when that day will be! Perhaps never.

If one party is consistently using very formal language, it may be a sign of disagreement. In other words, that party wants to keep a distance from you. Part Two of Lesson Nine is a very good example.

VII. Exerting Pressure on the Other Party

A commonly used tactic is to mention an offer from a third party.

说正经的，我今天能不能定货？**人家那边的日本公司**答应给我八折优惠。 *(L1)*

韩森： 恕我直言，你们的报价大大高于**我们考察的其他厂家**。如果你们坚持这么高的价格，恐怕成交的可能性微乎其微。 (L3)

Another tactic is to stress that time is of the essence.

请注意，这是说现在，再过几个月你可能就买不到了。 *(L5)*

韩森：可是，我们查了有关法规，你们必须在两个月内对申请作出答复。现在已经超过三个月了！ *(L8)*

Generally, using rhetorical questions can make your statements stronger while also exerting pressure.

现在腾云生产的皮鞋就是利用了桑德蓝的技术，你们对此难道没有责任吗？ *(L9)*

[Stronger than 你们是有责任的.]

不管是来自草药的天然T3还是用化学合成的人造 *T3*，反正都是T3，你能说没有关系吗？ *(L10)*

[Stronger than 这是有关系的]

如果康福德商标本身就有侵权的问题，那还有什么资格告别的公司侵权呢？ *(L10)*

[Stronger than 那就没有资格告别的公司侵权]

VIII. Talking During Business Meals

In China, dining venues are important places for talking business, and business meals (especially business banquets with liquor and wine) are important expenses for business operations. There are many fixed phrases or sentence patterns used on these occasions.

GROUP ONE: INVITING THE OTHER PARTY TO A MEAL

刘宁：我们甘肃这个地方也没有什么好东西，粗茶淡饭，不过酒泉的酒倒是很有名的，**请二位赏光**，来来，**我们边吃边谈吧**？ *(L3)*

今天晚上，龙厂长会在苏州最有名的姑苏饭店**设宴招待二位**，**请务必赏光**啊。 *(L3)*

艾琳：该是吃午饭的时候了，咱们一起去外面吃个简单的工作午餐吧。**我来作东**。 *(L6)*

晚上我**给你接风**，时间和地点一会儿我让秘书通知你。 *(L8)*

好，今天我们就**边吃边谈**，让二位品尝一下我们四川火锅的精华。**请入席**。 *(L16)*

GROUP TWO: PROPOSING A TOAST

为我们的合作，**干杯**！ *(L7)*

韩金刚：**我提议**，**为表示对**两位远道而来的客人**的敬意**，**先干一杯**。 *(L11)*

我提议，**大家举杯**，**祝愿**双方的合作能够更上一层楼。 *(L11)*

韩先生精神可嘉，我再**敬您一杯**。 *(L11)*

GROUP THREE: ACCEPTING INVITATIONS AND OFFERING THANKS

艾琳：好啊，**恭敬不如从命**。 *(L6)*

今天**承蒙**广厦的主要领导专门**设宴款待**，**十分过意不去**。 *(L11)*

Vocabulary Glossary

English	Simplified	Traditional	Pinyin	Lesson
a bottomless pit	无底洞	無底洞	wúdǐdòng	12
a favorable turn; a turn for the better	转机	轉機	zhuǎnjī	6
a fictional person known as a dwarf	武大郎	武大郎	Wǔ Dàláng	2
a guest will follow the arrangement of a host	客随主便	客隨主便	kèsuízhǔbiàn	11
a measure word for case, instance	起	起	qǐ	10
a merger of two strong companies	强强联合	強強聯合	qiángqiáng liánhé	12
a notch under	略差	略差	lüèchà	8
a province in Northeast China	辽宁	遼寧	Liáoníng	1
a province south of Shanghai	浙江	浙江	Zhèjiāng	1
abbr. of 深圳证券交易所	深交	深交	Shēnjiāo	6
abbr. of 纪律检查 disciplinary inspection	纪检	紀檢	jìjiǎn	11
about a year	一年半载	一年半載	yìniánbànzǎi	5
abstract	提要	提要	tíyào	10
accessory	附件	附件	fùjiàn	13
accountant	会计师	會計師	kuàijìshī	3
accumulate	累计	累計	lěijì	14
achievement and efficiency	绩效	績效	jīxiào	12
active ingredient; effective component	有效成份	有效成份	yǒuxiào chéngfèn	10
adjust	调节	調節	tiáojié	10
administration	管辖	管轄	guǎnxiá	8
Administration of Industry and Commerce	工商部门	工商部門	gōngshāng bùmén	7

ENGLISH	SIMPLIFIED	TRADITIONAL	PINYIN	LESSON
advantage and disadvantage	利弊	利弊	lìbì	4
advise (a polite way of warning)	奉劝	奉勸	fèngquàn	10
advisor	顾问	顧問	gùwèn	6
agenda	日程表	日程表	rìchéngbiǎo	15
agent	代理	代理	dàilǐ	4
agent; agency	中介公司	中介公司	zhōngjiè gōngsī	2
agreement	协议	協議	xiéyì	3
agreement; mutual understanding	共识	共識	gòngshí	11
ahead of schedule	超前	超前	chāoqián	15
aim	宗旨	宗旨	zōngzhǐ	3
alcohol content	度数	度數	dùshù	11
alcohol tolerance	酒量	酒量	jiǔliàng	11
alkaline battery	碱性电池	鹼性電池	jiǎnxìng diànchí	8
all aspects	全方位	全方位	quánfāngwèi	4
all one's life	一辈子	一輩子	yībèizi	12
allocate	支配	支配	zhīpèi	11
allowance; subsidy	津贴	津貼	jīntiē	13
aluminum	铝材	鋁材	lǚcái	3
American International Assurance Company	友邦	友邦	Yǒubāng	14
American Standard	美国标准	美國標準	Měiguó Biāozhǔn	5
amount of increase	升幅	升幅	shēngfú	5
an officially rated top national magazine	核心杂志	核心雜志	héxīn zázhì	2
an outstanding student	高才生	高才生	gāocáishēng	13
animation	动画	動畫	dònghuà	7
annihilative battle	歼灭战	殲滅戰	jiānmièzhàn	11
annual production	年产值	年産值	niánchǎnzhí	3
annuity	终身年金	終身年金	zhōngshēn niánjīn	14
answer; reply	答复	答復	dáfù	8
apartment	公寓	公寓	gōngyù	5
appearance	外表	外表	wàibiǎo	2
appetite	胃口	胃口	wèikǒu	7

ENGLISH	SIMPLIFIED	TRADITIONAL	PINYIN	LESSON
artificial; man-made	人造	人造	rénzào	10
as compared with the same period last year	同比	同比	tóngbǐ	14
assemble	组装	組裝	zǔzhuāng	1
assembly line	生产线	生產綫	shēngchǎnxiàn	3
assert; say with confidence	断言	斷言	duànyán	14
assist; help	协助	協助	xiézhù	9
assume sole responsibility for its own profits or losses	自负盈亏	自負盈虧	zìfù yíngkuī	12
at one's own expense	自费	自費	zìfèi	10
at public expense; paid by the government	公费	公費	gōngfèi	10
at some other time	另行	另行	lìngxíng	5
at the appointed time; by that time	届时	屆時	jièshí	14
atmosphere; ambience	气氛	氣氛	qìfēn/qìfèn	11
attempt	尝试	嘗試	chángshì	2
attend to numerous affairs every day	日理万机	日理萬機	rìlǐwànjī	6
attract business	招商	招商	zhāoshāng	7
attract investment	引资	引資	yǐnzī	12
auction (n./v.)	拍卖	拍賣	pāimài	5
authentic	正宗	正宗	zhèngzōng	16
automated	自动化	自動化	zìdònghuà	3
avoid as taboo	忌讳	忌諱	jìhuì	14
back	背部	背部	bèibù	1
backbone; mainstay	骨干	骨幹	gǔgàn	3
bacteria	细菌	細菌	xìjūn	8
bad debt	呆帐	呆帳	dāizhàng	12
banquet room	宴会厅	宴會廳	yànhuìtīng	3
base	基地	基地	jīdì	8
bathroom	卫生间	衛生間	wèishēngjiān	11
bathroom heating light bulb	浴霸	浴霸	yùbà	15
be allied with	为伍	爲伍	wéiwǔ	15
be baffled; baffling	莫名其妙	莫名其妙	mòmíngqímiào	13

ENGLISH	SIMPLIFIED	TRADITIONAL	PINYIN	LESSON
be confiscated; confiscate	没收	沒收	mòshōu	5
be hitched to a losing investment	套牢	套牢	tàoláo	6
be indebted to; receive the grace of	承蒙	承蒙	chéngméng	11
be located	坐落	坐落	zuòluò	5
be obvious to all	有目共睹	有目共睹	yǒumùgòngdǔ	9
be persistent	锲而不舍	鍥而不捨	qièrbùshě	14
be praised by all who know	有口皆碑	有口皆碑	yǒukǒujiēbēi	11
be tasked to; (do something) according to an order	奉命	奉命	fèngmìng	9
be the first to do sth.	率先	率先	shuàixiān	15
be the first; unprecedented	开先河	開先河	kāi xiānhé	15
be the host	作东	作東	zuòdōng	6
be worthy of; deserve to be called	不愧	不愧	búkuì	7
bear market	熊市	熊市	xióngshì	6
bear paw	熊掌	熊掌	xióngzhǎng	11
bear; undertake	承担	承擔	chéngdān	9
beef tripe	毛肚	毛肚	máodǔ	16
Beijing to Shijiazhuang	京石	京石	Jīngshí	4
Beijing to Tianjin	京津	京津	Jīngjīn	4
benefit	造福	造福	zàofú	8
beverage	饮料	飲料	yǐnliào	4
bid	竞标	競標	jìngbiāo	11
bidding	竞价	競價	jìngjià	6
bifurcation; distribution; divert	分流	分流	fēnliú	12
black gauze cap; a symbol of an official post	乌纱帽	烏紗帽	wūshāmào	8
blood pressure	血压	血壓	xuèyā	1
blueprint	蓝图	藍圖	lántú	16
blueprint	图纸	圖紙	túzhǐ	5
board chairman	理事长	理事長	lǐshìzhǎng	6
board of directors	理事会	理事會	lǐshìhuì	6

ENGLISH	SIMPLIFIED	TRADITIONAL	PINYIN	LESSON
bond	债券	債券	zhàiquàn	6
borrow (money)	筹借	籌借	chóujiè	11
borrow a hen to lay eggs	借鸡生蛋	借鷄生蛋	jièjiīshēngdàn	11
boundless beneficence	功德无量	功德無量	gōngdé wúliàng	8
boundless hospitality	盛情	盛情	shèngqíng	3
boundless; unlimited	不可限量	不可限量	bùkě xiànliàng	7
breach a contract	违约	違約	wéiyuē	9
bribe	打点	打點	dǎdiǎn	13
bribe	贿赂	賄賂	huìlù	8
brilliant	辉煌	輝煌	huīhuáng	11
bring suit; lodge a complaint	告状	告狀	gàozhuàng	10
bring up; foster	造就	造就	zàojiù	15
broadband cable	宽带电缆	寬帶電纜	kuāndài diànlǎn	7
broker	经纪人	經紀人	jīngjìrén	5
bubble	泡沫	泡沫	pàomò	7
budget	预算	預算	yùsuàn	4
building with an unfinished interior	毛坯房	毛坯房	máopīfáng	5
bull market	牛市	牛市	niúshì	6
bureaucratization	官僚主义	官僚主義	guānliáo zhǔyì	8
bury; overlook	埋没	埋沒	máimò	2
bus	巴士	巴士	bāshì	13
business accounting	核算	核算	hésuàn	12
business reality	实务	實務	shíwù	7
business reputation	商誉	商譽	shāngyù	12
buy in; buy over	收买	收買	shōumǎi	9
buy; purchase	收购	收購	shōugòu	2
can be predicted from the outset	始料可及	始料可及	shǐliàokějí	13
candidate	候选人	候選人	hòuxuǎnrén	2
cannot agree	不敢苟同	不敢苟同	bùgǎngǒutóng	15
cannot keep up with the situation	跟不上趟	跟不上趟	gēnbùshàngtàng	12
cannot restore order	不可收拾	不可收拾	bùkěshōushi	15

ENGLISH	SIMPLIFIED	TRADITIONAL	PINYIN	LESSON
Canon	佳能	佳能	Jiānéng	13
capable	得力	得力	délì	10
capital of Shandong Province	济南	濟南	Jǐnán	8
capital/fund management	资金运作	資金運作	zījīn yùnzuò	11
carry out (formalities)	办理	辦理	bànlǐ	16
carve	雕	雕	diāo	3
cash in	变现	變現	biànxiàn	15
caustic	尖刻	尖刻	jiānkè	13
CD; DVD	光盘	光盤	guāngpán	10
cease to be angry	息怒	息怒	xīnù	8
ceiling	天花板	天花板	tiānhuābǎn	11
cement; concrete	水泥	水泥	shuǐní	11
central theme/goal (of a text)	文案诉求	文案訴求	wén'àn sùqiú	4
centralized power structure/style	集权式	集權式	jíquánshì	15
centripetal force; loyalty to the company	向心力	向心力	xiàngxīnlì	13
CEO	首席执行官	首席執行官	shǒuxízhíxíngguān	2
ceremony	仪式	儀式	yíshì	4
chain restaurant	连锁店	連鎖店	liánsuǒdiàn	16
change; alter	变更	變更	biàngēng	9
change; be replaced	更换	更換	gēnghuàn	2
channel	渠道	渠道	qúdào	12
charitable organizations	慈善机构	慈善機構	císhàn jīgòu	12
cheap; low-cost	低廉	低廉	dīlián	7
chemical synthesis	化学合成	化學合成	huàxué héchéng	10
chief operating officer	总监	總監	zǒngjiān	2
chief; director	主任	主任	zhǔrèn	2
Chinese peppercorn	花椒	花椒	huājiāo	16
choice of persons	人选	人選	rénxuǎn	2
choose the wrong person for the job	用人不当	用人不當	yòngrén búdàng	9
CIF (Cost, Insurance and Freight)	到岸价	到岸價	dào'ànjià	3

ENGLISH	SIMPLIFIED	TRADITIONAL	PINYIN	LESSON
Cisco	思科	思科	Sīkē	12
civil (suit) (vs. 刑事 or criminal suit)	民事	民事	mínshì	10
clean/honest government	廉政	廉政	liánzhèng	8
click rate	点击率	點擊率	diǎnjīlǜ	7
clinical	临床	臨床	línchuáng	10
close down; go bankrupt	倒闭	倒閉	dǎobì	9
clothing; apparel	服饰	服飾	fúshì	7
collapse	坍塌	坍塌	tāntā	11
colleagues in the same professional field	同仁	同仁	tóngrén	16
college by TV; distance learning	电大	電大	diàndà	12
commitment; promise	承诺	承諾	chéngnuò	11
common sense	常识	常識	chángshí	9
communication	通信	通信	tōngxìn	2
company motto	厂训	廠訓	chǎngxùn	3
compare favorably with; rival	媲美	媲美	pìměi	6
compensate	赔偿	賠償	péicháng	10
compensation	赔偿金	賠償金	péichángjīn	11
compensation	赔款	賠款	péikuǎn	13
compensation	佣金	傭金	yōngjīn	3
completed construction	竣工	竣工	jùngōng	11
completely annihilated	全军覆没	全軍覆沒	quánjūnfùmò	15
comply with; go along with the tide	顺应	順應	shùnyìng	14
compose and write	撰写	撰寫	zhuànxiě	2
comprehensive	一揽子	一攬子	yīlǎnzi	14
computer	计算机	計算機	jìsuànjī	2
confirm	确认	確認	quèrèn	7
confuse truth and falsehood	颠倒黑白	顛倒黑白	diāndǎohēibái	10
consistently; always	一贯	一貫	yíguàn	9
construction	施工	施工	shīgōng	11
consumption; cost	消耗	消耗	xiāohào	13

ENGLISH	SIMPLIFIED	TRADITIONAL	PINYIN	LESSON
contact	接洽	接洽	jiēqià	5
content	含量	含量	hánliàng	1
contract (with)	承包	承包	chéngbāo	11
contradict oneself	自相矛盾	自相矛盾	zìxiāngmáodùn	13
contradictory	悖	悖	bèi	15
contribution	贡献	貢獻	gòngxiàn	3
control or manipulate the market	操盘	操盤	cāopán	6
convert	折合	折合	zhéhé	1
convinced	服气	服氣	fúqì	2
cooking	烹饪	烹飪	pēngrèn	2
cool	酷	酷	kù	5
copy; be modeled on; counterfeit	仿制	仿製	fǎngzhì	9
core	核心	核心	héxīn	15
core component	核心部件	核心部件	héxīn bùjiàn	3
corporate group; conglomerate	集团公司	集團公司	jítuán gōngsī	11
correspondence college	函授学院	函授學院	hánshòu xuéyuàn	2
corrupt officials	贪官	貪官	tānguān	8
counterfeit and low quality goods	假冒伪劣	假冒偽劣	jiǎmào wěiliè	10
countermeasure or plan	对策	對策	duìcè	7
courage and insight	胆识	膽識	dǎnshí	15
cover	覆盖	覆蓋	fùgài	4
co-worker [cl.]	搭档	搭檔	dādàng	7
create impetus	造出声势	造出聲勢	zàochū sēngshì	16
create positions on the basis of persons (in need of jobs)	因人设岗	因人設崗	yīnrén shègǎng	12
cross	跨	跨	kuà	3
crucial moment	紧要关头	緊要關頭	jǐnyào guāntóu	11
Daewoo	大宇	大宇	Dàyǔ	13
daggers drawn	剑拔弩张	劍拔弩張	jiànbánǔzhāng	13
daily work/routine	日常事务	日常事務	rìcháng shìwù	6
dairy product	乳制品	乳製品	rǔzhìpǐn	6

ENGLISH	SIMPLIFIED	TRADITIONAL	PINYIN	LESSON
data	数据	數據	shùjù	2
decisively	果断	果斷	guǒduàn	15
decline	走下坡路	走下坡路	zǒu xiàpōlù	4
decline to accept/admit	谢绝	謝絕	xièjué	5
decorate; interior finishing	装修	裝修	zhuāngxiū	5
deduct a percentage; draw a percentage	提成	提成	tíchéng	7
deeds of valor in battle (perform)	汗马功劳	汗馬功勞	hànmǎgōngláo	12
deep-fried mandarin fish in sweet sauce	松鼠鳜鱼	松鼠鱖魚	sōngshǔ guìyú	11
degree	程度	程度	chéngdù	3
delay	耽搁	耽擱	dāngē	2
deliver	递	遞	dì	10
dense willow trees and bright flowers (i.e., a beautiful scene opens up, obstacles are overcome)	柳暗花明	柳暗花明	liǔ'ànhuāmíng	7
department; section	处	處	chù	3
desert	沙漠	沙漠	shāmò	8
designated	指定	指定	zhǐdìng	11
detailed rules	细则	細則	xìzé	5
detailed/itemized accounts	明细帐目	明細帳目	míngxìzhàngmù	13
develop	开发	開發	kāifā	3
devise a way to	设法	設法	shèfǎ	8
difficulties that one is hard put to explain	苦衷	苦衷	kǔzhōng	11
digital	数码	數碼	shùmǎ	13
dinnerware	餐具	餐具	cānjù	11
director's chair; (leading) position	交椅	交椅	jiāoyǐ	2
disaster resulting in a total loss	灭顶之灾	滅頂之災	mièdǐngzhīzāi	15
disastrous	惨重	慘重	cǎnzhòng	13
discipline	纪律	紀律	jìlù	3
disclosure; make public	披露	披露	pīlù	2

ENGLISH	SIMPLIFIED	TRADITIONAL	PINYIN	LESSON
dispatch; delegate	派遣	派遣	pàiqiǎn	9
dispute; conflict	纠纷	糾紛	jiūfēn	6
divert; misappropriate	挪用	挪用	nuóyòng	9
divide 50/50; split down the middle	五五分成	五五分成	wǔwǔ fēnchéng	11
divide the spoils	分赃	分贓	fēnzāng	13
dizzy	晕	暈	yūn	1
dizzy	晕	暈	yūn	11
do a favor for; look after	关照	關照	guānzhào	16
do not know the complexity of things	不知天高地厚	不知天高地厚	bùzhī tiāngāodìhòu	8
do not mind traveling far	不远万里	不遠萬里	bùyuǎnwànlǐ	3
do shadow boxing (Tai-chi martial arts)	打太极拳	打太極拳	dǎ tàijíquán	12
does not meet the standard; below par	不对路	不對路	bú duìlù	16
don't bother to see me out	请留步	請留步	qǐngliúbù	16
double [cl.]	双料	雙料	shuāngliào	10
doubtful point; suspicious point	疑点	疑點	yídiǎn	13
download	下载	下載	xiàzǎi	7
drain off; omit	排放	排放	páifàng	8
driver's licence	驾驶执照	駕駛執照	jiàshǐ zhízhào	2
dry	干燥	乾燥	gānzào	3
Dupont	杜邦	杜邦	Dùbāng	12
dust-proof	防尘	防塵	fángchén	3
each one does his duty	各司其职	各司其職	gèsīqízhí	2
each shows his special skill	各显所能	各顯所能	gèxiǎnsuǒnéng	2
earnest	真诚	真誠	zhēnchéng	4
earthquake	地震	地震	dìzhèn	5
ecology	生态	生態	shēngtài	8
e-commerce	电子商务	電子商務	diànzǐ shāngwù	7
efficiency	效率	效率	xiàolǜ	2
elder brother	家兄	家兄	jiāxiōng	11
electric capacity	电力性能	電力性能	diànlì xìngnéng	8

ENGLISH	SIMPLIFIED	TRADITIONAL	PINYIN	LESSON
electrical appliances/ equipment	电器	電器	diànqì	3
electromagnetic loss	电磁损耗	電磁損耗	diàncí sǔnhào	3
eliminate	淘汰	淘汰	táotài	5
emaciated	消瘦	消瘦	xiāoshòu	1
employee	员工	員工	yuángōng	3
employee	职工	職工	zhígōng	3
encourage; urge	激励	激勵	jīlì	13
energy consumption	能耗	能耗	nénghào	8
enforest	植树造林	植樹造林	zhíshù zàolín	3
engineer	工程师	工程師	gōngchéngshī	2
enjoy a great reputation all around the world	享誉全球	享譽全球	xiǎngyù quánqiú	16
enlarge an army; expand personnel	招兵买马	招兵買馬	zhāobīngmǎimǎ	2
Enron	恩龙	恩龍	Ēnlóng	6
ensure; guarantee	保障	保障	bǎozhàng	9
enter (an auction, game, show, etc.)	入场	入場	rùchǎng	5
entrepreneur	企业家	企業家	qǐyèjiā	3
environmental protection	环保	環保	huánbǎo	8
equally effective	效力等同	效力等同	xiàolì děngtóng	11
equipment; facility	设施	設施	shèshī	3
essence	精华	精華	jīnghuá	16
every other day	隔日	隔日	gérì	4
exact; precise	精确	精確	jīngquè	7
examine and approve	审批	審批	shěnpī	3, 8
examine and test	检测	檢測	jiǎncè	10
examine for approval	审查	審查	shěnchá	4
excellent goods at modest prices	物美价廉	物美價廉	wùměi jiàlián	3
excess; surplus	过剩	過剩	guòshèng	12
exhibition; show	博览会	博覽會	bólǎnhuì	1
expand	拓展	拓展	tuòzhǎn	14
expand; expansion	扩建	擴建	kuòjiàn	11
expected value	期望值	期望值	qīwàngzhí	2

ENGLISH	SIMPLIFIED	TRADITIONAL	PINYIN	LESSON
expert	行家	行家	hángjiā	1
expire; run out	期满	期滿	qīmǎn	9
extensive; wide-ranging	广泛	廣泛	guǎngfàn	3
extent; stage	地步	地步	dìbù	9
exterior wall	外墙	外墙	wàiqiáng	11
extra	额外	額外	éwài	4
extremely clever; ingenious	绝妙	絕妙	juémiào	7
eye-catching; noteworthy	瞩目	矚目	zhǔmù	15
face value	面值	面值	miànzhí	6
factory address	厂址	廠址	chǎngzhǐ	3
fall through; evaporate	破灭	破滅	pòmiè	7
falling	坠落	墜落	zhuìluò	11
falsehood; phoniness	虚假	虛假	xūjiǎ	6
fame; reputation	声誉	聲譽	shēngyù	10
fame; reputation	信誉	信譽	xìnyù	5
fashion	时尚	時尚	shíshàng	1
fatal	致命	致命	zhìmìng	7
favorable (price); discount	优惠	優惠	yōuhuì	3
fax	传真	傳真	chuánzhēn	3
fax	电传	電傳	diànchuán	3
feasible plan	可行之计	可行之計	kěxíngzhījì	11
financial accounting	财务会计	財務會計	cáiwù kuàijì	6
financial crisis	金融危机	金融危機	jīnróng wēijī	5
firm; sturdy	坚固	堅固	jiāngù	5
first establish	初创	初創	chūchuàng	7
first lot	首批	首批	shǒupī	3
first rate; top	一流	一流	yīliú	3
five continents	五大洲	五大洲	wǔdàzhōu	3
flat-screen	平面直角	平面直角	píngmiàn zhíjiǎ	1
flaw; defect	缺陷	缺陷	quēxiàn	7
flexible; nimble	灵活	靈活	línghuó	13
FOB (Free on Board)	离岸价	離岸價	lí'ànjià	3
focus	焦点	焦點	jiāodiǎn	14
follow	跟进	跟進	gēnjìn	6

ENGLISH	SIMPLIFIED	TRADITIONAL	PINYIN	LESSON
follow fashion trends; be fashionable [cl.]	赶时髦	趕時髦	gǎn shímáo	7
follow; observe	依照	依照	yīzhào	8
foods cooked with medicinal herbs	药膳	藥膳	yàoshàn	16
Ford	福特	福特	Fútè	12
foreground; prospects	前景	前景	qiánjǐng	5
foreign coach	洋教头	洋教頭	yáng jiàotóu	15
foresight; farsightedness	前瞻性	前瞻性	qiánzhānxìng	2
forever in place	永驻	永駐	yǒngzhù	10
foundation	功底	功底	gōngdǐ	2
founding member	发起人	發起人	fāqǐrén	6
frame; structure	构架	構架	gòujià	15
full time	全职	全職	quánzhí	3
gain/lose	盈亏	盈虧	yíngkuī	13
galloping horse	奔马	奔馬	bēnmǎ	3
gamble	赌博	賭博	dǔbó	6
General Electric	通用电气	通用電氣	Tōngyòng Diànqì	12
general principle	总则	總則	zǒngzé	8
general situation	概况	概況	gàikuàng	8
generous treatment	款待	款待	kuǎndài	11
genius	奇才	奇才	qícái	7
get (something) off one's hands	脱手	脫手	tuōshǒu	6
get both	兼得	兼得	jiāndé	11
get involved	插手	插手	chāshǒu	10
get straight to the point	开门见山	開門見山	kāiménjiànshān	1
get the job done [cl.]	搞定	搞定	gǎodìng	11
give up at the halfway point	半途而废	半途而廢	bàntú'érfèi	6
give; provide	给予	給予	gěiyǔ	9
go bankrupt	破产	破産	pòchǎn	11
go to	赴	赴	fù	8
gold-lettered signboard; famous brand	金字招牌	金字招牌	jìnzì zhāopai	16
golf	高尔夫	高爾夫	gāo'ěrfū	5

ENGLISH	SIMPLIFIED	TRADITIONAL	PINYIN	LESSON
good	佳	佳	jiā	11
goose foot ivy	鹅掌藤	鵝掌藤	ézhǎngténg	10
governmental seals	公章	公章	gōngzhāng	8
grace with your presence; be present	光临	光臨	guānglín	4
grant (a title of); bestow	授予	授予	shòuyǔ	3
grant forgiveness/immense tolerance	海涵	海涵	hǎihán	11
grant instruction	赐教	賜教	cìjiào	9
great master	大师	大師	dàshī	4
group	团队	團隊	tuánduì	2
grow continuously	节节上升	節節上升	jiéjiéshàngshēng	6
guest and host; superior and inferior	宾主上下	賓主上下	bīnzhǔ shàngxià	11
guide	指南	指南	zhǐnán	2
guts; courage	魄力	魄力	pòlì	7
guy; rogue [cl. derogatory]	小子	小子	xiǎozi	5
gymnastics	体操	體操	tǐcāo	4
handover; dispatch one's responsibility	交代	交代	jiāodài	14
have a close relationship with the authorities	手眼通天	手眼通天	shǒuyǎntōngtiān	5
have a fine spirit or good intentions	精神可嘉	精神可嘉	jīngshén kějiā	11
have a traffic jam	堵车	堵車	dǔchē	2
have an affinity (by fate or good fortune)	有缘	有緣	yǒuyuán	5
have integrity and always work for the public interest	廉洁奉公	廉潔奉公	liánjiéfènggōng	8
have more hands than needed	人浮于事	人浮于事	rénfúyúshì	12
have successively held the posts of	历任	歷任	lìrèn	2
have superficial knowledge of	一知半解	一知半解	yìzhībànjiě	7
have used up one's talent	江郎才尽	江郎才盡	jiānglángcáijìn	15

ENGLISH	SIMPLIFIED	TRADITIONAL	PINYIN	LESSON
have well balanced facial features	五官端正	五官端正	wǔguānduānzhèng	2
head advisor of a class	班主任	班主任	bānzhǔrèn	2
head-hunting	猎头	獵頭	liètóu	2
helplessly; cannot help but	无奈	無奈	wúnài	8
high quality	上乘	上乘	shàngchéng	5
high-end customers	高端用户	高端用戶	gāoduān yònghù	15
high-pitch; high-profile	高调	高調	gāodiào	4
Hilton	喜来登	喜來登	Xǐláidēng	7
hit from above	砸	砸	zá	11
hold a banquet to welcome	接风	接風	jiēfēng	8
hold the post of	担任	擔任	dānrèn	2
Holland	荷兰	荷蘭	Hélán	11
home appliances and consumer electronics	家电	家電	jiādiàn	15
hot pot	火锅	火鍋	huǒguō	16
hotel	宾馆	賓館	bīnguǎn	3
house available now	现房	現房	xiànfáng	5
house on blueprint (before construction)	楼花	樓花	lóuhuā	5
house to be built	期房	期房	qīfáng	5
huge profit	暴利	暴利	bàolì	4
human resources	人力资源	人力資源	rénlì zīyuán	2
humidity	湿度	濕度	shīdù	3
hunt for; seek	搜寻	搜尋	sōuxún	2
hurry	匆匆	匆匆	cōngcōng	8
I; me	敝人	敝人	bìrén	1
idea; conceptualization	构想	構想	gòuxiǎng	7
imitate	仿	仿	fǎng	3
immature	幼稚	幼稚	yòuzhì	6
immeasurable	难以计数	難以計數	nányǐjìshǔ	10
implement	施行	施行	shīxíng	8
implement	实施	實施	shíshī	2
import	引进	引進	yǐnjìn	3
in a weak position	弱势	弱勢	ruòshì	12

ENGLISH	SIMPLIFIED	TRADITIONAL	PINYIN	LESSON
in alternation	交替	交替	jiāotì	4
in charge; superintend	主管	主管	zhǔguǎn	8
in one payment; in one lump sum	一次到位	一次到位	yícì dàowèi	11
in succession; one after another	相继	相繼	xiāngjì	14
in view of; seeing that	鉴于	鑒于	jiànyú	9
income is surpassed by expenses; running at a deficit	入不敷出	入不敷出	rùbùfūchū	12
income tax	所得税	所得稅	suǒdéshuì	12
income; profit	收益	收益	shōuyì	9
incoming letter	来函	來函	láihán	11
incur; suffer	蒙受	蒙受	méngshòu	2
index	索引	索引	suǒyǐn	10
index number	指数	指數	zhǐshù	6
indicator; mark; symbolize (n./v.)	标志	標志	biāozhì	6
indigenous industries	民族工业	民族工業	mínzú gōngyè	12
individual stock holder	散户	散戶	sǎnhù	6
industry; enterprise	实业	實業	shíyè	12
infer; deduce	推断	推斷	tuīduàn	9
information	情报	情報	qíngbào	11
infrastructure construction	基建	基建	jījiàn	13
initiate a project	立项	立項	lìxiàng	8
inner organs	内脏	內臟	nèizàng	16
innovation	创新	創新	chuàngxīn	3
inquiry	垂询	垂詢	chuíxún	7
insert	插	插	chā	4
insider	圈内人	圈內人	quānnèirén	7
insider information	内幕	內幕	nèimù	5
insider; expert	内行	內行	nèiháng	7
install	安装	安裝	ānzhuāng	7
instant noodle	方便面	方便麵	fāngbiànmiàn	11
instep; vamp	鞋面	鞋面	xiémiàn	9

ENGLISH	SIMPLIFIED	TRADITIONAL	PINYIN	LESSON
institute of technology	工学院	工學院	gōngxuéyuàn	2
instruction	指教	指教	zhǐjiào	8
Insurance Regulatory Commission	保监会	保監會	Bǎojiānhuì	14
integral counter and cabinet with appliances	整体橱柜	整體櫥櫃	zhěngtǐchúguì	15
intellectual property rights	知识产权	知識産權	zhīshí chǎnquán	10
interior finishing	装潢	裝潢	zhuānghuáng	11
interior wall	内墙	内墙	nèiqiáng	11
internet	因特网	因特網	yīntèwǎng	7
inventory	库存	庫存	kùcún	13
investigate and verify	查证	查證	cházhèng	9
investigate; verify	核实	核實	héshí	11
investigation; verify	核查	核查	héchá	10
invite applications for a job; recruit	招聘	招聘	zhāopìn	2
IPO (initial public offerings); listed on the stock market	上市	上市	shàngshì	2
iron chunks [cl.]	铁疙瘩	鐵疙瘩	tiěgēda	1
issue	发布	發布	fābù	8
issue	发行	發行	fāxíng	6
items of payments	款项	款項	kuǎnxiàng	5
it's a long story	一言难尽	一言難盡	yìyánnánjìn	13
jewelry	首饰	首飾	shǒushì	7
join in alliance	加盟	加盟	jiāméng	16
joint stock (system)	股份制	股份制	gǔfènzhì	3
joint stock company; incorporated company	股份公司	股份公司	gǔfèn gōngsī	2
judicial organ	司法机构	司法機構	sīfǎ jīgòu	9
jurisdiction	管辖权	管轄權	guǎnxiáquán	9
keep secret; confidential	保密	保密	bǎomì	2
keep watch on	监视	監視	jiānshì	13
key; crux	关键	關鍵	guānjiàn	7
kickback	回扣	回扣	huíkòu	3
kill	斩	斬	zhǎn	15

ENGLISH	SIMPLIFIED	TRADITIONAL	PINYIN	LESSON
kitchen and bathroom	厨卫	厨衛	chúwèi	15
knife and fork	刀叉	刀叉	dāochā	16
know well; have a good knowledge of	通晓	通曉	tōngxiǎo	2
Kodak	柯达	柯達	Kēdá	15
lamb hotpot	涮羊肉	涮羊肉	shuàn yángròu	16
last will and testament	遗嘱	遺囑	yízhǔ	14
latest style	新款	新款	xīnkuǎn	9
law firm	律师事务所	律師事務所	lùshī shìwùsuǒ	10
lay the foundation for	奠定	奠定	diàndìng	15
lead	带领	帶領	dàilǐng	3
leader; boss	上司	上司	shàngsī	2
leak out	泄露	泄露	xièlù	9
leather jacket	皮夹克	皮夾克	píjiákè	1
lecturer	讲师	講師	jiǎngshī	2
legal person; (corporate) representative	法人代表	法人代表	fǎrén dàibiǎo	3
let me be candid with you	实不相瞒	實不相瞞	shíbùxiāngmán	1
letter of intent; memorandum of understanding	意向书	意向書	yìxiàngshū	1
leveling	扁平化	扁平化	biǎnpínghuà	2
license plate	牌照	牌照	páizhào	13
life insurance	人寿保险	人壽保險	rénshòu bǎoxiǎn	14
like a raging fire	如火如荼	如火如荼	rúhuǒrútú	14
liquid assets	流动资产	流動資産	liúdòng zīchǎn	12
loose hole; careless mistake; slip-up	纰漏	紕漏	pīlòu	10
loosen	松动	鬆動	sōngdòng	11
lose a lawsuit	败诉	敗訴	bàisù	10
lose control of the whole situation	全局失控	全局失控	quánjúshīkòng	15
low	低迷	低迷	dīmí	6
ltd.	有限公司	有限公司	yǒuxiàngōngsī	2
lucky; auspicious	吉利	吉利	jílì	14
magic weapon	法宝	法寶	fǎbǎo	14

ENGLISH	SIMPLIFIED	TRADITIONAL	PINYIN	LESSON
maintenance	维护	維護	wéihù	3
maintenance	维修	維修	wéixiū	2
make a career change; job-hop	跳槽	跳槽	tiàocáo	2
make a special trip	专程	專程	zhuānchéng	11
make an additional allocation for (investment)	追加	追加	zhuījiā	11
make someone's acquaintance	结识	結識	jiéshí	5
make transparent	透明化	透明化	tòumínghuà	13
Malaysia	马来西亚	馬來西亞	Mǎláixīyà	1, 3
male lion	雄狮	雄獅	xióngshī	15
Manhattan	曼哈顿	曼哈頓	Mànhādùn	9
marble balls for hand exercise	健身球	健身球	jiànshēnqiú	1
maritime space	海域	海域	hǎiyù	8
massage	按摩	按摩	ànmó	1, 12
material	材料	材料	cáiliào	3
material consumption	物耗	物耗	wùhào	8
matter	事项	事項	shìxiàng	10
may I trouble you to	烦请	煩請	fánqǐng	16
means of livelihood	生计	生計	shēngjì	12
measure	测量	測量	cèliáng	1
measure word for a tall building	栋	棟	dòng	11
measurements; size	尺寸	尺寸	chǐcùn	7
mechanical engineering	机械工程	機械工程	jīxiè gōngchéng	2
mechanism	机制	機制	jīzhì	10
medical apparatus and instruments	医疗仪器	醫療儀器	yīliáo yíqì	2
medicine peddler [cl.]	药贩子	藥販子	yàofànzi	10
medicine that lowers high blood pressure	降压药	降壓藥	jiàngyāyào	10
medicine to be taken after dissolving in hot water	冲剂	沖劑	chōngjì	10

ENGLISH	SIMPLIFIED	TRADITIONAL	PINYIN	LESSON
member of the board of directors; trustees	董事	董事	dǒngshì	2
Mercedes Benz	奔驰	奔馳	Bēnchí	13
mergers and acquisitions	兼并	兼并	jiānbìng	2
metric system	公制	公制	gōngzhì	5
Mexico	墨西哥	墨西哥	Mòxīgē	1
Microsoft	微软	微軟	Wēiruǎn	12
middleman	中间商	中間商	zhōngjiānshāng	3
Milan	米兰	米蘭	Mǐlán	5
mini; micro	微型	微型	wēixíng	3
miscellaneous fees	杂费	雜費	záfèi	13
mock; sneer	耻笑	耻笑	chǐxiào	2
mode; model	模式	模式	móshì	2
money in hand [cl.]	手头	手頭	shǒutóu	11
more than	余	餘	yú	3
mortgage	按揭	按揭	ànjiē	5
move to	迁至	遷至	qiānzhì	6
multidimensional	立体化	立體化	lìtǐhuà	4
multifunctional	多功能	多功能	duōgōngnéng	1
music tea house	音乐茶座	音樂茶座	yīnyuè cházuò	16
must; be sure to	务必	務必	wùbì	3
mutual fund	共同基金	共同基金	gòngtóngjījīn	6
name of a city	苏州	蘇州	Sūzhōu	3
name of a place	浦东	浦東	Pǔdōng	6
name of a premier university in Shanghai	复旦	復旦	Fùdàn	10
name of a province	甘肃	甘肅	Gānsù	3
name of a province	江苏	江蘇	Jiāngsū	3
Napoleon	拿破仑	拿破崙	Nápòlún	15
natural	天然	天然	tiānrán	10
negotiate; talk things over	协商	協商	xiéshāng	9
net worth; net value	净值	淨值	jìngzhí	12
network	网点	網點	wǎngdiǎn	15
next to nothing	微乎其微	微乎其微	wēihūqíwēi	3

English	Simplified	Traditional	Pinyin	Lesson
no comment; have nothing to report	无可奉告	無可奉告	wúkěfènggào	8
no profit to be gained	无利可图	無利可圖	wúlìkětú	13
non-government enterprise	民营企业	民營企業	mínyíng qǐyè	3
not enough; cannot get by [cl.]	下不来	下不來	xiàbùlái	11
not sparing any cost; at any cost	不惜一切代价代价	不惜一切代價代價	bùxī yíqiè dàijià	11
not yet	尚未	尚未	shàngwèi	11
nourishing; imparting a medicinal effect	滋补	滋補	zībǔ	16
number one (in a profession/field)	龙头	龍頭	lóngtóu	11
nutritional science	营养学	營養學	yíngyǎngxué	4
obedience	从命	從命	cóngmìng	6
observe and study	考察	考察	kǎochá	8
obtain	获	獲	huò	2
offend	冒犯	冒犯	màofàn	8
offer a bribe	行贿	行賄	xínghuì	8
office building	写字楼	寫字樓	xiězìlóu	5
office of the factory director	厂办	廠辦	chǎngbàn	2
Oh my God [cl.]	我的妈呀	我的媽呀	wǒdemāya	1
omitted	从略	從略	cónglüè	5
on a grand scale; in a big way	大张旗鼓	大張旗鼓	dàzhāngqígǔ	5
on short notice; temporary	临时	臨時	línshí	6
on the verge of	濒临	瀕臨	bīnlín	12
on-the-spot investigation	实地考察	實地考察	shídì kǎochá	3
opening quotation (on the stock exchange)	开盘	開盤	kāipán	6
operate	运作	運作	yùnzuò	2
operation	操作	操作	cāozuò	13
opportunistic; speculative	投机	投機	tóujī	6
opportunity	契机	契機	qìjī	15

ENGLISH	SIMPLIFIED	TRADITIONAL	PINYIN	LESSON
optimization	最优化	最優化	zuìyōuhuà	2
order already issued	成命	成命	chéngmìng	10
original seasoning and taste	原汁原味	原汁原味	yuánzhīyuánwèi	16
outspoken	心直口快	心直口快	xīnzhíkǒukuài	11
outstanding	杰出	杰出	jiéchū	2
overland	陆路	陸路	lùlù	3
overstock	积压	積壓	jīyā	7
owe	拖欠	拖欠	tuōqiàn	12
ownership	属权	屬權	shǔquán	9
oxygen	氧气	氧氣	yǎngqì	1
pace back and forth	徘徊	徘徊	páihuái	6
paint	涂料	塗料	túliào	11
paint (oil)	油漆	油漆	yóuqī	11
Pakistan	巴基斯坦	巴基斯坦	Bājīsītǎn	3
pardon me for not seeing you out/off	恕不远送	恕不遠送	shùbùyuǎnsòng	8
pardon me for speaking frankly	恕我直言	恕我直言	shùwǒzhíyán	3
participate in	参与	參與	cānyù	2
partnership	伙伴关系	夥伴關係	huǒbàn guānxi	3
party in a dispute; legal client	当事人	當事人	dāngshìrén	10
pass	关	關	guān	15
passenger car	轿车	轎車	jiàochē	13
patent	专利	專利	zhuānlì	9
patience	耐心	耐心	nàixīn	8
pay a visit to	走访	走訪	zǒufǎng	6
pay in full	付清	付清	fùqīng	5
pay in installments	分期付款	分期付款	fēnqī fùkuǎn	5
pay tax	交税	交稅	jiāoshuì	5
pay tax	纳税	納稅	nàshuì	13
pay tribute	进贡	進貢	jìngòng	13
payroll office	劳资科	勞資科	láozīkē	2
penalty drink (that a loser is obliged to drink)	罚酒	罰酒	fájiǔ	10

ENGLISH	SIMPLIFIED	TRADITIONAL	PINYIN	LESSON
percentage of gold; quality	含金量	含金量	hánjīnliàng	2
perform; carry out	履行	履行	lǚxíng	9
performance	业绩	業績	yèjī	2
person of the same profession	同行	同行	tóngháng	10
pharmaceutical	制药	制藥	zhìyào	10
photocopy	影印	影印	yǐnyìn	9
physical nonexistence	虚拟	虛擬	xūnǐ	7
place; arena	场所	場所	chǎngsuǒ	6
plan	策划	策劃	cèhuà	4
plan and prepare	筹划	籌劃	chóuhuà	16
plan to build	筹建	籌建	chóujiàn	11
plan; prepare	筹备	籌備	chóubèi	2
planning	规划	規劃	guīhuà	2
plentiful	充沛	充沛	chōngpèi	4
police	警方	警方	jǐngfāng	9
pollution	公害	公害	gōnghài	8
poor-quality construction project	豆腐渣工程	豆腐渣工程	dòufuzhā gōngchéng	11
port	港口	港口	gǎngkǒu	3
portion; quota	额度	額度	édù	11
possess	拥有	擁有	yōngyǒu	5
postpone	暂缓	暫緩	zànhuǎn	11
postpone for the time being	暂缓	暫緩	zànhuǎn	11
pour hot water onto	冲	沖	chōng	11
powerful; strong	强劲	強勁	qiángjìng	14
precision	精密	精密	jīngmì	2
predetermined	预设	預設	yùshè	5
prescription	处方	處方	chǔfāng	10
primitive accumulation	原始积累	原始積累	yuánshǐjīlěi	15
principal	本金	本金	běnjīn	11
privacy	隐私	隱私	yǐnsī	14
procedure	程序	程序	chéngxù	5

ENGLISH	SIMPLIFIED	TRADITIONAL	PINYIN	LESSON
process in an orderly way; step by step	循序渐进	循序漸進	xúnxùjiànjìn	15
processing equipment	加工机具	加工機具	jiāgōng jījù	3
profession	行业	行業	hángyè	8
professional skill; specialty	一技之长	一技之長	yījìzhīcháng	2
profit [cl.]	油水	油水	yóushuǐ	1
profit; gain	盈利	盈利	yínglì	6
projector	投影机	投影機	tóuyǐngjī	13
promote	提拔	提拔	tíbá	2
promote sale	促销	促銷	cùxiāo	2
promote the sale of	推销	推銷	tuīxiāo	1
proof	验证	驗證	yànzhèng	15
propose a toast	举杯	舉杯	jǔbēi	11
proposed toast	敬酒	敬酒	jìngjiǔ	10
provide service	效劳	效勞	xiàoláo	5
provincial level	省级	省級	shěngjí	3
public relations	公共关系	公共關係	gōnggòng guānxì	3
public security	公安	公安	gōng'ān	11
pull the rug out from under	釜底抽薪	釜底抽薪	fǔdǐchōuxīn	11
purchase	采购	采購	cǎigòu	1
pure [cl.]	一水	一水	yìshuǐ	5
put (money) in place	到位	到位	dàowèi	11
put down in writing; record	记载	記載	jìzǎi	6
put the cart before the horse	本末倒置	本末倒置	běnmòdàozhì	13
pyramid	金字塔	金字塔	jīnzìtǎ	2
qualification	资格	資格	zīgé	3
qualified for or competent at	胜任	勝任	shèngrèn	2
quota; (market) share	份额	份額	fèn'é	3
quoted price; quote	报价	報價	bàojià	1
railway	铁路	鐵路	tiělù	3
raise funds	集资	集資	jízī	12
rank; row; column	行列	行列	hángliè	7

ENGLISH	SIMPLIFIED	TRADITIONAL	PINYIN	LESSON
reach	达成	達成	dáchéng	3
real (vs. 虚拟)	实体	實體	shítǐ	7
real estate	房地产	房地產	fángdìchǎn	5
receive first place	占了头筹	占了頭籌	zhànle tóuchóu	11
recite fluently	倒背如流	倒背如流	dàobèirúliú	11
recommend	推荐	推薦	tuījiàn	10
red jade	红玉	紅玉	hóngyù	3
register; record	登录	登錄	dēnglù	7
registered trademark	注册商标	注冊商標	zhùcèshāngbiāo	10
regular meeting of the Standing Committee	常务会议	常務會議	chángwù huìyì	8
reimburse (v.); reimbursement (n.)	报销	報銷	bàoxiāo	10
rely on; lean on	借助	借助	jièzhù	11
remedy; make up for	补救	補救	bǔjiù	11
remit money by bank transfer	银行汇款	銀行匯款	yínháng huìkuǎn	9
remove obstacles to keep channels open	疏通渠道	疏通渠道	shūtōng qúdào	8
remove somebody from a position	撤销	撤銷	chèxiāo	11
remuneration	待遇	待遇	dàiyù	2
renowned at home and abroad	驰名中外	馳名中外	chímíng zhōngwài	16
repeal; countermand	撤销	撤銷	chèxiāo	10
research and develop	研制	研製	yánzhì	3
research group	课题组	課題組	kètízǔ	2
residential area	住宅区	住宅區	zhùzháiqū	11
residential building	居民楼	居民樓	jūmínlóu	11
resist	抗	抗	kàng	5
respect; politeness	恭敬	恭敬	gōngjìng	6
restaurants, cafes, and bars	餐饮业	餐飲業	cānyǐnyè	6
restructuring	重组	重組	chóngzǔ	2
resumé	简历	簡歷	jiǎnlì	2
retail	零售	零售	língshòu	7
retrieve	挽回	挽回	wǎnhuí	11

ENGLISH	SIMPLIFIED	TRADITIONAL	PINYIN	LESSON
return merchandise	退货	退貨	tuìhuò	7
rhythm	节奏	節奏	jiézòu	2
rich and generous	丰厚	豐厚	fēnghòu	9
rich; be rich in	富含	富含	fùhán	10
right to speak	发言权	發言權	fāyánquán	13
rise	崛起	崛起	juéqǐ	15
rise from three-year college status to four-year college status	专升本	專升本	zhuānshēngběn	2
rising industry	朝阳产业	朝陽產業	zhāoyángchǎnyè	15
risk; gamble	搏	搏	bó	14
Rockefeller	洛克菲勒	洛克菲勒	Luòkèfēilè	12
rowing machine	划船机	划船機	huáchuánjī	1
salary and bonus	薪酬	薪酬	xīnchóu	2
sale	销售	銷售	xiāoshòu	2
Samsung	三星	三星	Sānxīng	3
sanitation	卫生	衛生	wèishēng	5
saturate; filled to capacity	饱和	飽和	bǎohé	14
sauna	桑拿	桑拿	sāngná	12
saving deposit type (of insurance)	帐户型	帳戶型	zhànghùxíng	14
say goodbye	告辞	告辭	gàocí	16
scandal	丑闻	醜聞	chǒuwén	6
scenic	景色秀丽	景色秀麗	jǐnsè xiùlì	5
scholar	秀才	秀才	xiùcái	7
scientific research	科研	科研	kēyán	2
screen	屏幕	屏幕	píngmù	6
screen and select	筛选	篩選	shāixuǎn	2
scrupulously abide by	恪守	恪守	kèshǒu	9
seafood	海鲜	海鮮	hǎixiān	16
search	搜索	搜索	sōusuǒ	11
search for; recruit	物色	物色	wùsè	14
seasoning	调味品	調味品	tiáowèipǐn	16
second-hand	二手	二手	èrshǒu	5

ENGLISH	SIMPLIFIED	TRADITIONAL	PINYIN	LESSON
secret; classified information	机密	機密	jīmì	9
secretary	秘书	秘書	mìshū	2
securities	有价证券	有價證券	yǒujià zhèngquàn	12
securities	证券	證券	zhèngquàn	6
seek rice to cook	找米下锅	找米下鍋	zhǎomǐxiàguō	11
segment; link	环节	環節	huánjié	8
select and match	选配	選配	xuǎnpèi	9
sell off (all of one's shares)	清仓	清倉	qīngcāng	6
sell; marketing	行销	行銷	xíngxiāo	7
selling point; point of attraction to consumers	卖点	賣點	màidiǎn	15
send on errands	打发	打發	dǎfa	4
send out goods	发货	發貨	fāhuò	7
sense of responsibility	责任心	責任心	zérènxīn	2
Seoul	汉城	漢城	Hànchéng	5
series	系列	系列	xìliè	3
series; (product) line	系列	系列	xìliè	9
session	届	届	jiè	1
setting up and debugging	调试	調試	tiáoshì	2
settle accounts	结算	結算	jiésuàn	7
settle out of court	庭外和解	庭外和解	tíngwài héjiě	10
sexy	性感	性感	xìnggǎn	4
shake hands and greet	握手寒暄	握手寒暄	wòshǒu hánxuān	3
Shanghai to Nanjing	沪宁	滬寧	Hùníng	4
share dividend	分红	分紅	fēnhóng	13
shareholder	持股人	持股人	chígǔrén	13
shareholder	股东	股東	gǔdōng	13
shareholder's equity	股本总额	股本總額	gǔběn zǒng'é	6
Sharp	夏普	夏普	Xiàpǔ	3
shipping by air or by sea	航运	航運	hángyùn	3
shipping by sea	海运	海運	hǎiyùn	3
shoe pattern	鞋模	鞋模	xiémó	9
shoes	靴鞋	靴鞋	xuēxié	9
show	出示	出示	chūshì	1

ENGLISH	SIMPLIFIED	TRADITIONAL	PINYIN	LESSON
show; display	显示	顯示	xiǎnshì	6
sign (an agreement)	签订	簽訂	qiāndìng	3
sign (an agreement) provisionally	草签	草簽	cǎoqiān	1
simple food and drink	粗茶淡饭	粗茶淡飯	cūchádànfàn	3
simply put	说白了	說白了	shuōbáile	4
sincerely	谨	謹	jǐn	13
sincerity	诚意	誠意	chéngyì	3
Singapore	新加坡	新加坡	Xīnjiāpō	3
sizable	可观	可觀	kěguān	7
size; scope	规模	規模	guīmó	1
slimming	减肥	減肥	jiǎnféi	4
smart idea	点子	點子	diǎnzi	4
so many hills and brooks lie ahead (i.e., many obstacles)	山重水复	山重水複	shānchóngshuǐfù	7
social security	社会保障	社會保障	shèhuìbǎozhàng	14
soft drinks	苏打水	蘇打水	sūdǎshuǐ	4
software	软体／软件	軟體／軟件	ruǎntǐ/ruǎnjiàn	7
sold afar	远销	遠銷	yuǎnxiāo	3
sole of a shoe	鞋底	鞋底	xiédǐ	9
solid; ample	雄厚	雄厚	xiónghòu	3
Sony	索尼	索尼	Suǒní	13
sorry; regret	遗憾	遺憾	yíhàn	6
soy protein	大豆蛋白	大豆蛋白	dàdòu dànbái	8
special appointment	特聘	特聘	tèpìn	2
special dining room in a restaurant	雅座	雅座	yǎzuò	11
special fund for a particular purpose	专款	專款	zhuānkuǎn	15
special need	特需	特需	tèxū	4
specific area; localized	局部	局部	júbù	1
speculate on stocks	炒股	炒股	chǎogǔ	6
speed is precious in war	兵贵神速	兵貴神速	bīngguìshénsù	11
split up; break down	分解	分解	fēnjiě	12

ENGLISH	SIMPLIFIED	TRADITIONAL	PINYIN	LESSON
sponsor	赞助	贊助	zànzhù	4
spread	传播	傳播	chuánbō	8
square foot	平方英尺	平方英尺	píngfāng yīngchǐ	5
square meter	平米	平米	píngmǐ	5
staff	人员	人員	rényuán	3
staff in charge of bonus distribution	奖励员	獎勵員	jiǎnglìyuán	2
stage; phase	阶段	階段	jiēduàn	7
stagnation	停滞	停滯	tíngzhì	15
stamp	盖	蓋	gài	8
standard; respectable [cl.]	正经	正經	zhèngjǐng	10
start	起步	起步	qǐbù	15
start	启动	啓動	qǐdòng	7
state-run non-profit (institution)	事业	事業	shìyè	6
stay young-looking; age-defying	青春养颜	青春養顏	qīnchūn yǎngyán	10
steel reinforcing bar	钢筋	鋼筋	gāngjīn	11
stereo	音响	音響	yīnxiǎng	13
sterilizing cabinet	消毒柜	消毒櫃	xiāodúguì	15
stipulate in explicit terms	明文规定	明文規定	míngwénguīdìng	4
stock exchange	交易所	交易所	jiāoyìsuǒ	6
stock option	股权	股權	gǔquán	15
stock options	期权	期權	qīquán	2
storage; warehousing	仓储	倉儲	cāngchǔ	7
strategize on paper (not realistic)	纸上谈兵	紙上談兵	zhǐshangtánbīng	6
strategy	战略	戰略	zhànlüè	2
strict and fair in meting out rewards and punishments	奖惩分明	獎懲分明	jiǎngchéngfēnmín	2
strictly according to the facts	如实	如實	rúshí	9
strike a deal	成交	成交	chéngjiāo	3
student advisor	辅导员	輔導員	fǔdǎoyuán	2
style	款式	款式	kuǎnshì	7

ENGLISH	SIMPLIFIED	TRADITIONAL	PINYIN	LESSON
submit; present	呈报	呈報	chéngbào	9
submit; turn in	呈交	呈交	chéngjiāo	5
subordinate	属下	屬下	shǔxià	9
subordinate	下属	下屬	xiàshǔ	2
subscribe	认购	認購	rèngòu	6
substantive	实质性	實質性	shízhìxìng	12
suddenly have a fantastic idea	突发奇想	突發奇想	tūfā qíxiǎng	7
sue	起诉	起訴	qǐsù	9
suffer from	苦于	苦于	kǔyú	16
suggest	拟	擬	nǐ	4
suit; formal written complaint	诉讼书	訴訟書	sùsòngshū	10
suite	套间	套間	tàojiān	5
suited to market demand	适销对路	適銷對路	shìxiāoduìlù	1
sunset industry; a declining industry	夕阳工业	夕陽工業	xīyáng gōngyè	12
supervise; superintend	监督	監督	jiāndū	6
support services	后勤	後勤	hòuqín	12
suppose; hypothetical assumption	假设	假設	jiǎshè	2
surplus	余额	餘額	yú'é	14
surplus; redundant	富余	富餘	fùyú	12
surrender	投降	投降	tóuxiáng	10
survey questionnaire	问卷调查	問卷調查	wènjuàn diàoch	1
sweep across; engulf	席卷	席捲	xíjuǎn	4
Switzerland; Swiss	瑞士	瑞士	Ruìshì	14
tableware	餐具	餐具	cānjù	16
take (medicine)	服用	服用	fúyòng	10
take a look (for approval)	过目	過目	guòmù	11
take a shortcut	抄近道	抄近道	chāo jìndào	2
take care of everything; monopolize	包	包	bāo	14
take one's seat at a banquet	入席	入席	rùxí	16
take out insurance	投保	投保	tóubǎo	14

ENGLISH	SIMPLIFIED	TRADITIONAL	PINYIN	LESSON
take out or provide a loan (v.); loan (n.)	贷款	貸款	dàikuǎn	5
take over; handle	接手	接手	jiēshǒu	4
tall and well built	人高马大	人高馬大	réngāomǎodà	1
target; quota	指标	指標	zhǐbiāo	2
task force structure	事业部制	事業部制	shìyèbù zhì	15
technician	技师	技師	jìshī	9
technology	工艺	工藝	gōngyì	8
telecommunications equipment	通讯器材	通訊器材	tōngxùnqìcái	13
tell the truth/bottom line [cl.]	交个底	交個底	jiāogedǐ	11
territory	领域	領域	lǐngyù	8
text	文本	文本	běnwén	9
The Art of War by Sunzi	孙子兵法	孫子兵法	Sūnzǐ Bīngfǎ	11
the customer comes first	用户至上	用戶至上	yònghù zhìshàn	3
the export of labor services	劳务输出	勞務輸出	láowù shūchū	12
the glint and flash of swords	刀光剑影	刀光劍影	dāoguāngjiànyǐng	15
The main hall of a Buddhist monastery; your esteemed place	三宝殿	三寶殿	sānbǎodiàn	10
the masses	群众	群衆	qúnzhòng	12
the other shore; goal	彼岸	彼岸	bǐ'àn	15
the profession one has engaged in for years [cl.]	老本行	老本行	lǎo běnháng	2
the State Council	国务院	國務院	Guówùyuàn	6
the title of a technical post	职称	職稱	zhíchēng	2
the worst plan/strategy	下策	下策	xiàcè	15
there is only one way (out of a predicament)—die	死路一条	死路一條	sǐlùyìtiáo	12
thin	清瘦	清瘦	qīngshòu	1
think-tank; committee of experts	专家库	專家庫	zhuānjiākù	2
those who return from abroad	海归	海歸	hǎiguī	2
thriving	蒸蒸日上	蒸蒸日上	zhēngzhēngrìshàng	16

ENGLISH	SIMPLIFIED	TRADITIONAL	PINYIN	LESSON
throw a banquet	设宴	設宴	shèyàn	3
throw; cast	掷	擲	zhì	15
throw; discard	抛	拋	pāo	12
Tiger Woods	老虎伍兹	老虎伍茲	Lǎohǔ Wǔzī	4
time-honored	历史悠久	歷史悠久	lìshǐ yōujiǔ	16
tiny profit	区区小利	區區小利	qūqū xiǎolì	8
tip-off; file complaint	举报	舉報	jǔbào	11
title	称号	稱號	chēnghào	3
to accept (an invitation)	赏光	賞光	shǎngguāng	3
to be	系	系	xì	3
to be rated number one	居……之首	居……之首	jū zhīshǒu	3
to be serious [cl.]	叫真儿	叫真兒	jiàozhēnr	3
to list	挂牌	挂牌	guàpái	6
to lose one's capital; run a business at a loss	赔本	賠本	péiběn	13
to make the final decision [cl.]	拍板	拍板	pāibǎn	12
to order (goods)	订货	訂貨	dìnghuò	3
to order; to buy	订购	訂購	dìnggòu	3
to pay back	偿还	償還	chánghuán	12
to talk (business) [formal]	洽谈	洽談	qiàtán	3
to use for a special purpose	专用	專用	zhuānyòng	3
TOEFL	托福	托福	Tuōfú	2
Tokio Marine and Fire Insurance Company	东京海上	東京海上	Dōngjīnghǎishàng	14
top leaders [cl.]	老总	老總	lǎozǒng	11
top-rated	上好	上好	shànghǎo	5
Toshiba	东芝	東芝	Dōngzhī	3
totally different	截然不同	截然不同	jiéránbùtóng	15
toward	冲	冲	chòng	1
township and village enterprise	乡镇企业	鄉鎮企業	xiāngzhèn qǐyè	7
Toyota	丰田	豐田	Fēngtián	13
training	培训	培訓	péixùn	3
transfer power to a lower level	权力下放	權力下放	quánlì xiàfàng	3

ENGLISH	SIMPLIFIED	TRADITIONAL	PINYIN	LESSON
transform	改造	改造	gǎizào	3
transformer	变压器	變壓器	biànyāqì	3
transformer for power network	电力变压器	電力變壓器	diànlì biànyāqì	3
transition	转型	轉型	zhuǎnxíng	12
transparency	透明度	透明度	tòumíngdù	6
travel expense	差旅费	差旅費	chāilǚfèi	13
treadmill	跑步机	跑步機	pǎobùjī	1
trend; direction	走向	走向	zǒuxiàng	6
trend; momentum	势头	勢頭	shìtóu	14
triangle debts	三角债	三角債	sānjiǎozhài	12
truck	卡车	卡車	kǎchē	3
trustworthiness	诚信	誠信	chéngxìn	14
trustworthiness	信用	信用	xìnyòng	7
turn a millstone	推磨	推磨	tuīmò	4
turn around a situation	扭转乾坤	扭轉乾坤	niǔzhuǎnqiánkūn	13
turnover (capital); circulation	周转	周轉	zhōuzhuǎn	11
two copies of one document	一式两份	一式兩份	yíshì liǎngfèn	11
two living rooms and two bathrooms	双厅双厕	雙廳雙厠	shuāngtīng shuāngcè	5
two-bedroom apartment	两居室	兩居室	liǎngjūshì	5
type	类型	類型	lèixíng	7
unable to do as one wishes	身不由己	身不由己	shēnbùyóujǐ	6
undertake	经手	經手	jīngshǒu	10
unexpected	意想不到	意想不到	yìxiǎngbúdào	13
unique	独特	獨特	dútè	11
unmatched; superb	绝	絕	jué	16
unreasonable; far-fetched [cl.]	离谱儿	離譜兒	lípǔ	10
unstoppable trend	大势所趋	大勢所趨	dàshìsuǒqū	12
urgent matter	当务之急	當務之急	dāngwùzhījí	7
use as reference; draw from others' experience or knowledge	借鉴	借鑒	jièjiàn	10

ENGLISH	SIMPLIFIED	TRADITIONAL	PINYIN	LESSON
vacation (v./n.)	度假	度假	dùjià	5
vague	模糊	模糊	móhú	7
value exceeds the price	物超所值	物超所值	wùchāosuǒzhí	2
value-added tax	增值税	增值稅	zēngzhíshuì	12
vegetable	蔬菜	蔬菜	shūcài	8
version; edition	版本	版本	bǎnběn	4
very cautious	慎之又慎	慎之又慎	shènzhīyòushèn	8
very experienced and qualified	资深	資深	zīshēn	6
very few; scarce	寥寥无几	寥寥無幾	liáoliáowújǐ	5
very skillful; do with bold strokes	大手笔	大手筆	dàshǒubǐ	15
viewership rate	收视率	收視率	shōushìlǜ	4
violate	侵犯	侵犯	qīnfàn	9
VIP; celebrity [cl.]	大腕儿	大腕兒	dàwànr	5
virgin forest	原始森林	原始森林	yuánshǐ sēnlín	1
visit in person	登门造访	登門造訪	dēngmén zàofǎng	8
visit in person	上门	上門	shàngmén	5
volume; bulk	体积	體積	tǐjī	3
walk through streets and lanes	走街串巷	走街串巷	zǒujiēchuànxiàng	10
walking stick	拐杖	拐杖	guǎizhàng	10
Wall Street	华尔街	華爾街	Huá'ěrjiē	6
Wal-Mart	沃尔玛	沃爾瑪	Wò'ěrmǎ	7
ward off	挡	擋	dǎng	8
waste (your time)	耽误	耽誤	dānwù	8
wasted money	冤枉钱	冤枉錢	yuānwàngqián	1
water park	水上乐园	水上樂園	shuǐshàng lèyuán	5
way; channel	途径	途徑	tújìng	6
we'll meet again someday	后会有期	後會有期	hòuhuìyǒuqī	16
wearproof; durable	耐磨	耐磨	nàimó	9
well arranged	妥善	妥善	tuǒshàn	9
well known to all	家喻户晓	家喻戶曉	jiāyùhùxiǎo	4
what course to follow	何去何从	何去何從	héqùhécóng	15
wheelchair	轮椅	輪椅	lúnyǐ	10

ENGLISH	SIMPLIFIED	TRADITIONAL	PINYIN	LESSON
when everything is all right	好端端	好端端	hǎoduānduān	14
whirlwind	旋风	旋風	xuànfēng	7, 14
wholesale	批发	批發	pīfā	1
wholly-owned	独资	獨資	dúzī	2
wild animal	野生动物	野生動物	yěshēng dòngwù	11
win a suit	胜诉	勝訴	shèngsù	10
win the bid	中标	中標	zhòngbiāo	5
win the championship in a competition	夺魁	奪魁	duókuí	15
wine made from wild grapes	野葡萄酒	野葡萄酒	yěpútáo jiǔ	11
Winterthur Swiss Insurance	丰泰	豐泰	Fēngtài	14
win-win; victory for both sides	双赢	雙贏	shuāngyíng	12
workshop; workplace	车间	車間	chējiān	3
www.amazon.com	亚马逊	亞馬遜	Yàmǎxùn	7
www.yam.com	蕃薯藤	蕃薯藤	Fānshǔténg	7
Yale University	耶鲁	耶魯	Yēlǔ	10
year by year	逐年	逐年	zhúnián	2
yearbook; annals	年鉴	年鑒	niánjiàn	14
yeast	酵母菌	酵母菌	jiàomǔjūn	8
yield one's position to someone more capable	让贤	讓賢	ràngxián	2
you all	诸位	諸位	zhūwèi	11
young and promising	年轻有为	年輕有爲	niánqīngyǒuwéi	6
your brilliant idea	高见	高見	gāojiàn	13
your esteemed	贵	貴	guì	3
zip code	邮政编码	郵政編碼	yóuzhèng biānmǎ	3